CALL SIGN CHAOS

CALL SIGN CHAOS

LEARNING TO LEAD

JIM MATTIS
and Bing West

RANDOM HOUSE

NEW YORK

Copyright © 2019 by James N. Mattis and Francis J. West
Maps copyright © 2019 by David Lindroth Inc.

Published in the United States by Random House,
an imprint and division of Penguin Random House LLC, New York.

RANDOM HOUSE and the HOUSE colophon are
registered trademarks of Penguin Random House LLC.

Hardback ISBN 978-0-8129-9683-8
Ebook ISBN 978-0-8129-9684-5

Printed in the United States of America on acid-free paper

randomhousebooks.com

2 4 6 8 9 7 5 3 1

FIRST EDITION

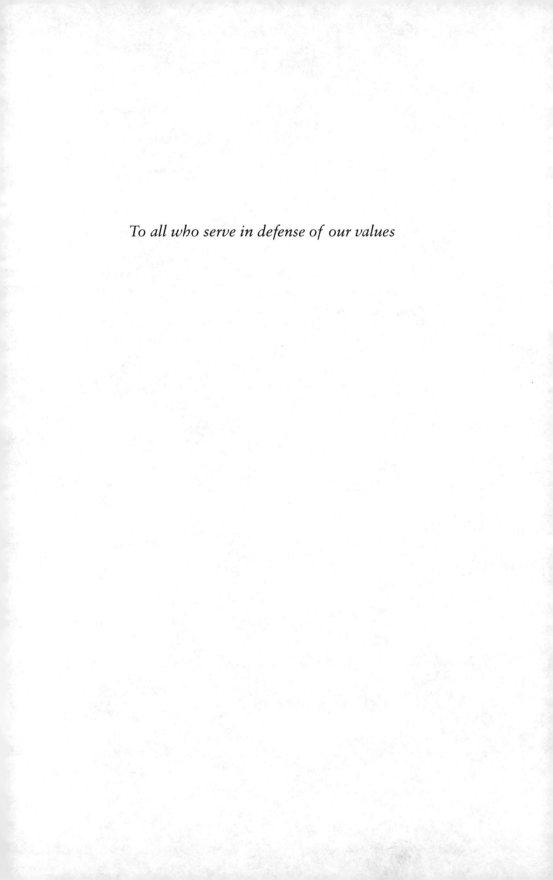

To all who serve in defense of our values

CONTENTS

PROLOGUE

In late November 2016, I was enjoying Thanksgiving break in my hometown on the Columbia River in Washington State when I received an unexpected call from Vice President–elect Pence. Would I meet with President-elect Trump to discuss the job of Secretary of Defense of the United States? I had taken no part in the election campaign and had never met or spoken to Mr. Trump, so to say that I was surprised is an understatement. Further, I knew that, absent a congressional waiver, federal law prohibited a former military officer from serving as Secretary of Defense within seven years of departing military service. Given that no waiver had been authorized since General George Marshall was made secretary in 1950, and I'd been out for only three and a half years, I doubted I was a viable candidate. Nonetheless, I flew to Bedminster, New Jersey, for the interview.

I had time on the cross-country flight to ponder how to encapsulate my view of America's role in the world. On my flight out of Denver, the flight attendant's standard safety briefing caught my attention: *If cabin pressure is lost, masks will drop. . . . Put your own mask on first, then help others around you. . . .* We've all heard it many times, but in that moment, these familiar words seemed like a metaphor: to preserve our leadership role, we needed to get our own country's act together first, especially if we were to help others.

The next day I was driven to the Trump National Golf Club

and, entering a side door, waited about twenty minutes before I was ushered into a modest conference room. I was introduced to the President-elect, the Vice President–elect, the chief of staff, and a handful of others. We talked about the state of our military, where our views aligned and where they differed. In our forty-minute conversation, Mr. Trump led the wide-ranging discussion, and the tone was amiable. Afterward, the President-elect escorted me out to the front steps of the colonnaded clubhouse, where the press was gathered. I assumed that I would be on my way back to Stanford University's Hoover Institution, where I'd spent the past few years doing research and guest lecturing around the country, and was greatly enjoying my time. I figured that my strong support of NATO and my dismissal of the use of torture on prisoners would have the President-elect looking for another candidate. Standing beside him on the steps as photographers snapped away and shouted questions, I was surprised for the second time that week when he characterized me to the reporters as "the real deal." Days later, I was formally nominated. That was when I realized that, subject to a congressional waiver and Senate consent, I would not be returning to Stanford's beautiful, vibrant campus.

During the interview, Mr. Trump had asked me if I could do the job of Secretary of Defense. I said I could. I'd never aspired to the job, and took the opportunity to suggest several other candidates I thought highly capable of leading our defense. Still, having been raised by the Greatest Generation, by two parents who had served in World War II, and subsequently shaped by more than four decades in the Marine Corps, I considered government service to be both honor and duty. In my view, when the President asks you to do something, you don't play Hamlet on the wall, wringing your hands. To quote a great American athletic company's slogan, you "just do it." So long as you are prepared, you say yes.

When it comes to the defense of our experiment in democracy and our way of life, ideology should have nothing to do with it. Whether asked to serve by a Democrat or a Republican, you serve. "Politics ends at the water's edge." This ethos has shaped and defined me, and I wasn't going to betray it no matter how much I was enjoying my life west of the Rockies and spending time with a family I had neglected during my forty-plus years in the Marines.

When I said I could do the job, I meant I felt prepared. By happenstance, I knew the job intimately. In the late 1990s, I had served as the executive secretary to two Secretaries of Defense, William Perry and William Cohen. I had also served as the senior military assistant to Deputy Secretary of Defense Rudy de Leon. In close quarters, I had gained a personal grasp of the immensity and gravity of a "SecDef's" responsibilities. The job is tough: our first Secretary of Defense committed suicide, and few have emerged from the job unscathed, either legally or politically.

We were at war, amid the longest continuous stretch of armed conflict in our nation's history. I'd signed enough letters to next of kin about the death of a loved one to understand the consequential aspects of leading a department on a war footing when the rest of the country was not. Its millions of devoted troops and civilians spread around the world carried out their mission with a budget larger than the gross domestic products of all but two dozen nations. On a personal level, I had no great desire to return to Washington, D.C. I drew no energy from the turmoil and politics that animate our capital. Yet I didn't feel inundated by the job's immensities. I also felt confident that I could gain bipartisan support for Defense despite the political fratricide practiced in Washington.

In late December, I flew into Washington, D.C., to begin the Senate confirmation process.

This book is about how my career in the Marines brought me to this moment and prepared me to say yes to a job of this magnitude. The Marines teach you, above all, how to adapt, improvise, and overcome. But they expect you to have done your homework, to have mastered your profession. Amateur performance is anathema, and the Marines are bluntly critical of falling short, satisfied only with 100 percent effort and commitment. Yet over the course of my career, every time I made a mistake—and I made many—the Marines promoted me. They recognized that those mistakes were part of my tuition and a necessary bridge to learning how to do things right. Year in and year out, the Marines had trained me in skills they knew I needed, while educating me to deal with the unexpected.

Beneath its Prussian exterior of short haircuts, crisp uniforms, and exacting standards, the Corps nurtured some of the strangest mavericks and most original thinkers I would encounter in my journey through multiple commands, dozens of countries, and many college campuses. The Marines' military excellence does not suffocate intellectual freedom or substitute regimented thinking for imaginative solutions. They know their doctrine, often derived from lessons learned in combat and written in blood, but refuse to let that turn into dogma. Woe to the unimaginative one who, in after-action reviews, takes refuge in doctrine. The critiques in the field, in the classroom, or at happy hour are blunt for good reason. Personal sensitivities are irrelevant. No effort is made to ease you through your midlife crisis when peers, seniors, or subordinates offer more cunning or historically proven options, even when out of step with doctrine.

In any organization, it's all about selecting the right team. The two qualities I was taught to value most in selecting others for promotion or critical roles were initiative and aggressiveness. I looked for those hallmarks in those I served alongside. Institutions get the behaviors they reward. Marines have no institutional confusion about their mission: they are a ready naval force designed to fight well in any clime or place, then return to their own society as better citizens. That ethos has created a force feared by foes and embraced by allies the world over, because the Marines reward initiative aggressively implemented.

During my monthlong preparation for the Senate confirmation hearings, I read many excellent intelligence briefings. I was struck by the degree to which our competitive military edge was eroding, including our technological advantage. We would have to focus on regaining the edge. I had been fighting terrorism in the Middle East during my last decade of military service. During that time and in the three years since I had left active duty, haphazard funding had significantly worsened the situation, doing more damage to our current and future military readiness than any enemy in the field.

I could see that the background drummed into me as a Marine would need to be adapted to fit my role as a civilian secretary. The formulation of policy—from defining the main threats to our country to adapting the military's education, budget, and selection of leaders to address the swiftly changing character of war—would place new demands on me. It now became even more clear to me why the Marines assign an expanded reading list to everyone promoted to a new rank: that reading gives historical depth that lights the path ahead. Slowly but surely, we learned there was nothing new under the sun: properly informed, we weren't victims—we could always create options.

Habits ingrained in me over decades of immersion in tactics, operations, and strategy, in successes and setbacks, in allied and political circles, and in dealing with human factors, guided by the Marine Corps's insistence that we study (vice just read) history, paid off. When I left active duty, I was reminded that I'd been fortunate in being allowed to serve so long, and fortunate in being in the right place at the right time on what had been an adventurous career path. When I told the President-elect I could do the job, I knew that those decades of study and watching the competent and incompetent deal with issues similar to what I'd face would greatly inform my work.

Looking back, some things are clear: the required reading that expanded with every rank, the coaches and mentors imposing their demanding standards, the Marine Corps emphasis on adaptation, team building, and critical thinking, and my years at sea and on foreign shores had all been preparation for this job, even if I'd never sought it. Fate, Providence, or the chance assignments of a military career had me as ready as I could be when tapped on the shoulder. Without arrogance or ignorance, I could answer yes when asked to serve one more time. While I intended to serve the full four years, I resigned at the halfway point. That is how my public service ended; now I will tell you how it began.

My purpose in writing this book is to convey the lessons I learned for those who might benefit, whether in the military or in civilian life. I have been fortunate that the American people funded my forty years of education, and some of the lessons I learned might prove helpful to others. I'm old-fashioned: I don't write about sitting Presidents. In the chapters that follow, I will pass on what prepared me for challenges I could not anticipate, not take up the hot political rhetoric of our day. I remain a steward of the public trust.

The book is structured in three parts: Direct Leadership, Executive Leadership, and Strategic Leadership. In the first part, I will describe my formative years growing up and then in the Corps, where the Vietnam generation of Marines "raised" me and where I first led Marines into battle. This was a time of direct, face-to-face leadership, when, alongside those I led, I had a personal, often intense bond with troops I frequently knew better than my own brothers.

In the second part, I will describe the broadening tours in executive leadership, when I was commanding a force of 7,000 to 42,000 troops and it was no longer possible to know the name of every one of my charges. I had to adapt my leadership style to best ensure that my intent and concern, filtered through layers of command below, were felt and understood by the youngest sailors on the deck plates and the most junior soldiers in the field, where I would seldom see them.

Finally, in the third section, I will delve into the challenges and techniques at the strategic level. I will address civilian-military interaction from a senior military officer's perspective, where military leaders must try to reconcile war's grim realities with political leaders' human aspirations, and where complexity reigns and the consequences of imprudence are severe, even catastrophic.

The habit of continuing to learn and adapt came with me when I joined the administration as a member of the cabinet, where my portfolio exceeded my former military role. Yet at the end of the day, driving me to do my best were the veterans of past wars I felt watching me, and the humbling honor of serving my nation by leading those staunch and faithful patriots who looked past Washington's political vicissitudes and volunteered to put their lives on the line to defend the Constitution and the American people.

Much of what I carried with me was summed up in a handwritten card that lay on my Pentagon desk these past few years, the desk where I signed deployment orders sending troops overseas. It read, "Will this commitment contribute sufficiently to the well-being of the American people to justify putting our troops in a position to die?" I would like to think that, thanks to the lessons I was taught, the answer to the Gold Star families of those we lost is "yes," despite the everlasting pain those families carry with them.

PART I

DIRECT LEADERSHIP

CHAPTER 1

A Carefree Youth
Joins the
Disciplined Marines

Like most twenty-year-olds, I thought I was invulnerable. Then, on a steep ridge in eastern Washington, in the winter of 1971, I fell toward my death. I was looking at the tiny figures of workers on a dam far below when my foot slipped and I plunged down an icy sheet toward the Columbia River. I threw my body back to avoid pitching headlong into space, sliding on my back down the steep slope. I tried to dig in my heels, but my boots slid off the rocks. My pack tore loose as I accelerated down the slope. I had a Ka-Bar in my belt, a fighting knife given to me by a Marine veteran. I pulled it and stabbed at the sheet ice, only to find it torn from my hands. I kept sliding, picking up speed. I twisted over and frantically clawed and scratched. But I wasn't slowing down.

I bounced off a big rock and tumbled sideways, slamming into a boulder that broke my fall. When I came to, I was bleeding from my nose, but not from my ears, and I wasn't vomiting, so I knew my skull wasn't fractured. I lay there, testing various body parts. My ribs ached when I breathed, but I could flex my arms and legs. I hadn't impaled myself.

I was lucky, and it certainly wasn't my alpine skills that had saved me. It took me a few hours of slipping and sliding to make it to a rocky ravine and down the slope. A worker saw me hobbling along and gave me a lift across the Priest Rapids Dam. He offered to drive me the forty miles back to my home.

"I appreciate it," I said, "but I'd like to heal up a bit first."

He gave me an understanding look. A working man, he was outdoors every day. He knew the type. If I chose to take my time before returning home, that was my business.

I camped for two days, waiting for the bruising to go down. During the day I was flat on my back with nothing to do but admire the sleet on the sagebrush. At night I dozed more than slept. With bruised, probably cracked ribs, each time I rolled over I was jolted wide awake.

The summer before, I had gone through the rigors of Marine Officer Candidates School. I remembered what one tough sergeant told us. Years earlier, his platoon had to take a hill under fire. Everyone was nervous; the North Vietnamese knew how to shoot. He told us how his platoon commander had settled them down.

"We don't get to choose when we die," he said. "But we do choose how we meet death."

My fall on the ice had driven home to me that I wanted to spend my career among men like that: men who dealt with life as it came at them, who were more interested in living life fully than in their own longevity. I didn't care about making money. I wanted to be outdoors—and in the company of adventurous people. For me, the Marines had the right spirit and the right way of looking at life. My fall would serve as a metaphor for my subsequent career in the Marines: You make mistakes, or life knocks you down; either way, you get up and get on with it. You deal with life. You don't whine about it.

I grew up in Richland, Washington. Back in the 1940s, it was a dusty farming community of a couple hundred on the Columbia River. During World War II, the Army Corps of Engineers brought the emerging nuclear age, harnessing the Columbia's hydroelectric power to build the Hanford reactors. It was part of the Manhattan Project, the race to build the atomic bomb. In the process, Richland became a solidly middle-class town, without enclaves of wealth or poverty. Our community of seventeen thousand engineers, technicians, construction workers, and merchants had been shaped by the trials of the Depression and World War II—hardworking, civic-minded, family-oriented, and patriotic. Nobody threw their weight around. Years later, I read the epitaph on Jackie Robinson's tombstone: "A life is not important except in its impact on other lives." That sentiment captured the credo of the generation that raised me.

My dad was a seafarer, a chief engineer in the Merchant Marine who had sailed to dozens of countries in the 1930s and '40s. My mother, valedictorian of her high school class and daughter of a Canadian immigrant family, served as a civilian in U.S. Army intelligence in Washington, D.C., and Pretoria during World War II. She met my dad aboard ship on her way to Africa. They introduced their three sons to the free competition of ideas, a world not to be feared but to be explored. Their curiosity about life guides me to this day.

Growing up, I loved the freedom I had. Between family camping trips in the mountains and hunting rabbits with my .22, accompanied by my dog Nikki or friends, I had my family's full permission to wander the great outdoors. How many parents would drive their teenager to the highway outside town so that he could hitchhike across the West?

I never enjoyed sitting in classrooms. I could read on my own at a much faster rate. Instead of a television, at home we had a well-stocked home library. I devoured books—*Treasure Island, Captains Courageous, The Last of the Mohicans, The Call of the Wild, The Swiss Family Robinson.* . . . Hemingway was my favorite author, followed closely by Faulkner and Fitzgerald. Reading about the Lewis and Clark expedition, I was fascinated that they had canoed on the Columbia River and had passed through our neighborhood.

I had started hitchhiking in 1964, when I was thirteen. I had an insatiable penchant to see what was out there. The highways provided a means of exploring far beyond the backcountry of the Cascades. My parents had no problem with my forays. It was a simpler time back then, with a stronger sense of trust in one's fellow Americans. I wandered across a wide swath of the western United States, enjoying the rough and ready life. I was in good shape, accustomed to sleeping outdoors, and equally curious about books, people, and open country.

Like anyone who has wandered far and wide, I got into a fair number of scrapes. In Montana, I tangled with three local boys. I was getting the worst of it when a tall sheriff wearing a silver star and a white cowboy hat showed up in a pickup—a figure right out of the movies. He gave me a jail cell and early the next morning drove me to the rail yard to hop an eastbound freight.

"Three against one," he said. "Tough to win against those odds."

At Central Washington State College in 1968, I was a mediocre student with a partying attitude. After I caroused too much one night, the local judge ordered me to spend weekends in jail—punishment for underage drinking.

One inmate, Porter Wagner (not the famous singer), had jumped bail in Maryland. One Saturday night he saw me hoisting myself up to look out the barred window, eager to see what I was missing outside.

"What do you see, Jimmy?" he said, lying back on his bunk.

"A muddy parking lot."

"From down here, I see stars in the night sky," he said. "It's your choice. You can look at stars or mud."

He was in jail, but his spirit wasn't. From that wayward philosopher I learned that no matter what happened, I wasn't a victim; I made my own choices how to respond. You don't always control your circumstances, but you can always control your response. The next day I volunteered to sweep the jail, wash police cars, and pick up food at the local restaurant for the other prisoners so I could change my circumstances as fast as possible, getting a day and a half of credit for each day served.

I was spending summers in officer candidate training in Quantico, Virginia, and loved the challenge of that environment. We were evaluated and molded by corporals and sergeants fresh from Vietnam battlefields, determined that we aspiring lieutenants would make good officers—or be sent home. Those sergeants never accepted that we were giving our best effort; rather, they always pushed us to do more. Either you kept up with them on the steep, muddy hill trails, completed the obstacle course in the allotted time, and qualified on the rifle range or you went home. They dangled airline tickets home to entice us to quit, to take the easy way out. In Vietnam, Marines were dying while we were training. Trying didn't count; you had to deliver. Well over half the class got screened out over the course of two sweltering summers.

In early 1972, after a little over three years in college, I was commissioned as a second lieutenant in the Marines. My first stop was seven months at Basic School in Quantico. Unique among the four services, every Marine officer is initially trained as an infantry officer. He will later attend other schools to become a pilot, a logistician, or what have you. But all officers begin their service together, learning the same set of basic skills and being shaped into one culture. Every Marine is first and foremost a rifleman and must qualify on the rifle range. Lieutenants learn that everything they will go on to do in the Corps, no matter the rank or the job, relates back to the private who is attacking the enemy. This initiation and common socialization has a strong impact on the Marine Corps, permeating every facet of its warfighting ethos.

Later that year I was sent to Okinawa to join my first infantry unit. I was lucky: I had joined the 2nd Battalion, 4th Marine Regiment, where most of the key leaders had spent years fighting in rice paddies, mountains, and jungles. They knew their stuff. Far from being standoffish because they had seen combat, they were tough and friendly, and they readily shared their combat knowledge. I didn't have to earn their support; it was mine to lose, not to gain.

At the same time, each of us was establishing an individual professional reputation. Whether you stayed in the Corps for four years or forty, that reputation would follow you: Were you physically fit? Were you tactically sound? Could you call in artillery fire? Could you adapt quickly to change? Did your platoon respond to you? Could you lead by example? You had to be as tough as your troops, who weren't concerned with how many books you'd read. I tried to work out with the most physically fit and learn from the most tactically cunning.

The early seventies were a disruptive time in American history, with riots, political chicanery, and a divisive war. The military wasn't isolated from this unrest in society. As the draft ended, our unpopular military ranks included an increasing number of dropouts and petty criminals. Racial tension, disobedience, and drug use caused disruption and division in the ranks. So we had our fair share of racists and druggies. They would try to infect others. If a junior officer didn't lead by firmly displaying force of personality, that number would grow. Due to war casualties and a barracks environment that drove too many good men out of the Corps, my platoon initially numbered only twenty-six. My platoon sergeant was twenty-one-year-old Corporal Wayne Johnson, an immigrant from British Guyana nicknamed "John Wayne." With only three years in the Corps, all overseas, he was doing the job designated for a staff sergeant who had ten years' training and experience. He tolerated no guff or slackness from his teenage charges.

"Lieutenant," Corporal Johnson told me, "you have to be harder than petrified woodpecker's lips." He reiterated that some in the platoon weren't up to Marine standards and that if I wanted my troops to follow me, I had to be as tough as my toughest men. At one point, I was out in the jungle with my platoon. We had been pushing hard for several days, sweaty, stinking, sleep-deprived, exhausted—the usual fare for grunts. One guy, the biggest malcontent in the platoon, muttered that he'd like to kill his "fucking hard-ass lieutenant." When Corporal Johnson brought him over to me, I decided he wasn't going to ruin the trust in our tight-knit platoon. I told him to follow me back through the jungle to the company command post. At the end of the hike, I told him that he could have shot me in the back. But he didn't have the guts.

I could have written up formal charges. Instead I took him to First Sergeant Mata, the senior NCO (noncommissioned officer) in our company. As a second lieutenant, I outranked him, but that was only a formality. The company first sergeant guided us young officers. He told me to return to my platoon—he would take care of the matter.

"That shitbird," he said a few days later, "is no longer in our Corps, Lieutenant."

Boom. The man was gone. Packed up and shipped out. Every lieutenant needs a First Sergeant Mata, a man with twenty-five years of experience and a hundred friends at other duty stations. Where did the malcontent go? Who cared; he was out. He was representative of the challenges junior officers faced in those days, and such summary dismissals of bad actors were necessary for dealing with the turbulent times. The Marine Corps would not lower its standards. Called "expeditious discharge," it was a critical policy set for a time that, happily, is in our distant past.

Thanks to first sergeants like Mata, and a young battalion commander who would one day become Commandant of the Marine Corps, in our battalion the number of bottom-feeders rapidly decreased in number and in influence. Fence-sitters quickly got the message and straightened up. Why? Because there are few fates worse than public rejection and summary dismissal. Everyone needs a friend, a purpose, and a chance to belong to something greater than themselves. No one wants to be cast aside as worthless.

As a naval force, the Marines are organized to embark on Navy ships for landings on hostile shores. We would embark with only a forty-pound seabag and our combat gear and live out of that for months at a time. We lived a physically demanding life that created a rough good humor among us. I grew to know my 180 men as well as I knew my brothers back home. We would run countless laps on the flight deck when we weren't practicing amphibious landings. We read everything from *Starship Troopers* to *The Battle of Okinawa*. We would blow off steam and weeks of pay during a couple of rambunctious days ashore in Hong Kong, Seoul, Singapore, Manila, and a dozen other cities, sometimes to the chagrin of our commanders. And what I learned about the complexities of amphibious operations on numerous shipboard deployments in the Pacific and Indian Oceans would pay off enormously in the future.

In my first dozen years in the Marines, I commanded two platoons and two companies, deploying to thirteen countries on a half dozen ships. Everywhere we sailed, at every landing and every exercise in foreign countries, I was introduced to the enormous value of allies. In Korea, their marines served as my advisers and proved their toughness in the freezing hills. The New Zealand force in Malaysia demonstrated their Maori warrior spirit and taught us jungle warfare, just as the Philippine troops did on their islands. The high-spirited, competent Australians and the quietly competent Japanese Self-Defense Force troops showed us different but effective fighting styles. These and more showed me the irreplaceable benefit of learning from others.

The Vietnam veterans taught me that you don't win firefights by being kind. In the Vietnam jungles, the enemy tactic was to sneak as close as possible to Marine lines so that we couldn't employ our indirect fires. In response, the Marines became skilled at registering fire sacks—identifying critical terrain features to be struck. With a simple code word, a series of shells would unleash hell on the enemy.

To give an example of the mentoring I received as a young officer, one of our company commanders, Andy Finlayson, tutored me in the fine art of fire support. On a live-fire range in the Philippines, he rehearsed with me how to employ a series of artillery strikes, bringing them ever closer to our position. I tried to reciprocate Andy's faith in me by reading the books he recommended, including *Lee's Lieutenants,* by Douglas Freeman, and Liddell Hart's *Strategy.* He urged me to expand my horizons, and I adopted that same mentoring technique throughout my career.

On the final day of our training, I expected Andy to control the artillery fires. Nope. He left me alone to control the artillery, mortar, and machine guns as the troops advanced. I had one mortar series plotted to land two hundred yards to the front of the troops. I was sure the coordinates and timing were correct, so I spoke the code word and the shells slammed in. The earth shook as a parallel sheaf of 81mm shells impacted and the troops continued advancing. Andy nodded and walked away. I got the message: Have faith in your subordinates after you have trained them.

Ever since, I've tried to ingrain in generations of Marines the effective employment of supporting arms. You don't send a grunt with a rifle when a five-hundred-pound bomb will do the job. Firepower brings to bear America's awesome technologies, giving our grunts a decided edge. Coupled with the power of the junior officers' expectations, confidence that their leader knows his job and won't waste their lives is key to gaining full commitment from our troops. The resulting attitude of confidence is the strongest weapon available to us.

Six years later, Andy and I were serving together in a battalion out of Hawaii. We were on board amphibious ships in the Indian Ocean, sent there by President Carter after the Soviets moved into Afghanistan. At the same time, Iran was holding captive fifty-two members of the American embassy staff in Tehran. A commando team was about to launch a rescue attempt, and our mission was to distract the Iranians and react to any other contingency. We could divert the attention of the Iranian military by seizing something critical to them.

Our battalion designed an amphibious assault to seize a large Iranian facility. This was supposed to be a feint. But after we refined and rehearsed the plan, we were confident that we would defeat the several thousand Iranian soldiers guarding the facility. Although we'd be outnumbered, we were trained shock troops with the advantage of surprise. Our carrier-based fighters and naval guns would stun the defenders, and then we would overrun them. That may sound presumptuous, but history is filled with examples— like Stonewall Jackson in the Shenandoah Valley—where audacity coupled with sound planning has prevailed over numbers. The rescue mission ultimately failed to reach Tehran, and we were never given the signal to launch, which I regret—the Iranian zealots needed a lesson in humility.

I chose to find a home among warriors because I was drawn in by the cocky, exuberant, devil-may-care spirit of grunts. I loved being with the troops, gaining energy from their infectious, often sardonic enthusiasms. We were all volunteers, and patriotism was found more in our DNA than in our words; most of us hadn't signed up because of a national cause. We seldom felt our country was united behind us on a war footing, and we identified principally with one another. We shared what F. Scott Fitzgerald called "riotous excursions with privileged glimpses into the human heart." I never committed for the long term. My aims were modest. I thought, *Maybe I'll make captain*. It freed me up to not worry about my next command and focus instead on doing the best job I could in the one I had. Each week in the Fleet Marine Force was considered the last week of peace. As a gunnery sergeant put it, "Be ready. Next week we'll be in a fight."

My early years with my Marines taught me leadership fundamentals, summed up in the three Cs.

The first is *competence*. Be brilliant in the basics. Don't dabble in your job; you must master it. That applies at every level as you advance. Analyze yourself. Identify weaknesses and improve yourself. If you're not running three miles in eighteen minutes, work out more; if you're not a good listener, discipline yourself; if you're not swift at calling in artillery fire, rehearse. Your troops are counting on you. Of course you'll screw up sometimes; don't dwell on that. The last perfect man on earth died on a cross long ago—just be honest and move on, smarter for what your mistake taught you.

Battles, conventional or irregular, turn on the basics of gaining fire superiority and maneuvering against the enemy. Fire and maneuver—block and tackle—decide battle. The Corps exists to win battles. That is inseparable from making Marines who stand for its values in tough times. Anything that doesn't contribute to winning battles or winning Marines is of secondary importance. Regrettably, too many of the men I've seen killed or wounded failed to perform the basics. War is fraught with random dangers and careless missteps. Clear orders and relentless rehearsals based on intelligence and repetitive training build muscle—not once or twice, but hundreds of times. Read history, but study a few battles in depth. Learning from others' mistakes is far smarter than putting your own lads in body bags.

Physical strength, endurance, calling in fire, map reading, verbal clarity, tactical cunning, use of micro-terrain—all are necessary. You must master and integrate them to gain the confidence of your troops. A good map-reading lieutenant is worthless if he can't do pull-ups.

Second, *caring*. To quote Teddy Roosevelt, "Nobody cares how much you know, until they know how much you care." In a family, you watch out for your younger brother. You're interested in him—how he grows, how he learns, who he wants to be. When your Marines know you care about them, then you can speak bluntly when they disappoint you. They are young, but they did volunteer for the Marines, so don't patronize them. They know they're not in a life insurance company. Be honest in your criticism, but blow away the bad behavior while leaving their manhood intact.

Show no favoritism. Value initiative and aggressiveness above all. It's easier to pull the reins back than to push a timid soul forward. Consistently maintain a social and personal distance, remembering that there is a line you must not cross. But you should come as close to that line as possible—without surrendering one ounce of your authority. You are not their friend. You are their coach and commander, rewarding the qualities essential to battle-field victory.

You get to know them as individuals—what makes them tick and what their specific goals are. One is striving to make corporal, another needs a letter of recommendation for college, another is determined to break eighteen minutes for three miles. A Marine knows when you are invested in his character, his dreams, and his development. Men like that won't quit on you.

Third, *conviction*. This is harder and deeper than physical courage. Your peers are the first to know what you will stand for and, more important, what you won't stand for. Your troops catch on fast. State your flat-ass rules and stick to them. They shouldn't come as a surprise to anyone. At the same time, leaven your professional passion with personal humility and compassion for your troops. Remember: As an officer, you need to win only one battle—for the hearts of your troops. Win their hearts and they will win the fights.

Competence, caring, and conviction combine to form a fundamental element—shaping the fighting spirit of your troops. Leadership means reaching the souls of your troops, instilling a sense of commitment and purpose in the face of challenges so severe that they cannot be put into words.

After several years of commanding small units, I had a good sense of what the Marine Corps expected of me. Whether in a command billet or a staff job, I was operating inside an organization of mission-oriented sailors and Marines who were straightforward in describing the tasks that would be done. How the mission was to be accomplished was left up to me, but it was clear that I was to deliver results.

I spent many months in the seventies and early eighties on amphibious ships in the Pacific and Indian Oceans. When crises arose, American naval task forces were placed on alert and sailed to the region of unrest. That was what first propelled me into Middle Eastern waters in 1979. With the intelligence officers providing in-depth briefings, I had a ringside seat from which to observe how quickly flashpoints spread across this increasingly violent arena.

Much of the security challenge we deal with today grew out of 1979. That year, a radical Sunni splinter group seized the Grand Mosque in Mecca, Saudi Arabia, Islam's holiest site. In a battle that unnerved the Muslim world, hundreds were killed before the group was eradicated. Ayatollah Khomeini's revolutionary regime took hold in Iran by ousting the Shah and swearing hostility against the United States. That same year, the Soviet Union was pouring troops into Afghanistan to prop up a pro-Russian government that was opposed by Sunni Islamist fundamentalists and tribal factions. The United States was supporting Saudi Arabia's involvement in forming a counterweight to Soviet influence. The reverberations of these cataclysmic events were swiftly felt: within a year, Iraq's President, Saddam Hussein, had launched an inconclusive eight-year war against Iran that would claim nearly a million lives.

The reverberations of that tumultuous year continue to be felt today. As a young infantry officer sailing back to Pearl Harbor from the North Arabian Sea, I didn't know then that these tectonic shifts would define my next forty years.

CHAPTER 2

Recruit for Attitude, Train for Skill

IF YOU WANT AN ELITE FORCE, selection is critical. Like any organization, the Marine Corps has to recruit to get the talent it needs. In the mid-1970s, I served the first of two tours on recruiting duty.

In the post-Vietnam environment, after the draft went away, it wasn't easy convincing a young man to devote years to the Marine Corps. In those fractious times, the Corps had taken in too many dropouts and criminals exempted from jail by judges who thought a stint in the Marines would straighten them out. By my second tour of recruiting, recognizing that we could be only as good as the raw material we brought in, we began sending only our most competitive NCOs as our recruiters—infantrymen, artillery, aviation technicians, tank crewmen, etc. Our best were charged with bringing in the best they could find.

The Marine philosophy is to recruit for attitude and train for skills. Marines believe that attitude is a weapon system. We searched for intangible character traits: a quest for adventure, a desire to serve with the elite, and the intention to be in top physical condition. The strenuous task of the recruiter was to find young men and women with the right stuff to send to boot camp. There, the drill instructors worked their magic to turn recruits into Marines.

I found that each recruiter had moved his family to a faraway town, where he usually worked alone or with several others in small teams spread across the country. Every day, he had to reassure some mother that the Marine Corps was the right organization for her son, or persuade a counselor with grave reservations about the Marines to let him talk to his or her students. Every night, he brought his work home, answering phone calls from anxious parents. He worked long hours and experienced frequent frustrations, not the least being hostile faculty. Alongside my recruiters, I learned the art of persuasion, creating common ground where none seemed to exist and gaining the confidence of a young person terrified of the legendary Marine drill instructor.

In the mid-1980s, when I was brought back to command a recruiting station that covered Oregon, Idaho, and part of Washington, plus eventually Hawaii and Guam, my station was near the bottom among the eight recruiting stations on the West Coast. In a brief meeting with my commanding officer, he made it clear that I was expected to turn things around—to "get things going," as he said. I welcomed the challenge. From my hitchhiking days, I knew they were out there: the young, high-spirited, cocky, and often rebellious ones whom the Marine spirit would appeal to.

As I was walking out of that meeting, I met the operations officer.

"Lieutenant," I said, "give me the address of each recruiter's office."

I was taking command of a platoon of overachievers—NCOs with six to twenty-eight years of service. They had done well in their previous jobs, and now they were literally out on their own. In the next two weeks, I drove and flew more than two thousand miles, meeting individually with each of the thirty-eight NCOs, who worked in various towns. My message was simple.

"You and I," I said to each recruiter, "have a clear goal: four recruits a month who can graduate from boot camp. Anything you need from me, I'll get you. We will succeed as a team, with all hands pulling their weight."

I had learned in the fleet that in harmonious, effective units, everyone owns the unit mission. If you as the commander define the mission as your responsibility, you have already failed. It was *our* mission, never *my* mission. The thirty-eight recruiters were my subordinate commanders. "Command and control," the phrase so commonly used to describe leadership inside and outside the military, is inaccurate. In the Corps, I was taught to use the concept of "command and feedback." You don't control your subordinate commanders' every move; you clearly state your intent and unleash their initiative. Then, when the inevitable obstacles or challenges arise, with good feedback loops and relevant data displays, you hear about it and move to deal with the obstacle. Based on feedback, you fix the problem. George Washington, leading a revolutionary army, followed a "listen, learn, and help, then lead," sequence. I found that what worked for George Washington worked for me.

It's all about clear goals and effective coaching. At the Portland headquarters, I was blessed with two first-rate young officers. My twenty-four-year-old operations officer was action-oriented and sharp enough to do my job. With the small headquarters staff implementing my intent and orchestrating the team according to my vision, I spent most of every month out coaching my recruiters. I traveled so much that hotel desk clerks from Pocatello, Idaho, to Honolulu called me by my first name.

Headquarters Marine Corps had issued a strict set of selection standards that usually worked. It allowed for case-by-case waivers for a few who, like me, had had a run-in with the law or some other infraction. In one case soon after I arrived, my staff turned down the request for a young man who had been arrested for a single use of cocaine. The recruiting sergeant was convinced it was a one-time mistake in judgment.

The judge who sent me to jail as a nineteen-year-old taught me a lesson, but he didn't ruin my future. There's a huge difference between making a mistake and letting that mistake define you, carrying a bad attitude through life. When I was informed about the rejection for a waiver, I called in my staff.

"Look," I said, "the sergeant on-scene endorsed that young man. He sees character in that guy. Unless you know something the recruiter is missing, your duty is to advocate so that headquarters grants the waiver." That recruiter was on the line to see that recruit graduate from boot camp. The recruit was accepted and proudly became a Marine.

In return for eighty-hour workweeks, the recruiter had to believe that his success in recruiting people who graduated would advance his career. A written fitness report on each sergeant—an assessment of his or her performance and potential for promotion—

was then required twice a year. Computers and word-processing apps were in their infancy in 1985. To submit seventy-six "fitreps," it was tempting to fall back on a standard template to fill in the blanks. "Shows initiative," "consistently works hard," "does an excellent job," etc. With specially selected recruiters working extraordinary hours, I wanted to write fitness reports that would break them out from the pack.

With the help of my officers, a thesaurus, and caffeine, we chipped and hammered sentence after sentence until each fitrep reflected the individual personality and his accomplishments. Keeping in mind that the evaluator at the other end had never met this particular sergeant, I strove to describe each Marine accurately as an individual, the same way any of us would want to be evaluated. If we wanted ethical recruiting of top-notch applicants, I had to make sure that those who gave 100 percent to the mission received the promotions their commitment earned.

It wasn't all smooth sailing. Early on, one recruiter walked into my office and said, "Sir, I'm not going to do this. I'm not going to work these hours."

His words and attitude had made the rounds. One of my seasoned gunnery sergeants had told me, "The whole station is watching how you handle this, Major."

I told the man, "You can be a quitter or you can be a Marine. But you can't be both." I busted him and ended his career.

Partial commitment changes everything—it reduces the sense that the mission comes first. From my first days, I had been taught that the Marines were satisfied only with 100 percent commitment from us and were completely dissatisfied with 99 percent. You can't have an elite organization if you look the other way when someone craps out on you.

The bottom line was that I learned to hold everyone to the same standard. I told each recruiter, "If at any time you can't meet the quota, call and I'll send somebody to help you." Soon the team was hitting its stride, and for thirty-nine months it was rated the top recruiting station in the western district. Most of my recruiters received meritorious promotions or commendations. They had learned the art of persuasion, according to the Marine Corps training program for recruiters. They were able to find common ground, even with those high school teachers for whom anti-Vietnam sentiment had blossomed into anti-military attitudes. For me, the education I'd received in the skills of persuasive leadership would prove critical to my effectiveness.

Beyond that, for the rest of my career, I aggressively delegated tasks to the lowest capable level. I made sure missions were clearly understood. Ethics and honesty held everyone to the same standard. I grew comfortable delegating authority to people I saw only once or twice a month. Decision-making was decentralized. Thirty-eight junior and senior sergeants spread out over thousands of miles operated as a team without seeing one another. This showed me that this approach could unleash subordinate initiative in any organization.

Recruiting duty also introduced me to a useful paradox. On the one hand, success was quantitatively measurable. You couldn't fake it. Speaking crisply or having a tight haircut did not make a leader. Collectively, I and my thirty-eight sergeants had a monthly quota to make. It wasn't enough to deliver warm bodies. A recruiter was evaluated on the performance of his candidates. If he had a top graduate, the recruiter attended graduation to be publicly praised along with his recruit. But if his recruits failed, the recruiter's fitrep would reflect that. Because I was held to a rigorous quantitative standard, I learned to value clear output goals.

On the other hand, achieving those quantitative results depended upon qualitative skills that defied mere mathematical evaluation. I was the coach for those on the front lines, and I had to understand their problems, their strengths and weaknesses, and how they could improve. None of that was quantitative. Finally, I understood what President Eisenhower had passed on.

"I'll tell you what leadership is," he said. "It's persuasion and conciliation and education and patience. It's long, slow, tough work. That's the only kind of leadership I know."

CHAPTER 3

Battle

By 1990, I was a "totus porcus" (whole hog) Marine. While I hated some tasks that came with my jobs in the Corps, like crawling through minefields, I reveled in the camaraderie of men crawling through them with you, biting their lip the whole time. Before I knew it, I'd spent eighteen years deploying around the globe and reached the rank of lieutenant colonel, and, by early 1990, I was commanding the 1st Battalion of the 7th Marine Regiment, or 1/7.

This was a humbling assignment. In the military, unit legacies matter, and this battalion had a proud legacy indeed. The renowned Chesty Puller had commanded 1/7 in the epic World War II battle of Guadalcanal. In the Korean War, Ray Davis had earned the Medal of Honor leading my battalion in its critical fight at the "Frozen Chosin" Reservoir, freeing the 1st Marine Division from the Chinese Communist trap.

I was also energized because I was up to the job. I had been trained well by the Marines: between Quantico and my shipboard deployments, I had mastered fire-and-maneuver and amphibious operations—the fundamentals to a Marine officer. The Vietnam veteran whetstone had sharpened my edge and taught me how to build confidence in the men I led. In the preceding year I'd served under a uniquely capable combat leader, Colonel Carlton Fulford, so I understood the man above me. The day I took command on a windy parade deck at Twentynine Palms, California, I was eager to coach a new team, passing on the lessons I'd been taught.

The word *battalion* originated in the sixteenth century, derived from the Italian word for "battle," *battaglia*. The battalion is the last command where the leader has a face-to-face, direct relationship with the troops. It is large enough to fight for a sustained period on its own, and small enough to ensure a close relationship between the commander and the troops. Inside a nine-hundred-man battalion, the sergeants and officers know one another. A company commander will know every one of his 180 men. A battalion is so small and tightly meshed that, like a football or soccer team, it develops a distinct personality. This is called the command climate, and it reflects the tone set by the battalion commander, the sergeant major, the company commanders, and their first sergeants. Taken together, these men know the personalities, strengths, and weaknesses of every man in their battalion.

My battalion was under strength, numbering fewer than 500 instead of the normal 860-man complement. Although this was not what I expected, it was also an opportunity. I'd been taught an approach when I was a second lieutenant in command of a half-strength platoon. The battalion sergeant major told us lieutenants to focus on training the young Marines we had, not worry about the ones we didn't have. That way, we would have a cadre we could shape who could instruct the new recruits when they joined us. Now I was in command of an under-strength battalion in the desolate base of Twentynine Palms, California. There, I set about shaping a cadre.

Because a unit adopts the personality of its commander, just as a sports team adopts the personality of its coach, I made my expectation clear: I wanted a bias for action, and to bring out the initiative in all hands. I would make do with what I had, and not waste time whining about what I didn't have.

In the spring of 1990, we conducted two months of amphibious training in the eastern Pacific. In June, we returned to Twentynine Palms. There, in the Mojave Desert's blistering heat, we evaluated another battalion's mechanized training. Then we flew four hundred miles north to the remote Mountain Warfare Training Center, located among the ten-thousand-foot high peaks of the Sierras.

For four weeks, my squads hiked, rappelled, navigated, and competed against one another night and day. Our only distraction was the soaring, stunning scenery. We slept in tents or on the open ground, patrolled constantly, and climbed sheer cliffs, with not one day off, no television or phone calls. My primary objective in the demanding, unforgiving mountain terrain was to build small-unit leaders focused on brilliance in the basics. Small units of a dozen men operating together, facing conditions that demanded every ounce of physical strength, bred trust in one another. Day by day, I saw my squads physically harden, develop tighter bonds, and grow in confidence as we built from the ground up.

The isolation provided the ideal setting for me to learn the personalities of my Marines. My job was to know which leaders should be assigned to which tasks. What do I mean? Had Custer been one of my subordinate commanders, I wouldn't put him on point; I'd put him in trace—behind a more calculating commander—so I could unleash Custer's hell-for-leather style into a developed situation. After a month together, I knew the strengths and weaknesses of my company commanders. One, a former enlisted artillery observer in Vietnam, was mature and cool. I would use him as my reliable point man. Another had an active, even agitated mind. He thought of one thing even when talking about the next, the words tumbling out. I would employ his aggressiveness once the situation had sorted itself out. A third was quiet, authoritative and cunning. He would do well busting up an enemy position. I matched personalities to anticipated tasks, whether amphibious assault, mechanized war, or mountain fighting, because I had watched them in all three domains.

The Iraqi Army under the dictator Saddam Hussein invaded Kuwait in August 1990. Saddam claimed that Kuwait was a province of Iraq. Believing that no nation would come to the defense of tiny Kuwait, he intended to take over its rich oil fields, adding billions to his coffers. He misread America, believing we were indifferent. President George H. W. Bush spoke out strongly against the aggression, declaring, "This will not stand." While this was going on, I was in the backcountry of the Sierras, far away from any television news, concentrating on a three-day march to a dirt airstrip.

My regimental commander called at midnight. Colonel Carl Fulford was a Vietnam veteran. A true southern gentleman, firm yet unfailingly polite, he never had to raise his voice. He simply assumed you would meet his high standards. And you did—because you did not want to disappoint him. In the midst of one exercise, for instance, he told the battalion commander that he and all his officers had been killed. That required the sergeants to direct the live fires and seize the objectives. The exercise was a success and all officers in the regiment learned the lesson. It wasn't how well any one of us performed; our test was how well the unit functioned without us.

"Jim," Colonel Fulford said, "get your battalion back here."

"Sir," I said, "we're stepping off for a fifty-mile trek. I'll arrive on base in about four days."

There was silence on the phone as the colonel contemplated being saddled with the least astute battalion commander in the Marine Corps.

"I expect your advance party here by morning," he said. "Everyone else tomorrow. And you may want to read a newspaper. We're going to war."

I'd just received a blunt education about any unit commander's role as the sentinel for his unit: You cannot allow your unit to be caught flat-footed. Don't be myopically focused on your organization's internal workings. Leaders are expected to stay attuned to their higher headquarters' requirements. In the military, we exist to be prepared.

For me and my men, it was time to stand and deliver.

PREPARATIONS

A fellow battalion commander, Nick Pratt, was tasked with bringing me up to strength. He sent me his top 125 performers—squad leaders, snipers, and top-notch infantrymen who immediately filled our gaps. When you have to give up personnel, the tendency is to hang on to your best. Nick's example stuck with me: When tasked with supporting other units, select those you most hate to give up. Never advantage yourself at the expense of your comrades. Thanks to Nick's support, I was able to fill critical leadership gaps, reinforcements joining us literally on the way to the airport. Subsequently, when my unit was tasked with attaching an infantry company to a tank battalion, I sent my best.

Two weeks after leaving the Sierra Nevadas, my battalion was arrayed in the blistering, humid desert of Saudi Arabia. For five long months, the mission was to defend the kingdom in case the Iraqis attacked south out of Kuwait. We were superbly fit when we landed, but the suffocating heat and the constantly blowing sand in our eyes, noses, and mouths caused dysentery. It was crude living, without any creature comforts. Going over tactical plans, rehearsing and patrolling, we gradually ground down. I wasn't unique in losing twenty pounds.

In mid-November, the mission changed to forcing Saddam out of Kuwait. Our diplomats were sending the message *Get out.* If that didn't work, the alliance assembled by President Bush would shift to offense and throw out the Iraqi Army. The strategy was simple. After our air had bombed the Iraqi forces, our ground forces would attack. Two Marine divisions would charge straight north from Saudi Arabia into Kuwait, fixing the Iraqi Army in place. While the Iraqis fought us, U.S. Army and allied divisions would swing around to the west and deliver a knockout left hook against the exposed Republican Guard divisions on the Iraqi flank.

The 1st Marine Division had assigned our regiment the responsibility for breaking through the Iraqi forward defensive lines. Colonel Fulford organized the assault. My beefed-up battalion of 1,250 Marines, sailors, and Kuwaiti troops, mounted in Humvees and amphibious tracked vehicles and supported by eighteen tanks, would open corridors through two obstacle belts and associated minefields. Then we would overrun the front lines of the dug-in, armored enemy.

I chose my two most cunning captains to open parallel breaching lanes through which thousands of Marines would follow. Each captain's team had tanks, engineers, and infantry. I organized the battalion into thirteen elements, melding infantry platoons with tanks and organizing minefield-breaching and anti-armor teams. Once in the fight, I would not rearrange the organization. If a team bogged down or took heavy casualties, I would flank the enemy using another team. Strangers don't fight well together, and it's a precept with me not to reorganize in combat. I wanted the members of every team to know one another so well that they could predict each other's reactions.

Most of the troops would be buttoned up inside dark vehicles with no portholes and no glimpse of what was going on around them. In training, I saw my sergeants throwing rocks at the amtracs so that the Marines inside would grow accustomed to hearing shrapnel rattling off their vehicles. The assault element leaders peering out their hatches would decide how close they could get to the enemy before the vehicles became targets rather than protection. They would then drop the ramps for my young wolves to pile out and attack while our air and artillery pounded the enemy.

We planned our maneuvers every Sunday, rehearsed in the desert for six days, and refined the plan the next Sunday. It was a methodical rhythm as each week the blade got sharper. Colonel Fulford came by occasionally, but he ran on trust. He assumed your professionalism was equal to his. His quiet confidence and competence were infectious throughout the regiment, which was called Task Force Ripper. The Marine Corps is a general-purpose fighting force, but this time we would not be fighting on a beach or in a jungle. This would be the Marines' first mechanized assault against a fully dug-in, armored enemy. Fulford stressed one thing: *Do not bog down once in the attack. If one thing isn't working, change to another. Shift gears. Don't lose momentum. Improvise.* His message was simple: *Do it.* My fellow battalion commanders and I were absorbing the sure-footed spirit of this understated yet fierce warrior. Fulford left me confident that once the battle began, I wasn't expected to call back for instructions. Use your aggressive initiative according to his intent.

I and the assault element leaders practiced mechanized maneuvers until we could do them in our sleep. To save fuel and wear and tear on mechanized vehicles, the commanders would drive a handful of much lighter Humvees into the desert, where we'd spread out and talk over our tactical radio nets as if we were commanding our entire units. We worked out our command kinks without wasting the time of our subordinates, who were relentlessly rehearsing. I had the battalion break camp and move every few days so that everyone was accustomed to immediately reassembling in battle order, night or day.

I adapted a technique used by Roman legions, which built rectangular camps. I organized our camp (or laager) in a triangular shape so that every man knew where he fit. The triangle always pointed north toward the enemy. Day or night, regardless of where we made camp, everyone knew the exact locations of the mortar pits, the communications tent, the fuel compound, and his command element. We were oriented toward the enemy, so all hands could roll out in battle formation at a moment's notice. Having only a few night vision goggles and GPS sets, the compass was our navigation tool. We practiced night movement until our breaching techniques were second nature. Frequently, I had our air controllers run Marine jets over our laager site. When an F-18 roars over your head at five hundred miles an hour, you know what's going to happen to your enemy.

We continued this routine for months, sleeping on the ground without cots. At night we sat together like Horatio Nelson's lieutenants, arguing tactics by moving rocks to simulate units. Sitting on sand dunes, I pulled out books I carried in my rucksack that revealed how others had handled desert warfare. They allowed me to image chaos and what could go wrong.

On elaborate sand tables, some as large as football fields, every platoon commander and squad leader walked through his tasks. Covered by our air and artillery fire, our engineers explained how they would detonate explosives to open a path through the minefield. One lance corporal explained how, following the lead tanks, he would drive his armored bulldozer to cover the enemy trenches. All sergeants would keep their "bump plans," detailing which troops switch to another vehicle when one is knocked out. The infantry assault leaders described how they'd widen the breach in the enemy lines. The corpsmen and doctors described the medevac procedures to pull wounded Marines from knocked-out vehicles in the minefields. We rehearsed each drill and contingency ad nauseam, until my troops were glaring at me as if I thought they were idiots. We all knew one another's jobs so well that we could adapt to any surprise. My intent was to rehearse until we could improvise on the battlefield like a jazzman in New Orleans. This required a mastery of the instruments of war, just as a jazz musician masters his musical instrument.

Colonel Fulford took me aside during our Christmas Eve service. From the shadows we watched our troops singing Christmas carols, laughing and smiling. They'd been five months in the desert, living rough a long way from home. I had told them this would be their best Christmas or their worst—it was up to them what attitude they adopted. They decided to make it their best. Colonel Fulford quietly warned me of what lay ahead.

"The Army has run a series of test exercises for breaching the Iraqi obstacle belts," he said. "Anticipate taking very heavy casualties when you assault."

I asked how many.

"Nearly half killed and wounded."

The regiment on call would have numerous aircraft and more than forty-eight artillery tubes to bombard the Iraqis overwatching their minefields. We had constructed a fire plan that we thought was sufficient to isolate the breaching point, in the shape of an inverted U to our left, right, and front. But Colonel Fulford's words had sobered me. I lay awake in my sleeping bag after he left.

On Christmas Day, I called in my fire support team. Proud of their plan, they were dismayed and dumbstruck when I ripped it in half. I wanted to disprove those test results about heavy casualties in the minefields.

"Start over," I said. "Inside that U, I want everything dead, including the earthworms."

PSYCHOLOGICAL TUNING

My battalion was trained infantry. But, other than a dozen Vietnam vets, they hadn't experienced actual battle. Combat involves a level of intensity that is difficult to prepare for even with the most grueling training. How do you prepare your men for the shock of battle? For one thing, you need to make sure that your training is so hard and varied that it removes complacency and creates muscle memory—instinctive reflexes—within a mind disciplined to identify and react to the unexpected. And once your men have been trained, you need to ensure that they are in the same unit long enough to know their brothers and develop trust and confidence in one another. Once this building block is accomplished, the next training step is rehearsal as they focus intently on the skills that will constitute their repertoire in battle. Mentally, this is a step beyond combat skills training, one that must continue during any pause in combat, whether before a patrol or before a deliberate attack. We would use any opportunity to rehearse.

I was conscious of what George Washington wrote to the Congress early in our war for independence: "Men who are familiarized to danger meet it without shrinking; whereas troops unused to service often apprehend danger where no danger is."

The key to preparation for those who hadn't yet been in battle was imaging. The goal was to ensure that every grunt had fought a dozen times, mentally and physically, before he ever fired his first bullet in battle, tasted the gunpowder grit in his teeth, or saw blood seeping into the dirt.

I wanted my troops to imagine what would happen, to develop mental images, to think ahead to the explosions, yelled orders, and, above all, the deafening cacophony. Battle is so loud that it is hard to hear—let alone make sense of—what someone is trying to direct you to do in the midst of the chaos. At that instant, the muscle memory of training and rehearsals must kick in; swift decisions have to be made with inadequate information. Every warrior must know his weapon, his job, and his comrades' reactions so well that he functions without hesitation. A hitter has a quarter of a second to gauge the arc of a curveball and swing his bat. He doesn't have time to think. He has practiced so many times that calculating whether to swing is automatic, grooved into his muscle memory. The same is true of the grunt engaged in close combat.

Verbal clarity requires the same intense practice. We have all heard recordings of 911 calls by frantic people who are talking incomprehensibly. Imagine, then, trying to give clear, terse, accurate descriptions and orders over the radio when you are under fire. So, day after day, I had my platoon sergeants and platoon commanders on the radio, responding to sudden scenarios designed to inject stress.

In the Saudi desert, there was no end to the workday, no weekend off, and no email. I walked the lines at night; troops will tell you things when they're on guard duty in the dark. Back home, television news and graphics about the anticipated casualties were disturbing to the families. Mail call fed that back to my Marines and Navy corpsmen.

Everyone has a plan, Mike Tyson said, until he gets punched in the mouth. The prepared fighter knows he's going to be rocked back on his heels. He's anticipated that before the brawl begins. So I expressed out loud to my troops how our assault might be screwed up. "What if I went down?" I asked them in informal sessions. "What if radio communications are lost at night during a chemical attack?"

"Corporal, your fire team is advancing behind the cover of a tank, bullets bouncing off the armor. To your left, you see a bulldozer throw a track. What do you do? Who do you notify?"

By having all hands share a mental model, each man learned the bigger picture and could adapt to changing circumstances. By walking through sand tables and imaging through setbacks, casualties, and chemical attacks, we built grim confidence in our ability to adapt. I've found this imaging technique—walking through what lies ahead, acclimating hearts and minds to the unexpected—an essential leadership tool.

To show how our casualties would be cared for, I gathered my battalion to watch a rehearsal. Sand dunes were our amphitheater. With Sergeant Major Dwight Walker holding a stopwatch to time the procedure, our medical staff drove up in two trucks. Our two surgeons hopped out, followed by the battalion cooks, who established a defensive perimeter while the Navy corpsmen set up the tents and generators. Inside twenty minutes, the battalion aid station was ready to receive patients. I wanted to demonstrate that no Marines would languish without immediate aid.

All this preparation gave me confidence in my men, but no less important was making sure they had confidence in me. Even as letters and magazines from home foretold heavy losses, especially for the first in, we knew we were more cunning and better prepared than the enemy.

FOCUSED TELESCOPES

Although in the flat desert I could see most of my units, I still delegated tactical command to the lowest capable level. Once in the attack, I wasn't going to shout orders to corporals. The leaders of each element knew my intent: Open the lanes through the minefields and, once in close combat, kill the enemy. When they were maneuvering, they would also be calling for fires and evacuating casualties.

Keeping me informed would be a lower priority. By listening over their tactical radio nets, I could gather information without interfering. But I needed more than that. Using a technique I had found in my reading, I intended to gather information that bypassed normal reporting channels by means of "focused telescopes." I copied this technique from Frederick the Great, Wellington, and Rommel, among others.

From my readings, I knew I needed to know more than I could expect distracted commanders engaged against the enemy to deliver. I wanted to know the fatigue level of my subordinate commanders, the morale of their units, and the enemy situation. I used officers who had sound tactical judgment, unfailing tact, initiative, and empathy in order to deliver to me impartial reports in concise terms, bypassing normal reporting channels.

There is no battalion unit that uses the call letter *J*. So I designated my focused-telescope officers with the military phonetic "Juliet." For instance, I had reassigned my personnel section to help with the incoming casualties. That left my adjutant, who understood my battle plan and my intent, without a job. He would act as a Juliet officer. I selected three Juliets, who met with me many mornings. They knew our plan and understood what information I needed, so I wouldn't be caught off-balance. Understanding my intent, they'd then circulate among my dispersed elements. Their sole priority was to keep me informed while also putting a human face to my intent. If you have multiple avenues of information coming to you and you're out and about yourself, you develop an enhanced understanding.

Every commander and chief executive officer needs tools to scan the horizon for danger or opportunities. Juliets proved invaluable to me by providing a steady stream of dispassionate information. I chose men who I was confident would maintain trust. What kept the Juliets from being seen as a spy ring by my subordinate commanders was their ability to keep confidences when those commanders shared concerns. They knew that information would be conveyed to me alone.

KNOW YOUR STRENGTHS . . .
AND YOUR WEAKNESSES

In war, even the greatest victory is salted with tragedy. It's not like business—or losing money in the market or missing a sales quota. The human and moral dimension is paramount. In combat, Napoleon once said, the moral is to the physical as three is to one. The combination of intangible qualities—confidence, trust, harmony, and affection for one another that build on each man's physical strength, mental agility, and spiritual resilience—produces cohesive units capable of dominating the battlefield. But death is ever present.

To risk death willingly, to venture forth knowing that in so doing you may cease to exist, is an unnatural act. To take the life of a fellow human being or to watch your closest comrades die exacts a profound emotional toll. In Michael Shaara's novel *The Killer Angels,* Robert E. Lee says, "To be a good soldier you must love the army. But to be a good officer you must be willing to order the death of the thing you love. This is . . . a very hard thing to do. No other profession requires it. That is one reason why there are so very few good officers. Although there are many good men."

To maintain my emotional equilibrium, I knew I couldn't be informed about casualties, let alone their names, while fighting. I instructed my staff not to report the names or the number of casualties to me unless their mission was jeopardized. The doctors and corpsmen, with the cooks as stretcher-bearers, would care for the wounded and swiftly evacuate them. I would remain focused on accomplishing the mission. On some level, I knew every one of my men, and I didn't want to think of his face if he was hit.

As the leader, anticipating heavy casualties, I had to compartmentalize my emotions. Otherwise I would distract myself from what had to be done. The mission comes first. Personal solace must wait for another day. I knew my limitations. Sort it all out later on the banks of the Columbia.

INTO THE ATTACK

Homer described the Trojan War as wild and confused, a storm of dust and smoke, hoarse screaming and bloody swords, cacophony and irrationality. Ever since then, in their imaginations commanders have searched in vain for the orderly battlefield that unfolds according to plan. It doesn't exist.

General Ulysses S. Grant, who knew a thing or two about war, had criteria for leaders, which boiled down to humility; toughness of character, so one is able to take shocks in stride; and the single-mindedness to remain unyielding when all is flying apart but enough mental agility to adapt when their approach is not working. This was how I pictured my Marines fighting. In doing so, they would present the enemy with a cascading series of disasters, shattering his coherence and creating a state of confusion and an inability to concentrate his mind or his forces.

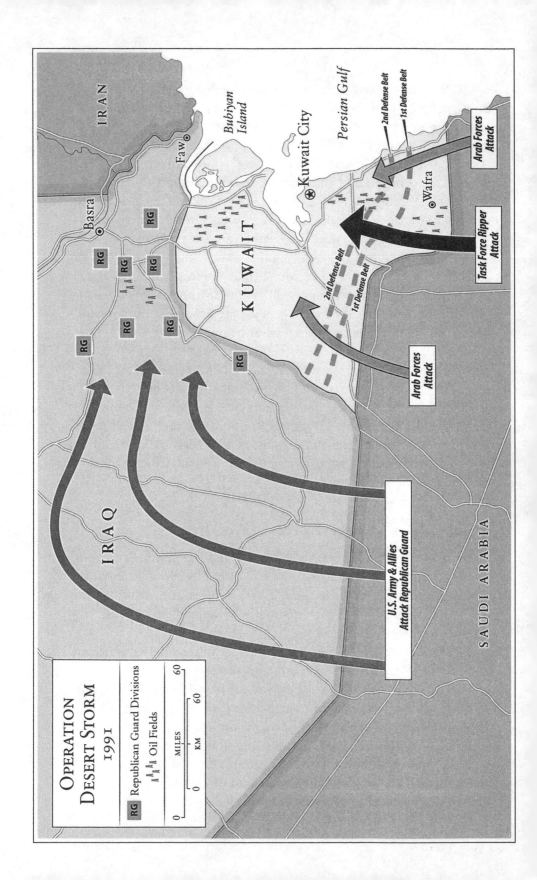

After more than a month of bombing, we launched our ground attack before dawn on February 24, 1991. The Iraqis had torched hundreds of oil wells, and ugly smog covered the landscape, shutting out the sun. After moving through the night, at dawn we closed on the first obstacle belt. The Iraqi engineers had constructed robust defenses composed of complex minefields, barbed wire, deep trenches, and flame obstacles, all covered by their dug-in troops and artillery.

As our artillery and air support provided covering fire for us, the engineers, covered by our tanks, sprinted forward, firing rocket-propelled explosives to detonate the mines and blast lanes through the minefields. Then our tanks and armored bulldozers moved up and "proofed" the lanes, shoving aside any mines that remained. Once the lanes were proofed, tanks and infantry went through to take out the enemies in the trenches. As we hurried on to the second belt, we had opened a path for the twenty thousand Marines behind us. In training, our fastest breach had taken twenty-one minutes. In the actual fight we did it in eleven. The relentless rehearsals had paid off. Our incessant bombing had sapped the Iraqis' will to fight. Their artillery fires were desultory and random. Direct fire from their tank cannons and machine guns was half-hearted. As cowed Iraqi soldiers were herded off the battlefield, I felt admiration for those few who continued to fight. As we moved forward, my troops knew that the tougher obstacle belt lay ahead.

During the assault, I did not want my company commanders wasting time passing information to me that I could gain simply by staying adjacent to them. From the hatch of my command vehicle, I could see my units in the open desert around me. I'm sure it was an odd sight for our Vietnam veterans, who had been unable to see ten feet in the jungle. I monitored the assault company radio nets while occasionally talking on my battalion net or updating regiment on its net. Listening to the tone in their voices, I could sense what was going on from their perspectives. Having sliced through the enemy's forward-most positions, we rushed on to the second, tougher obstacle belt, nine miles farther north. I knew that speed was of the essence; the Iraqis now knew the approximate location where we would strike their main line of resistance. We didn't want to give them time to reinforce that sector of the line.

At the second belt, a more determined enemy fought harder; mines knocked out several tanks and other vehicles, and we took casualties. Artillery fire slowed us but could not stop us. At one point I flopped into a crater; crouched down inside it, I noticed an ant trying to crawl out. When I scooped away a little dirt, the ant fell back into the hole and resumed climbing. Again, I scooped away some dirt.

"Don't go out there, Mr. Ant," I told him. "You're safer in here."

Once our air and artillery had silenced the enemy's guns, we pushed on. At an agricultural station called Emir's Farm, a dug-in Iraqi battalion was holding its ground, firing mortars. Bravo Company dropped ramps at six hundred fifty yards from the entrenched enemy. The Marines were rushing forward, and the Iraqis, having recovered their courage, were shooting back. Then an F-18 roared over our heads and dropped a five-hundred-pound bomb. That was it. The survivors streamed toward my Marines with their hands in the air.

Across the entire southern front, the coalition attack was accelerating. The basic building blocks of planning and rehearsals, the iterative discussions, the generals' sharing of the overall strategy, the heavy bombing, the simultaneous breaching of multiple lanes through the minefields—all had come together in violent harmony. By afternoon, the Marines were far ahead of schedule. The high command had assumed that poison gas, land mines, and direct fire would inflict heavy casualties on the assault battalions, so my battalion didn't have an assigned follow-on mission. I had to rein in my lead elements because we were so far ahead of expectations.

On the third day, we picked up even more momentum, charging toward Kuwait International Airport. With dozens of oil rigs ablaze, the smoke was so thick that we could see only a few hundred yards. At midday, I had to turn on a flashlight to read my map. By employing my focused telescopes and listening to the radio nets and my staff, I could keep abreast of events without calling a halt for meetings. We were not slowing down. I gave few orders, letting the assault leaders make the decisions.

It was a rout. When any enemy combustion engine was turned on, it emitted a heat signature that glowed in our thermal sights. Every vehicle and piece of armor became a target. We advanced in dense, oily smoke reminiscent of Dante's *Inferno,* Cobra gunship helicopters flying low overhead. Iraqi tanks and armor were scattered, crushed, pulverized, or ripped apart as though a tornado had swept through, casting aside broken vehicles and dismembering bodies. Few of the corpses resembled human beings. Most were scorched black and shrunken to half their size.

I was with my forward elements as we drew abreast of a large quarry, squeezing us tightly on our right flank. We moved toward high-tension power lines still standing in the middle of a desolate, featureless desert. I'd had little rest in three days, and nothing out of the ordinary clicked in my fatigued mind as we moved past the quarry. Suddenly the horizon ahead of us lit up with flashes, plus streams of green tracers. The power lines had served as the waiting enemy's perfect target reference point, their tanks and machine guns locked on and ready to fire. At that same moment, an Iraqi mechanized company hidden inside the quarry we had passed rushed out to attack my logistics elements, following to my rear. There are happier times than being ambushed, and nothing was a better reminder that I was not von Clausewitz than having my battalion surrounded in the open desert.

In the midst of the enemy attack, I saw Lieutenant Chris Woodbridge maneuvering to my front, standing in the turret of his Humvee. A burly rugby player with a perpetual grin, Woody was leading an antitank platoon. As I watched, his Humvee disappeared in a column of sand and smoke—a direct hit from a tank round. The concussion rolled past me as sand and smoke enveloped Woody's vehicle.

I looked away, shoving the direct hit out of my mind. I ordered units to shift farther right to gain maneuver room, bringing our tanks into the fight. When I glanced to the rear, I saw red star flares. Our logistics train, commanded by Lieutenant Jeff Hooks, was signaling that it was under attack. Fortunately, every third day for six months, Jeff and Gunnery Sergeant Kendall Haff had trained their corpsmen, cooks, drivers, engineers, clerks, and mechanics to fight as infantry. Their training paid off as they tore into the enemy.

They were now knocking out enemy vehicles while our mortars were firing both south and north, on the enemy in the quarry and to our front. As the Iraqis emerged, cooks and engineers energetically responded with machine-gun fire and anti-armor rockets that knocked out the Iraqi vehicles. The fight was over in twelve minutes, and grinning corpsmen and mechanics welcomed the reinforcing infantry. I had rushed back to join them. My men had gotten me out of a jam. But because they had the muscle memory and the nerve, they had also smashed the enemy, turning inside the enemy's decision loop.

As we continued our attack, some Iraqis offered resistance, but most quickly surrendered. In midafternoon, Colonel Fulford called his commanders together: we were to continue the attack and break through to Kuwait City before dark, days ahead of schedule. After a quick order, I turned back toward my Humvee.

"Learn anything today, Jim?" Fulford asked quietly.

We both knew my Marines had bailed me out at the quarry.

"Yes, sir."

"Good," he said as he walked away. He didn't belabor the point.

When I arrived back at my battalion, I called together the combat leaders for a quick order brief. Woody joined us, disheveled, covered in grime, but intact and still smiling hugely.

"I thought you were dead," I said.

"So did I, sir." Woody grinned. "That shell threw a ton of dirt on us."

After the explosion, I had forced Woody and his men out of my mind. The human mind, though, is a wonderful mystery. As I write about Woody a quarter of a century later, the sense of relief is as strong now as it was when he grinned at me all those years ago.

After a month of bombing and one hundred hours of ground attack, the Iraqi Army was thoroughly beaten and thrown out of Kuwait. I learned not to put much stock in estimates about an enemy until we've fought him. Although my battalion had a dozen wounded, I felt a huge relief that not one Marine, sailor, or Kuwaiti had been killed. I would not be so fortunate in the future. Seeing the Kuwaiti people's relief and joy showed us all what victory looks like. And though I didn't realize it at the time, the capabilities, morale, and confidence of the 1st Battalion, 7th Marines, provided me with a measuring stick to apply when training units in future wars. I knew what confident men looked like when they went into the assault.

In the months following my return to the United States, I grew increasingly displeased with the lack of individual recognition my men were receiving. Frontline service in the military brings with it the dignity of danger, and recognizing valor is critical. Against the advice of a senior officer who told me that protesting the actions of seniors would end my career, and determined to gain appropriate awards for my troops, I wrote to the MEF commander, Lieutenant General Robert Johnston, with my concerns. I immediately received a lesson in the power of a general officer: General Johnston personally called me, assuring me that he would correct the situation. Within a week I was receiving welcome news of appropriate recognition. There would come a time when that general's responsive example would guide me in similar situations that were brought to my attention. Delays or parsimonious award action for frontline troops must be overcome if we're going to pay respects to those who go toe-to-toe with our enemies. (See Appendix A.)

The ultimate auditor of military competence is war. The campaign was victorious. Our casualties were far fewer than anyone had projected. Much credit must be given to the astonishing improvements in air-to-ground target detection and destruction. More broadly, the American military, in the two decades since Vietnam, had developed a doctrine for fighting mechanized warfare that maximized our advantages in maneuver and mobility. At the geopolitical level, President George H. W. Bush had demonstrated a trifecta of statesmanship. On the diplomatic front, he had pulled together a coalition of Western and Arab states; on the military front, he had provided his generals with the forces and policy direction they needed; and on the political front, he had avoided overreach once he achieved his objective of freeing Kuwait.

"This will not stand," he had said.

With impressive resolve, America backed up those words, throwing Saddam out of Kuwait.

In my military judgment, President George H. W. Bush knew how to end a war on our terms. When he said America would take action, we did. He approved of deploying overwhelming forces to compel the enemy's withdrawal or swiftly end the war. He avoided sophomoric decisions like imposing a ceiling on the number of troops or setting a date when we would have to stop fighting and leave.

He systematically gathered public support, congressional approval, and UN agreement. He set a clear, limited end state and used diplomacy to pull together a military coalition that included allies we'd never fought alongside. He listened to opposing points of view and guided the preparations, without offending or excluding any stakeholder, while also holding firm to his strategic goal.

Under his wise leadership, there was no mission creep. We wouldn't discipline ourselves to be so strategically sound in the future.

CHAPTER 4

Broadening

A FTER MY EIGHT MONTHS IN THE GULF WAR, I returned to a new global setting. To many, it seemed the "end of history" was at hand. There would be no more wars between major powers. Liberal democracy had defeated communism. Saddam was back in his cage, and our troops enjoyed a massive ticker-tape parade down Broadway in New York City, an event that has not been repeated in the quarter century since. The Warsaw Pact fell apart, followed by the disintegration of the Soviet Union. In the fall of 1992, President Bush and Russia's President Boris Yeltsin declared that the Cold War was over. America and NATO had held the line as internal contradictions rotted the Soviet Union from the inside out and Afghanistan bled the Soviet Army. The U.S. Senate ratified significant mutual reductions in the numbers of U.S. and Russian nuclear warheads.

The next few years were more mixed. On the positive side, twelve states in Western Europe pulled closer together and formed the European Union. Eastern Europe pulled toward the West, and a military coup in Russia failed. On the negative side, Yugoslavia collapsed into a civil war and China conducted nuclear tests to upgrade its strategic weaponry. The newly elected President Bill Clinton pulled U.S. peacekeeping forces from Somalia after eighteen American soldiers were killed. Reality was giving rude hints of the disorder to come.

Inside the U.S. military, our national assessment of the global situation had a major impact. No major wars were looming on the horizon, and pressure for a "peace dividend" resulted in a severe cut in the Pentagon budget as we came home from the Gulf War. Having relinquished command of my battalion, I was assigned to Headquarters Marine Corps, in the Pentagon. This was the normal rotation in an officer's career, with tours split between the supporting establishment and the operating forces, with a year of school thrown in every four or five years. I was responsible for assigning specific jobs to all active-duty and enlisted Marines. My branch had to approve the retention of every enlisted Marine who wanted to stay in the Corps. That was tough duty. The Marine Corps was in the act of swiftly reducing our forces, from more than 189,000 to 172,000. Nine percent of all serving Marines had to retire or leave, whether they wanted to or not.

People join us to be part of a small, elite tribe, "the few, the proud." Within the Pentagon, the Marine budget was less than 10 percent of the total. We do with little, because for centuries we've sailed around the world limited by what we can carry on ships. We deploy in all oceans, guard all our embassies—and we are eager to be first to fight, anytime, anywhere. We're the service youngest in age, with two-thirds of our forces serving only one tour, while our longer-serving officer and NCO corps are kept lean. We improvise to overcome operational obstacles and aging equipment. But improvisation cannot overcome serious budget cuts, and I had to cut thousands of veterans fresh home from war from our ranks. I had to decide which NCOs were assigned to what posts, who would be promoted, and who would be told to retire.

A decade earlier, I had driven around the Pacific Northwest, encouraging sergeants to recruit Marines; only months before, I had thanked the Lord for the sergeants who had bailed me out when I made a mistake in combat. Those same men who had helped me along the way, crawled through minefields, and faced other hazards now had to gather their families, load U-Haul trailers, and head down the road. Marines with four, fourteen, or twenty-four years of faithful, brave service had to be let go. Those with twenty years had pensions, but most didn't. That wasn't the determining factor. In a society that equates a person's value with the size of their paycheck, the military has a different social contract with those who serve. If you commit to the defense of this country, giving a blank check to the American people payable with your life, you expect a career path in return. Now every rank and age had to be trimmed back to keep a balanced force, ensuring that our ranks didn't stagnate in the post–Cold War period. As I traveled to Marine Corps bases with my NCOs to explain the bad news, it was hard to look the people we were forcing out in the eye.

The war was over. Those we forced out would be missed following the surprise attack on September 11, 2001.

READ, READ, READ

I was forty-three when I attended the National War College. Over the course of the previous twenty years, I had trained in probably twenty-five countries and had served in a dozen different assignments. Each job broadened my skill set. This is standard in our military. Every officer and noncommissioned officer goes through that same maturing process. The military is a "closed labor" system, and we take responsibility for educating our leaders. I would have gladly paid for that privilege.

Most of us at the War College had reached the rank of colonel. Up to this point, we had focused our attention principally down the chain of command. Step by step, rank by rank, we had accumulated the skills necessary to command a warship or to lead a battalion of eight hundred troops or a squadron of aircraft costing hundreds of millions of dollars. Each of us had been promoted based upon a mastery of tactical and operational skills. The War College curriculum in strategy, history, and economics broadened me. Guest lecturers included senators, cabinet members, foreign officers, and historians. When we left, after a year of study and reflection, many of us were assigned to jobs that required executive rather than direct leadership.

I learned this as an officer candidate, when a hard-nosed sergeant would correct my tactical mistake by sarcastically saying, "Good job, candidate—you just got your Marines killed." Several years later, I was training in the jungles of northern Okinawa when, without warning, I was temporarily put in command of a 180-man company. On a Saturday morning, the sergeant major requested that I drop by for a quiet discussion. Technically, I outranked him, but no lieutenant with his wits about him is slow to respond when his top noncommissioned offer wants to talk with him alone.

"You are a very persuasive young man," he said, handing me a book about a Roman centurion, "but it would be best if you did your homework first."

Before going into battle, you can learn by asking veterans about their experiences and by reading relentlessly. Lieutenants come to grasp the elements of battle, while senior officers learn how to outwit their opponents. By studying how others have dealt with similar circumstances, I became exposed to leadership examples that accelerated my expanding understanding of combat.

The Marines are known for their emphasis on physical toughness. But I well recall an Israeli exchange officer, on a sweltering run in the Virginia woods, bellowing at me that the physically vigorous life is not inconsistent with being intellectually on top of your game. "Read the ancient Greeks and how they turned out their warriors," he said.

Reading is an honor and a gift from a warrior or historian who—a decade or a thousand decades ago—set aside time to write. He distilled a lifetime of campaigning in order to have a "conversation" with you. We have been fighting on this planet for ten thousand years; it would be idiotic and unethical to not take advantage of such accumulated experiences. If you haven't read hundreds of books, you are functionally illiterate, and you will be incompetent, because your personal experiences alone aren't broad enough to sustain you. Any commander who claims he is "too busy to read" is going to fill body bags with his troops as he learns the hard way. The consequences of incompetence in battle are final. History teaches that we face nothing new under the sun. The Commandant of the Marine Corps maintains a list of required reading for every rank. All Marines read a common set; in addition, sergeants read some books, and colonels read others. Even generals are assigned a new set of books that they must consume. At no rank is a Marine excused from studying. When I talked to any group of Marines, I knew from their ranks what books they had read. During planning and before going into battle, I could cite specific examples of how others had solved similar challenges. This provided my lads with a mental model as we adapted to our specific mission.

Reading sheds light on the dark path ahead. By traveling into the past, I enhance my grasp of the present. I'm partial to studying Roman leaders and historians, from Marcus Aurelius and Scipio

Africanus to Tacitus, whose grace under pressure and reflections on life can guide leaders today. I followed Caesar across Gaul. I marveled at how the plain prose of Grant and Sherman revealed the value of steely determination. E. B. Sledge, in *With the Old Breed,* wrote for generations of grunts when he described the fierce fighting on Okinawa and the bonds that bind men together in battle. Biographies of Roman generals and Native American leaders, of wartime political leaders and sergeants, and of strategic thinkers from Sun Tzu to Colin Gray have guided me through tough challenges. Eventually I collected several thousand books for my personal library. I read broadly and selected a few battles and areas where I was weak to study deeply. Asked by a fellow Marine to provide specific examples, I sent him a list of my favorite books. (See Appendix B.)

Coming out of the War College, I took command for the next two years (1994–96) of Colonel Fulford's old regiment, the 7th Marines, stationed in the Mojave Desert. This included more than six thousand Marines and sailors organized into six battalions. I had hit the point where I could no longer lead by hands-on, direct, eye-to-eye contact. My directives were filtered through officers and staffs, and my direct contact with junior troops required increased effort to sustain.

Once he's removed from direct interaction with his troops, a commander must guard most rigorously against overcontrol, compounded by the seduction of immediate communications. That is, any senior officer or staff member can dash off a query and numerous officers will hasten to respond. Digital technology—instant questions demanding instant responses—conveys to higher headquarters a sense of omniscience, an inclination to fine-tune every detail below. When you impose command via that sort of tight communications control, you create "Mother may I?" timidity.

Once subordinate commanders sense that, they hesitate. The very brittleness of detailed orders that cannot possibly anticipate unknowns sucks the initiative out of them, suffocating their aggressiveness and slowing operational tempo, a problem doubled if hobbled by risk aversion. Success on the battlefield, where opportunities and dangers open and close in a few compact and intense minutes, comes from aggressive junior officers with a strong bias for action. Unleashing this quality among junior leaders, disciplined by my commander's intent, was always my vision. Trust up and down the chain must be the coin of the realm.

To instill that trust, the Marine Corps demanded that, as young officers, we learn how to convey our intent so that it passed intact through the layers of intermediate leadership to our youngest Marines. For instance, you may say, "We will attack that bridge in order to cut off the enemy's escape." The critical information is your intent, summed up in the phrase "in order to." If a platoon seizes the bridge and cuts off the enemy, the mission is a success. But if the bridge is seized while the enemy continues to escape, the platoon commander will not sit idly on the bridge. Without asking for further orders, he will move to cut off the enemy's escape. Such aligned independence is based upon a shared understanding of the "why" for the mission. This is key to unleashing audacity.

Developing a culture of operating from commander's intent demanded a higher level of unit discipline and self-discipline than issuing voluminous, detailed instructions. In drafting my intent, I learned to provide only what is necessary to achieve a clearly defined end state: tell your team the purpose of the operation, giving no more than the essential details of how you intend to achieve the mission, and then clearly state your goal or end state, one that enables what you intend to do next. Leave the "how" to your subordinates, who must be trained and rewarded for exercising initiative, taking advantage of opportunities and problems as they arise.

The details you don't give in your orders are as important as the ones you do. With all hands aligned to your goals, their cunning and initiative unleashed, you need only transparent sharing of information (*What do I know? Who needs to know? Have I told them?*) to orchestrate, as opposed to "control" or "synchronize," a coordinated team.

Subordinate commanders cannot seize fleeting opportunities if they do not understand the purpose behind an order. The correct exercise of independent action requires a common understanding between the commander and the subordinate, of both the mission and the commander's intent of what the mission is expected to accomplish.

If a corporal on the front lines could not tell me what my intent was, then I had failed. Either I had not taken the time to be clear or my subordinates were not effectively conveying it down the chain of command. Instillation of personal initiative, aggressiveness, and risk-taking doesn't spring forward spontaneously on the battle-field. It must be cultivated for years and inculcated, even rewarded, in an organization's culture. If a commander expects subordinates to seize fleeting opportunities under stress, his organization must reward this behavior in all facets of training, promoting, and com-mending. More important, he must be tolerant of mistakes. If the risk takers are punished, then you will retain in your ranks only the risk averse.

Viscount Slim was the finest British field commander in World War II. In 1941, the Japanese had driven the British out of South-east Asia. In his book *Defeat into Victory,* Slim explains how he reinvigorated his beaten forces and outmaneuvered the Japanese. I was struck by how he directed units that were far away in deep jungles, even out of radio contact for days and weeks.

Slim wrote: "Commanders at all levels had to act more on their own; they were given greater latitude to work out their own plans to achieve what they knew was the Army Commander's intention. In time they developed to a marked degree a flexibility of mind and a firmness of decision that enabled them to act swiftly to take ad-vantage of sudden information or changing circumstances without reference to their superiors. . . . This acting without orders, in an-ticipation of orders, or without waiting for approval yet always within the overall intention, must become second nature in any form of warfare."

"Acting without orders . . . yet always within the overall inten-tion." That was how Colonel Fulford had led the 7th Marine Regi-ment in Operation Desert Storm. Looking back, I realized that in the open desert of Kuwait, he had ideal communications. Yet he rarely called me, and his staff stood ready to help my battalion, not badgering me for information. From Slim to Fulford—both pro-moted to four-star general—came the same message: at the execu-tive level, your job is to reward initiative in your junior officers and NCOs and facilitate their success. When they make mistakes while doing their best to carry out your intent, stand by them. Examine your coaching and how well you articulate your intent. Remember the bottom line: imbue in them a strong bias for action.

Let me give a concrete example. My regimental base at Twenty-nine Palms, near Palm Springs, comprised a maneuver area only slightly smaller than Rhode Island. On one exercise in 1995, my regiment faced a cunning Red Force enemy dispersed across six hundred square miles of deep canyons and sharp ridgelines. I took a page from Colonel Fulford's book about issuing mission-type orders. I removed the boundary lines between my battalions, widening their fire and maneuver area, giving increased opportunity for their initiative while intentionally necessitating increased collaboration. Within minutes, the lieutenant colonels began coordinating over my regimental radio net. For the rest of the exercise, I listened as they swiftly maneuvered, saying things like "You shoot artillery left of that hill and we'll move to the right." The tempo of thousands of Marines picked up, swiftly exploiting the successes of units on their left and right. By decentralizing authority to take full advantage of opportunities on the broader front, we maneuvered faster than the enemy, getting inside his decision-making loop. Guided by my intent, they acted, and the feedback loops kept me attentive to anticipated decision points. My subordinates taught me a lot that day.

It was a lesson in team building and tempo; they knew my intent and didn't seem to notice I was gone from the radio net. (Actually, maybe they benefited!) So in the weeks after, I tried to dispense my wisdom by way of a short note here and a subtle suggestion there. I saw myself passing on advice from a combat-tested colonel, light hands on the steering wheel guiding the regiment. Then, one day, I walked into the operations office. There before the blackboard stood my operations officer, chalk in hand. Lieutenant Colonel John Toolan, with his thick Brooklyn accent and a busted nose, was still playing in the rugby scrum in his forties. He often made wry comments, accompanied by a disarming Irish smile. On the board, in capital letters, he had written: C H A O S.

Curious, I asked him what he was thinking. He handed me the chalk.

"Does," he asked, "the Colonel Have Another Outstanding Solution?"

Thus did Chaos become my call sign. Rumors later claimed that Chaos referred to my desire to inflict bedlam in the enemy ranks. That was true. But the underlying reality is that my often irreverent troops assigned me the call sign. There's always a Toolan waiting out there to keep your ego in check, providing you keep the risk takers and mavericks at your side.

In 1996, I was selected to serve as executive secretary to Secretary of Defense Dr. William Perry and his successor, Senator William Cohen. I reviewed pounds of paperwork, signed off on reports, and found it amazing to see the diverse issues they dealt with, from running the largest corporation in the world to a small newsmaking story. In the morning, the SecDef might meet with a king, decide about a billion-dollar aircraft carrier, and cope with a story about a corporal in trouble on Japan. In the afternoon, he would meet with congressional leaders, plan how to visit seven countries in seven days, and parse every word of a speech he would deliver before a global audience. I was struck by the speed of decision-making, given the limited amount of time available even for weighty matters.

While Washington duty was not my cup of tea, I gained an abiding respect for those with whom I served and from whom I learned a new skill set. I received a pragmatic introduction to Article I of the Constitution, which assigns Congress responsibility "to raise and support armies and to provide and maintain a navy." I watched how funding for defense was allocated and listened to earnest debate about deploying troops to the Balkans and what qualities were needed in senior uniformed officers. Often I was dealing with my civilian counterparts at the State Department, at the CIA, and on the National Security staff in the White House. They were consistently helpful in guiding me through the unimaginably complex interagency process.

I had a front-row seat to policymaking as it was supposed to work. Weekly meetings between my boss, the Secretary of Defense, the National Security Adviser, and the Secretary of State kept foreign policy aligned. The NSC coordinated the inputs from the agencies, and the cabinet officers met to work out their differences in both planning and execution. The process was necessarily messy, and required ugly compromises. The view from the top of the Pentagon further informed my understanding—I watched, listened, and learned, with no idea how relevant this on-the-job training would prove in time.

In 1998, I returned to Headquarters Marine Corps to direct our personnel planning and was promoted to brigadier general. At first, I questioned why an infantry officer should be assigned to superintend personnel policy. By the time I left, I understood why the job demanded a warfighter's focus. If an organization gets the behavior it rewards, promoting warriors fit for war is where the rubber hits the road.

This is no less true for selecting generals, because that says what a service values. Each year in the Marine Corps, a board of senior generals is convened to select fewer than a dozen new brigadier generals from about two hundred eligible colonels. Each board member is given the records of ten or more colonels, covering their decades of service. After several days of study, the board member briefs the case for every colonel in his group, ranking them in a rough order. The board as a whole takes a vote—who is out and who is still in the running.

This goes on day after day, until the board has whittled down the candidates to the final twenty or thirty. You choose the best from the warfare specialties: the best infantry, artillery, aviation, and logistics officers. At that cutoff point, chance plays a large role. If the final picks were on a plane that crashed, the next in line would be promoted, with no difference in overall performance, such is the quality of our colonels, winnowed by years of service and previous selections, their professional reputations known by members of the selection board.

All Marines are coequal in their commitment to carrying out the mission when they face the enemy. I never thought, as a general, that I had more commitment than my nineteen-year-old lance corporals; I could see it in their eyes. Because a Marine's greatest privilege is to fight alongside a fellow Marine, we respect one another regardless of rank. Yet the popular culture treats generals as above everyone else. The Pentagon sends them to a special course, called Capstone. There they are instructed by retired generals about their new roles. The Vietnam vets put their stamp on us, reminding us that once you made general, you never had a bad meal and you never again heard the truth. From the men we called "graybeard generals," we heard firsthand about their mistakes and their lessons learned. But in this course and others I would attend over my next dozen years as a general, the graybeards also taught us humility and dedication to maintaining our professional ethics.

In 2000, I returned to the Pentagon as the senior military assistant to the Deputy Secretary of Defense. Over the course of two separate tours, first as a colonel and now as a brigadier general, I would spend a total of three years in the executive suites of the Pentagon. I got a PhD-level course in running large organizations, witnessing how civilian control of the military actually works. The Secretary of Defense most often had to choose the least bad option. If it was an easy decision with good options, that decision had already been made. I sat in more meetings than I can count, and the whole experience brought home to me in an even more elevated context how critical it is to delegate decision-making authority or face paralyzing chaos.

I stayed in the Corps to be with the troops. At the Pentagon, I did my best to support my civilian bosses, and I learned a great deal. My faith in our form of government and the motives of the civilian leadership and the Congress was reinforced. That said, I couldn't wait to get out of that job. I wasn't cut out for Washington duty. I didn't get my energy from behind a desk. I had the privilege of supporting men who cared deeply about the defense of our nation, even as the chorus for a peace dividend grew louder: Secretaries Perry, Cohen, and Donald Rumsfeld, Deputy Secretaries John White, John Hamre, Rudy de Leon, and Paul Wolfowitz. Whether or not one agreed with their points of view, their dedication was beyond question.

In July 2001, I happily reported back at Camp Pendleton, north of San Diego, as the deputy commander of I Marine Expeditionary Force (I MEF)—forty thousand sailors and Marines in camps across southern California and Arizona. I was elated to be back with grunts. Throughout my time in service I'd always assumed each promotion would be my last. So I was pretty sure I'd conclude my career back where I started, among Marines. Then I'd go back home to the Cascade Mountains on a high note, having served one last time with the operating forces.

Looking back now, I see how mistaken that assumption was and why learning and mastering your job must never stop. I had changed in the ten years since Desert Storm. My involvement in downsizing the Marine Corps, studying at the War College, leading a large regiment, and learning how to make bureaucracy work for the warfighters would all combine to ensure I was ready for the tests ahead.

CHAPTER 5

Rhino

A̲T SIX IN THE MORNING ON SEPTEMBER 11, 2001, I was driving to work at Camp Pendleton and thinking about an upcoming exercise in Egypt. Over the radio, I heard that one of the Twin Towers had been hit.

They got through was my first thought.

I was certain it was Osama bin Laden. Al Qaeda had declared war on America in the mid-1990s. The group killed more than two hundred people in the 1998 attacks upon two American embassies in Africa and killed eighteen sailors on the USS *Cole* while she was refueling. Our intel community knew the Islamist terrorist network was thriving in Afghanistan, hosted by the radical Islamist Taliban government. I immediately thought that our military and intelligence services had let down our country. But I forced that out of my mind. Before I pulled into my parking space, I was thinking how to hunt them down to the end of the earth, in this case to Afghanistan. Having been in and out of the Middle East since 1979, I was keenly aware that it wouldn't be a fast fight, and that the maniacs who thought that hurting us would scare us would have to be proven wrong.

On 9/11, Al Qaeda destroyed the Twin Towers, murdered three thousand innocent civilians from ninety-one countries, and injured more than six thousand in New York City, Pennsylvania, and Washington. President George W. Bush and Secretary of Defense Donald Rumsfeld insisted upon swift retaliation, with CIA operatives and

Army Special Forces linking up with Afghanistan's Northern Alliance to call in air strikes against the exposed Taliban and Al Qaeda forces.

I assumed that my Marines and I would get into the fight, but that it would take some persuasion. General Tommy Franks had rejected the initial Marine offer of assistance, explaining to his staff, "No doubt about it, guys—this son of a bitch is definitely landlocked. We can't make use of the Marines' amphibious capabilities." Because Afghanistan was four hundred miles from the ocean, some at Central Command headquarters assumed that Marines could not be employed. As a CENTCOM planner explained, "We don't have access from the sea anyway, and it's going to have to be introduced by air, then let's just introduce the Army. . . . So, quickly we went away from—at least initially—consideration of the Marines."

This was a classic example of being trapped by an outdated way of thinking. The Marines don't need to be anywhere near a beach to land from ships. We had long-range, air-refuelable helicopters and transport aircraft. We were expeditionary, able to fight at a moment's notice in forward-deployed, self-contained combat packages.

At Camp Pendleton the month prior, I'd taken command of the 1st Marine Expeditionary Brigade, planning to deploy to Egypt for an annual multinational exercise called Bright Star. Even though we were at war, it was critical that we maintain our military-to-military contacts, conducting exercises with dozens of friendly nations. When I arrived in the Egyptian desert, I felt at home. I was accustomed to living in sweltering heat, under cramped, austere conditions. My Marines shared with soldiers from eight other nations a vast encampment of tents, plywood offices, and flies. The exercise was thoroughly scripted, crafted as much to display political unity as military training. So once my staff and I had memorized our parts, I had ample time to study the Afghanistan situation.

I liked prodding the young guys. You always learned something. Besides, I enjoyed the pained expressions at staff meetings when I brought up a lance corporal's latest recommendation. If you can't talk freely with the most junior members of your organization, then you've lost touch.

"How's it going, lads?"

"Oorah! Fine, sir, terrific. Living the dream . . ."

I never accepted that stock reply.

"Nah. We both know that's bullshit. We're stuck in the middle of nowhere while we want to be killing Al Qaeda. Level with me. Give me something I can fix."

On one occasion, the troops pointed to the porta-johns they shared with soldiers from other nations, some with what we considered gross hygiene habits. To fix that, I sent a sergeant eighty miles to Alexandria. To the cheers of the troops, he returned with a truckful of toilet paper, issuing every man a roll. Sometimes the basic things in life are the most important.

A commanding officer is always a sentinel for his unit, alert to danger. One senior officer was irate that I had ordered my Marines to carry live ammo at all times. He announced that I was out of step and that live ammo was not permitted. Having notified seven families that their sons had been killed in the Beirut bombing in 1983, I insisted that we Marines were always responsible for our own security. We were carrying our ammo with us. Only a month after 9/11, it amazed me that I had to make my case at all.

Of course, Murphy's Law was always in play. That same day, two Marines negligently discharged their weapons, causing no casualties except apoplexy at senior staff levels. Again I was pressured to disarm all Marines. Again I refused, arguing that it was imprudent. The two junior offenders were busted down one rank. Their two acts of negligence had jeopardized the trust of the high command in the discipline of four thousand other Marines. For the rest of the deployment, they would not carry loaded weapons—a singular disgrace. That was the end of it.

Once the exercise was under way, my friend Major General John "Glad" Castellaw, in charge of Marines in the Middle East, and I had time to sit under a camouflage net and talk about how to fight Al Qaeda. He conjectured that we could bring two afloat Marine units and a small command staff together in the North Arabian Sea. He got me thinking. Returning to my bivouac, I told my staff to identify remote locations in Afghanistan where we could land and then went back to conducting the exercise.

When the exercise concluded, I received orders to fly to Bahrain, a tiny island nation in the Persian Gulf. Since the 1940s, Bahrain had always stood with us, always punching above its weight. It provided the home port for the U.S. Navy's Fifth Fleet, commanded in 2001 by three-star Vice Admiral Willy Moore. Upon arrival in Bahrain, I had checked in with him, and later that night he called me back to his office. He pointed to a wall map, indicating that the Taliban and Al Qaeda were under crushing attack in the north, where our CIA and Special Forces were stationed alongside Afghan tribes.

Willy Moore had done his homework. He told me the southern half of the country remained the Taliban's home turf and that our bombing campaign in the north was forcing more Taliban toward the south. Kabul had never been successfully defended in five hundred years. Willy knew where they were going: to Kandahar, Afghanistan's second-largest city and the spiritual capital of the Taliban. We had estimates of tens of thousands of fighters scattered across several provinces, with more fleeing south. Their leader, Mullah Omar, was sheltered among the two million Pashtuns living there. With Taliban concentrating in the region as winter set in, bombing would put at risk two million innocents. Holding off, however, would mean that by spring Omar could organize a formidable defense. Willy's envisioned second front would prevent that from happening.

Kandahar was a thousand miles northeast of Willy Moore's office, on the far side of barren deserts and Baluchistan's mountain ranges. To further complicate matters, Pakistan lay between the North Arabian Sea and landlocked Afghanistan. But Willy Moore was a warrior unintimidated by distance or number of enemies, and one who didn't wait for directions; rather, he could see opportunities where others saw only obstacles.

"There is a gift," Napoleon wrote in his memoirs, "of being able to see at a glance the possibilities offered by the terrain. . . . One can call it coup d'oeil [to see in the blink of an eye] and it is inborn in great generals."

"It really is the commander's coup d'oeil," Clausewitz agreed, "his ability to see things simply, to identify the whole business of war completely with himself, that is the essence of good generalship. Only if the mind works in this comprehensive fashion can it achieve the freedom it needs to dominate events and not be dominated by them."

Admiral Moore had that gift, embodied in a forceful countenance. If he'd been born two hundred years earlier, I could see him attacking a ship, swinging down with a cutlass in hand and a black patch over one eye. He put the question to me.

"Can you pull together Marines," he said, "from the Mediterranean and Pacific fleets, land in Afghanistan, and move against Kandahar?"

"Yes, I can do that," I said. "I need a few days to plan and recon."

"Okay, go figure out what you need, and I'll get you a plane for your recon," he said.

From my years at sea to a discussion under a camouflage net in Egypt to an admiral who could seize opportunity, it had all come together.

At his request, CENTCOM had authorized Moore to plan raids, and he had rather liberally stretched what that meant. If we struck fast from an unanticipated angle, the Taliban would crumble. Moore saw that in the blink of an eye.

So here I was—offered an opportunity. Biographies of executives usually stress achievement through hard work, brilliance, or dogged persistence. By contrast, many who achieve less point to hard luck and bad breaks. I believe both views are equally true. Following the attacks on 9/11, when Al Qaeda and the Taliban in Afghanistan became the target, I was the next up to deploy. As Churchill noted, "To each there comes in their lifetime a special moment when they are figuratively tapped on the shoulder and offered the chance to do a very special thing, unique to them and fitted to their talents. What a tragedy if that moment finds them unprepared or unqualified for that which could have been their finest hour." Thanks to the Vietnam veterans, at this "special moment" I was prepared and qualified "to do a very special thing." While six months earlier, it would have been someone else leading our Marines into Afghanistan, mastering your chosen vocation means you are ready when opportunity knocks.

As I walked out of the admiral's office, I could already see the shape of the operation in my mind. Granted, we had to penetrate four hundred miles, and what Willy Moore had in mind took poetic license with doctrine. But doctrine is the last refuge of the unimaginative. The Marines taught me that it is a guide, not an intellectual straitjacket. Improvise, adapt, and overcome; I was going to do whatever it took to carry out the admiral's intent.

The first thing we had to deal with was the tyranny of distance. Thanks to decisions made in the 1950s, the Marine Corps has its own KC-130 refuelers and its own helicopters fitted for refueling in flight. Thanks to Navy ships, we could haul thousands of troops thousands of miles without requiring access to bases in foreign nations. Admiral Moore's authority alone was sufficient.

I could pull together two Marine expeditionary units (MEUs), each consisting of one reinforced infantry battalion, more than two dozen fixed-wing aircraft and helicopters, and fifteen days of warfighting supplies packed on board three ships. For three days, my three-man "staff" and I pushed around the numbers—distances, weather, fuel, altitudes, lift weights for helicopters, fire support, and the like. We concluded that leaping four hundred miles from the sea could be done. You can never allow your enthusiasm to exceed your unit's capabilities, but my assessment was governed by the principle of calculated risk.

After I explained my plan, Admiral Moore said, "Good. I'm putting you in charge of Task Force 58—the ships and the landing force."

Task Force 58 consisted of six amphibious ships and occasionally allied escorts, carrying more than four thousand Marines. It was humbling that a senior Navy officer with whom I'd never before served had vested me, a Marine, with that responsibility. This was the first time in nearly two hundred years that any Navy ship had been placed under the command of a Marine. Willy Moore took some Navy flak. But he was unperturbed. His attitude meshed with mine: *Just do it.*

I walked out of Admiral Moore's office keenly conscious of the trust he had reposed in me. It never entered my mind that we might fail. Marines don't know how to spell the word. I knew that our air could deliver and our lads were ready for the brawl, ready to bloody those who had attacked our country or supported them. My immediate job was getting my Marines from the ocean into the Taliban's backyard.

Outside the admiral's office, I bumped into a friend, Navy Captain Bob Harward. His SEALs, stuck in Bahrain for lack of airlift, couldn't get into the fight. With his shaved head and muscular frame, Bob looked like the stereotype of a SEAL. As a youth he had lived in Iran, he was fluent in Farsi, and he had an encyclopedic knowledge of the Middle East. I knew him to be a cunning, competitive, and flexible leader who led by example. I stuck out my hand. "Welcome to war. I've got aircraft. We'll go together." We shook hands, striking a partnership that would endure over decades of war.

Already conducting raids across southern Afghanistan was Army Major General Dell Dailey's Joint Special Operations Task Force. For weeks, Dell had been launching raids into the southern region, primarily flying small units from the deck of the USS *Kitty Hawk* in the North Arabian Sea. His operational tempo was constrained by the enormous distances they were flying under daunting conditions. One minute after Dell and I met, he heartily endorsed landing Task Force 58 in southern Afghanistan. A forward base meant more flexibility for Dell and his men. A few weeks before I arrived, his Rangers had pulled a gutsy night raid against a remote dirt strip called Rhino, ninety miles outside Kandahar. He recommended that I land my Marines there. Once we had that lodgment, both Special Operations Forces and Marines would launch raids in all directions. No one really knows an enemy until he fights them, and Dell had been fighting them. He sensed Rhino was the right target, and it became my objective, putting Admiral Moore's vision into motion.

My next stop was an air base in Saudi Arabia, to meet with Air Force Lieutenant General Michael Moseley, the overall commander of air operations in the Middle East and Afghanistan. As I explained the concept, he gauged the scale of miles on a map. He looked up and asked, "Are you really going to do this?" I said yes. Pushing the map back across the table to me, he said, "If you get in trouble, I'll put every airplane you need over your head."

Taking the measure of this man, I knew he could deliver. For the first time in my career, I decided not to bring artillery in my assault waves. While doctrine rightly points out that artillery ashore is key to promoting high-tempo round-the-clock operations, I judged that our helo insertion, enemy threat, and air support gave me license to adapt. In this specific case, I could increase the buildup ashore by bringing in artillery later.

But I still had to figure out how to get across Pakistan. Using Admiral Moore's plane, I flew to Islamabad to meet with our diplomats and the Pakistani military.

"What is a Marine doing here?" Ambassador Wendy Chamberlin asked when I entered her office.

"Madam Ambassador," I said, "I'm taking a few thousand of my best friends to Afghanistan to kill some people." She smiled and said, "I think I can help you." Never before had I personally experienced a diplomat's impact so directly.

I needed to cross Pakistani airspace to attack Al Qaeda and their Taliban allies in Afghanistan. On the spot, this highly regarded diplomat arranged the right introductions. I met with Major General Farooq Ahmed Khan, the planning chief for the Pakistani military. After losing several wars with India, to its east, Pakistan was determined to exert leverage over any government in Kabul in order to avoid any threat from the west. But the Taliban were sheltering Al Qaeda. Now, given the Taliban's refusal to break with the Al Qaeda operatives they were sheltering, the Pakistanis knew that I would be attacking the Taliban, with whom they had come to an accommodation.

When we met, General Farooq launched into a litany of grievances about decades of American foreign policy. I heard him out. Pakistan's relationship with America was marked by disappointments on both sides. Smoldering resentment was the result.

Once General Farooq was finished, I said, "General, I'm not a diplomat. I'm going to Afghanistan. I want to know if you will help me."

Farooq understood, and the discussion shifted. He agreed to air corridors over Pakistan. While the initial assault troops would seize Rhino, going in by air-refuelable helicopters, the reinforcements would fly into Rhino later.

By seizing the initiative, a commander forces the enemy to react, throwing him off-balance. Once we landed, Rhino could be defended against any ground attack with air support. Conversely, once we had boots on the ground, we could control the roads and isolate Kandahar while preparing to seize it.

In his fast-moving campaigns during the Civil War, Union General William T. Sherman habitually sought to threaten two objectives before he attacked. This forced the Confederate generals to split their forces, giving Sherman a decisive advantage when he made his lunge. Admiral Moore was thinking in similar terms. Once my brigade had a lodgment at Rhino, the Taliban were placed on the horns of a dilemma: keep the bulk of their forces to defend in the north or shift them south to hold Kandahar against us.

To do this, we had to move quickly. History gives us ample precedents for making decisions at the speed of relevance. In 1943, General Douglas MacArthur was planning a landing in the Southwest Pacific. He wrote to Admiral William Halsey, in charge of the South Pacific, asking for a naval campaign to divert the Japanese forces. Only two days later, Halsey wrote back, pledging his support. (See Appendix C.) There was no need for extended exchanges between staffs. The shared objective was to shatter the Japanese forces. All else was secondary. Two strong-willed commanders collaborated to unleash hell upon our enemy.

Compared with that giant endeavor, our effort in 2001 was small in scale. It nonetheless demanded the same speed of decision; we had to move against Kandahar before the enemy had time to reinforce its defenses. Bureaucratic, organizational, and political frictions were cast aside. In the space of a few days, a Navy admiral, an American ambassador, a SEAL commodore, an Army Special Forces general, an Air Force general, and a Marine brigadier general had determined how best to invade southern Afghanistan. We had a shared spirit of collaboration that enabled swift decisions. We shook hands and committed to one another's success, confident that each of us would do his part. Trust remains the coin of the realm.

A LEAN STAFF

I had flown into Bahrain with a staff of three: my super-efficient aide, Lieutenant Warren Cook, my clever planner, Major Mike Mahaney, and my operational brain, Lieutenant Colonel Clarke Lethin. Admiral Moore had appointed me commander of Naval Task Force 58, and we went to work. The TF 58 designation had a hallowed lineage going back to World War II. Relying upon speed and deception, TF 58 was the hammer that struck at one Japanese-controlled island after another. At the Battle of Iwo Jima, in 1945, Task Force 58 included eighteen aircraft carriers and eight battleships—more firepower than any navy in history.

We took a quick inventory and determined that our 2001 version of TF 58 would comprise six amphibious ships, plus escorts; 3,100 sailors and 4,500 Marines; plus KC-130s, Harrier fighters, and helicopters. While tiny by comparison with World War II, an operation of this size required more than a staff of three.

By doctrine, a deployed brigade could have a staff exceeding two hundred. For what we had in mind, we drastically cut down staff size by employing "skip-echelon," a technique I learned in discussions with a voluble English-speaking Iraqi major my battalion had captured in the 1991 Gulf War. In most military organizations, each level of command—or echelon—has staff sections with the same functions, like personnel management, intelligence gathering, operational planning, and logistics support. As the Iraqi major explained, such duplication wasted time and manpower and added no value.

I wanted my staff at the top to do only what we alone could do, delegating as much authority as possible to proven Marine and Navy commanders below me. Assuming that my boss knew how to run Fifth Fleet and that my subordinates knew how to run their ships or outfits, I did not replicate their staffs. I decided we didn't need our own chaplain or public affairs officer or a host of other officers repeating functions that were being carried out at lower levels. Ashore at fleet HQ, when I was dealing with a legal issue, I consulted the Navy lawyer on Admiral Moore's staff. At sea, I'd consult with a lawyer on the Marine staff. Once we were ashore in Afghanistan, I decided my senior enlisted adviser would be the senior noncom in our Coalition Special Forces. He kept me informed of any broad issues bothering the troops, regardless of nationality, through his network of NCOs across Navy, Marine, and allied elements. Throughout my career, I've preferred to work with whoever was in place. When a new boss brings in a large team of favorites, it invites discord and the concentration of authority at higher levels. Using skip-echelon meant trusting subordinate commanders and staffs. I chose to build on cohesive teams, support them fully, and remove those who didn't wind up measuring up.

By eliminating redundant functions, I kept my own staff exceedingly small. Rather than two hundred, it numbered thirty-two, including Navy officers and Marines plus an Air Force Special Tactics captain and a CIA officer. When someone answered a phone, he dealt with each question tersely and generally on the spot.

Business management books often stress "centralized planning and decentralized execution." That is too top-down for my taste. I believe in a centralized vision, coupled with decentralized planning and execution. In general, there are two kinds of executives: those who simply respond to their staffs and those who direct their staffs and give them latitude, coaching them as needed to carry out the directions. I needed to focus on the big issues and leave the staff to flesh out how to get there. Guided by robust feedback loops, I returned to three questions: *What do I know? Who needs to know? Have I told them?* Shared data displays kept all planning elements aligned.

Everyone on my staff, in Marine parlance, filled sandbags. No one was exempt from the simplest tasks. We answered our own phones, brewed our own coffee, and slept six hours when lucky. Meals were operational discussions. I kept my commander's intent brief and to the point. After I communicated my intent, subordinate commanders, along with their Navy and Marine staffs, drafted plans for how they would execute their parts of the mission.

I kept my door open. If anyone needed guidance, he'd walk in and say, "Sir, here's the issue. What's your intent?" I had studied the British experience in Burma in World War II. To keep the numerically superior Japanese forces off-balance, in 1943 Brigadier General Orde Wingate led a long-range penetration force, called the Chindits, behind enemy lines. I was confident we could do the same and, importantly, sustain our forces four hundred miles deep in enemy territory.

At the end of each day, we'd all discuss how we had done so far. I'd sum up the meeting by saying, "Okay, I like this. Now let's do that." The next morning, my Navy and Marine operations officers would inform me, "Here is where we now are." It was a constant dialogue, and hundreds of fleet exercises were now paying off in real time. Absent those years of integrating Navy and Marine exercises and complex operations, I could not have executed this operation.

I took an eight-hour reconnaissance flight over southern Afghanistan in a Navy P-3, a long-legged, long-loitering airplane designed to find submarines. Its sophisticated technologies made my observations easy. We detected no enemy units near our intended insertion point. The Taliban had left their back door open. Memo to young officers: I can appear brilliant if I fight enemy leaders dumber than a bucket of rocks.

WHAT CAME BEFORE

Military men have long memories about failures. In 1915, the British tried to seize the Dardanelles strait in order to force Turkey, fighting on the side of Germany, out of the war. But the amphibious landing at Gallipoli proved catastrophic. Two hundred thousand troops were pinned on the beachhead. The allies lost forty-four thousand killed and a hundred thousand wounded. When World War I ended, historians emphasized the futility of assaulting from the sea.

Six years later, Major Pete Ellis, a true Marine Corps maverick, anticipating war with Japan, urged the Commandant of the Marine Corps to develop amphibious techniques to seize advanced land bases across the Pacific. In Navy/Marine experiments in the Caribbean, the amphibious forces were honed to a razor's edge. Amphibious assaults proved key to winning World War II: Germany held Western Europe in an iron fist until the 1944 landing at Normandy, while in the Pacific, the seizure of islands isolated and doomed Japan. The frontal assaults on Japanese-held islands cost tens of thousands of Marine casualties.

When the Korean War broke out, in 1950, General Douglas MacArthur ignored Washington's advice and ordered the Marines to land behind the North Korean army and seize Seoul, the enemy-held capital of South Korea.

"The amphibious landing," MacArthur explained, "is the most powerful tool we have to employ. We must strike hard and deep into enemy territory. The deep envelopment, based upon surprise, which severs the enemy supply lines, is and always has been the most decisive maneuver of war." MacArthur's brilliance in Korea lay in moving the Marines hundreds of miles by sea to land in the rear of the unsuspecting North Korean army, and resulted in far fewer friendly casualties.

After the Korean War, the Navy constructed helicopter carriers, designed like aircraft carriers. Several years later, the Marines modified the rugged C-130 Hercules to provide aerial refueling of both fighter aircraft and helicopters. In the late sixties, Marines deployed the CH-53 helicopter, a 46,000-pound monster that, fully loaded, could haul troops and cargo hundreds of miles.

Each generation fights with the tools shaped by preceding generations. So in 2001, I had a tool kit unimaginable in prior wars. Some military and political leaders still envisioned amphibious warfare in terms of landing on Iwo Jima. The minute Admiral Moore pointed to a map showing landlocked Afghanistan, hundreds of miles from the sea, I knew I could land there with thousands of Marines. The planning would take only a few weeks, because I had the right tools at hand. Over five decades, farsighted men, both military and civilian, had contributed the pieces that I was assembling into Task Force 58.

But having a plan counts for nothing unless those above you are made confident that you can execute. As the leader, you maintain communications connectivity up, not just down. This can be hard when you introduce the phrase "amphibious operation" to people whose mental image has not progressed beyond World War II landings at Normandy and in the Pacific.

By the second week in November, small teams of CIA operatives and Special Operations Forces in northern Afghanistan were providing air support for tribal militias that were routing the Taliban. Convinced that our plan for seizing Rhino was solid, Admiral Moore decided to put the issue before Central Command to approve or disapprove, basically a "go" or "no go" decision. CENTCOM convened a video teleconference call with Moore, Dell Dailey, and me speaking, plus a host of others listening in. CENTCOM had envisioned the Marines launching small raids, as the Special Operations Forces were doing.

Actually, we were proposing an invasion. Admiral Moore suggested we not emphasize this. So in my brief, I explained that seizing Rhino provided a forward base for raids. I left out any mention of withdrawing my forces, because I did not intend to do so. Once ashore, I wanted to stay there and tear the enemy apart. To my surprise, no one asked me about withdrawing.

I had assessed this admittedly complex operation through the lens of calculated risk. But as I briefed the MEU's plan for a nighttime heliborne assault into Rhino, followed by Marine KC-130s landing on the dirt strip with reinforcements, CENTCOM's central concern became obvious. On the screen, I watched the expressions of two senior CENTCOM generals, both aviators who had logged thousands of hours in the cockpit. They were keenly aware of the dangers associated with nighttime refueling, and they fully understood that our proposed operation required many moving parts: ships steaming full-speed from the Mediterranean; helicopters launching at night, needing to rendezvous with KC-130 tankers hundreds of miles inland; and SEALs, hiding for days deep inside enemy territory, communicating with the ships at sea. All that said, I was confident that every piece of the plan was well within our capability.

Videoconferences may speed decision-making, but they have a downside. You can see only the participants selected by the camera. You can't read the body language of the others. In addition to the two generals, there were others listening in that conference room in Tampa, plus more than a dozen other stations, from Bahrain to Washington to Hawaii. I knew I had only a few minutes to win CENTCOM's approval. A negative consensus can lock in without a word being spoken. By now I had shifted my location from fleet headquarters in Bahrain to my flagship in the North Arabian Sea. I wanted to send a message to the ships at sea and the Marines on board that we were going, but as I watched, I had no idea which way CENTCOM's decision would go.

The silence was broken by a question about potential friction between the Special Ops Task Force SWORD and TF 58. The TF SWORD commander, quietly watching from his tent, interrupted immediately.

"I am in total support of what Task Force 58 is proposing," he said firmly. "We have deconflicted in time and space. I fully support this operation."

He put it over the top. We were cleared hot to invade.

OPERATION ENDURING FREEDOM—NOV 2001

PURPOSE: Working in concert with TF SWORD, Amphibious Raid Forces will maintain constant pressure on Taliban/Al Qaida forces, creating chaos and destabilizing enemy control of southern Afghanistan.

I intend to exploit the enemy's focus on active ground operations in northern Afghanistan. Coordinating, integrating, and deconflicting with TF SWORD, Amphibious Raid Forces will attack the Taliban in southern Afghanistan with repeated raids designed to destroy the enemy's sense of security and shatter his will. Amphibious Raid Forces will exploit TF SWORD's successes and maintain the momentum gained by SWORD attacking targets that compel the enemy to react, exposing him to our combined arms.

END STATE:

- Taliban/Al Qaida Leaders in disarray, facing an operational dilemma on how to allocate their forces (northern front or southern Afghanistan).
- Freedom for TF-58 to operate on the ground at the time and place of our choosing.
- Destroy Taliban leadership's confidence that they maintain any control over southern Afghanistan.

A few days after Thanksgiving, I stood on the deck of a helicopter carrier a few dozen miles off the Pakistani coast. Clangs of gunfire were reverberating inside the hangar deck as Marines test-fired their rifles into the sea. Grunts in full armor were clambering up the catwalks with hundred-pound packs. Red lighting splayed their shadows, thick and gorilla-like, against the bulkheads. Topside on the dark flight deck, Marines were following guides with blue chemical lights up the ramps of CH-53 helicopters the size of tractor trailers. Teams of sailors and Marines in colored jerseys were carrying out precision tasks, fueling and arming the aircraft while moving the troops along in orderly files.

America's war machine was stirring, each cog sliding into place. With deafening rotor blades whirling overhead, the seemingly chaotic yet choreographed deck was no place for the untrained. Every step had been rehearsed.

During the day, AV-8B Harrier aircraft had taken off from the USS *Bataan* to strike targets outside Kandahar. The SEALs, in hide sites overlooking Rhino, had sent the call sign "Winter," signaling no enemy on the objective. Now, as I watched, seven gunships and six giant CH-53s had lifted off from the flight deck of the USS *Peleliu* for the four-hour flight. As they flew northeast over Pakistan, they were refueled in the air by four KC-130s.

At 9 P.M., the first wave hit the deck at Rhino. The first helicopters to touch down stirred up thick dust as fine as talcum powder, causing a plume that drifted hundreds of feet into the sky. This was what every aviator feared on landing—being enveloped in a total brownout. Minutes later, the Marines in the second wave felt like they were in a runaway elevator, descending and ascending like a yo-yo. Unable to see, the pilots gingerly fluttered up and down until they felt the ground. Within an hour, 170 grunts had taken up defensive positions without an accident, and Air Force Captain Mike Flatten's Special Tactics Team had the dirt strip ready to receive the KC-130s.

After 9/11, no nation could respond as America did. Wars, like hurricanes, recur without advance warning. Some you cannot avoid. If you want the fewest big regrets when surprise strikes, you must provide, ahead of time, the doctrine and resources to respond. A few months before, I had observed this very unit rehearsing a raid from their ships off the Californian coast deep into the Mojave Desert in California. I was confident they could do it.

For several nights before the assault, we had quietly staged Marines and vehicles. The assault wave launched from the ships, and by dawn, four hundred more Marines, plus gun trucks, had landed. Our team had just achieved the deepest amphibious assault from the sea in history.

From start to finish, it had taken our team—Navy, Marine, Army Special Operations, State Department—just twenty-eight days to conceive, plan, persuade, and execute the invasion of Afghanistan. Operations occur at the speed of trust.

On November 26, D-Day + One, the Taliban moved against Rhino by launching an armored convoy from Lashkar Gah, fifty miles to the northwest. Navy F-14s and Marine Cobra gunships made short work of them. They didn't get close, and didn't live to return to the town named for Alexander the Great's army, which had invaded Afghanistan 2,400 years ago.

Lieutenant General Gregory Newbold, Director of Operations for the Joint Chiefs of Staff, was later asked about opening a second front in the war. "The insertion of Task Force 58," he said, "had a deep psychological impact on the Taliban and Al Qaeda—they were confronted with a military situation which unhinged any hope they had for a gradual pullback from the north and a chance to hold from the barrier of greatest strength. Task Force 58 funda-

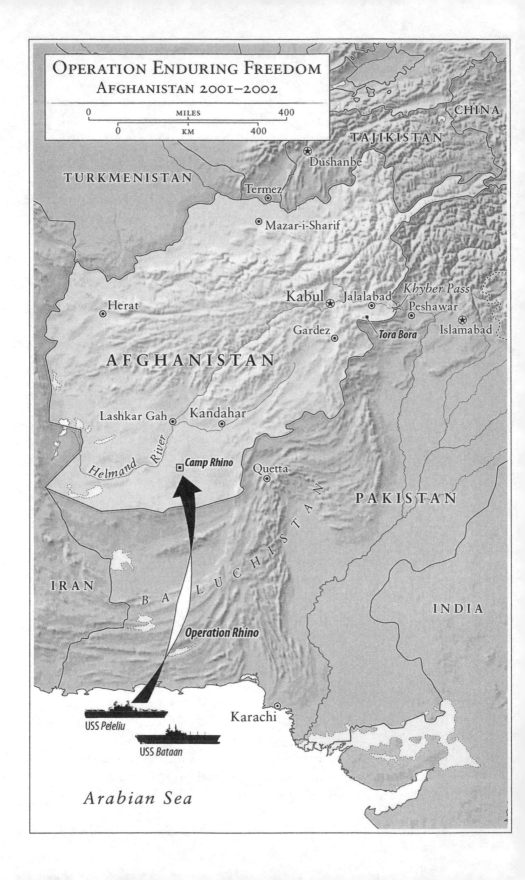

mentally changed the equation for the enemy from one of grim hope to hopelessness."

My goal at Rhino was to swiftly build up our combat power and take the offensive.

Rhino had only one advantage as a forward operating base: it was in Afghanistan. Aside from that, it was a distinctly unpleasant place, a dry lake bed where high winds covered us with dust. As you tromped through it, it enveloped you, clogging your eyes, nostrils, ears, and mouth. No blade of grass or scrub tree marred the landscape; it was brown to the horizon. All water was flown in, so we couldn't wash. We had to chip through calcified rock to dig in. The troops were constantly hacking up phlegm.

It was meant to be a jumping-off spot. We steadily built up our combat power, fuel, and medical supplies during our first week on the ground. Commodore Harward was amassing special forces from several nations alongside his SEALs. Very soon, we were ready to push against Kandahar.

Our aviators were performing at the outer edge of the envelope for man and machine. Allies were rushing in to come to America's aid—Australia, Canada, Germany, Jordan, New Zealand, Norway, Romania, Turkey, and the UK. I tightened a bit as I listened to landings in zero visibility. Mishaps in brownout conditions were inevitable. One CH-53 sucked debris into its air intake, lost power, and crash-landed, thankfully without injuries. A Huey lost power on takeoff and rolled over, consumed by flames. On a night takeoff, a taxiing C-130 hit the rotor blade of another CH-53. Again, we sustained no injuries. Twenty-four hours a day, Air Force Captain Mike Flatten and his dozen men kept the runway open, supported by thirty-nine sailors from the Navy Construction Battalion, the famous "Seabees," constantly grading and compacting the runway. Air Force C-17s, some flying 3,600 miles from Germany, kept us supplied.

Shortly before I had left the USS *Peleliu* for Rhino, I was directed by higher headquarters to speak with reporters on board ship. Without thinking much about it, I told them, "The Marines have landed. We now own a piece of Afghanistan and are going to give it back to the Afghan people."

When it showed up in the headlines, it read, "We now own a piece of Afghanistan." Secretary of Defense Rumsfeld didn't contact me personally, but he would genially reprimand me in a press conference by saying, "Don't do that again." He went on say that I was "clearly exuberant." While the headline caused consternation at CENTCOM headquarters, it wasn't my problem, and I went ashore.

Toward the end of the first week at Rhino, I grew impatient. We were still on hold.

General Franks was opaque. "We may well use assets from [Rhino] to interdict the roads. . . . It is not an invasion. As soon as our work is finished, it [Rhino] certainly will be removed. And yes, we may well use it to bring humanitarian assistance to the people in Afghanistan."

Not an invasion? Well, here we were—hundreds of Marines and Special Operations troops, caked in dust, cleaning their weapons four times a day. In September, the President had described CENTCOM's war plan as requiring ground troops to "hunt down remaining Taliban and Al Qaeda fighters." We had come to Rhino to destroy the terrorists who had murdered three thousand civilians. Admiral Moore had told me to land and shatter the Taliban's last hope of defending themselves. His clear-eyed vision, coupled with his force of personality, gave me at least one steady anchor point on which to plan and conduct the operation. His example would be a model to me in the years ahead.

Despite Franks's perplexing statement, I remained focused on building up combat power to quickly seize Kandahar, ninety miles away. Back at the Pentagon, General Richard Myers, chairman of the Joint Chiefs, said, "Kandahar, it's sort of the last bastion . . . of Taliban resistance. . . . They'll dig in and fight, and perhaps to the end." The chairman had clearly stated the right mission for Task Force 58, for we were within striking distance of their "last bastion." Maneuver warfare had taught us to shatter the enemy's capacity to make coherent decisions. The Taliban's command center in Kandahar didn't know what to do. It was time to put Mullah Omar out of his misery and tear apart the Taliban and their Al Qaeda allies. Don't give them the time and space to reconstitute.

Yet we were hunkered down, not knowing what we were waiting

to do. Although Admiral Moore was doing his best to get us into the fight, TF 58 was stuck, ordered to hold fast. It was maddening. One of my Marines from New York City summed up our frustration. "This is a perfect war, General," he said. "They want to die, and we want to kill them. Let's get this on!"

A week after we landed, General Franks held a press conference, saying, "The Marines . . . I will not characterize the intent of them being there [at Rhino] as a force to attack Kandahar. That's simply not the case. That's not why we put them there."

Now I was baffled. A negative statement is not a mission. Simply sitting at Rhino, we were sucking up resources and risking accidents, without moving against the enemy. Why were we there?

The news had gotten worse on November 28, our third day at Rhino. Admiral Moore informed us that CENTCOM had decided to limit our total force to one thousand personnel. Moore and I were not told why CENTCOM had unilaterally prevented me from bringing more of my troops to Rhino to move against the Taliban, whose numbers were estimated at twenty thousand. I still had 3,500 Marines waiting on board ships, deployed to my command by orders from CENTCOM and the Secretary of Defense. But on shore, I also needed support personnel like the Seabees to maintain the dirt airstrip. So as a result of the arbitrary limit, to bring in the Seabees, I had to send combat troops back to the ships.

On November 30—the sixth day after landing—control of Task Force 58 forces ashore at Rhino transferred from Admiral Moore to the U.S. Army Forces Central Command (ARCENT), located in Kuwait. Each night, I sent an "intentions message" to Moore and to ARCENT, updating recent activities and laying out my intent and the operations for the following days. I kept extending our patrol areas, some sixty miles from Rhino. I was confident in the skills of these small mounted units, and we were looking for a fight. But the enemy, knowing we were there, chose not to engage.

Loose control of operations is ingrained in Marine and Navy culture, and years of teamwork have us highly aligned. The Army approach provides more detailed oversight by the higher-level staffs. ARCENT was eager to support TF 58, but they needed coordination time and a deluge of information. Strangers who haven't trained together don't work smoothly together. Once in the fray, they need to work out the kinks. Ideally, they rehearse repeatedly before an operation such as ours. ARCENT brought a large staff with a deliberate and very thorough planning process.

From their perspective, they were exhibiting a thirst to contribute. But they needed data, a lot of data: what we were doing, what we needed, and details about what we were planning, when, where, how. Much of this my lean staff didn't know, because we never asked such questions of our subordinate units. The volume of demands for data was overwhelming us. The senior land component staff could transmit much more than my handful of staff could assimilate.

My operations officer told his ARCENT counterpart, "Sir, there is one of me and dozens of you. I'm working twenty-two hours a day, and I can't answer all of your action officers. I can answer *your* questions, but not everyone on your staff."

In response, ARCENT sent us a more generalized instruction: "Be prepared to interdict enemy lines of communication [roads] west of Kandahar."

That was clear and succinct. So we launched patrols far and wide. One night, a mounted patrol was in an ambush site about eighty miles from Rhino. After they shot up the lead vehicle of a Taliban convoy, a few hundred yards to the rear, enemy fighters hopped out of a dump truck to outflank our unit. Watching this through night vision goggles, the patrol called in an air strike. The enemy fighters climbed back into their truck just as a Navy F-14 dropped its bomb, killing a dozen of the unluckiest Taliban in Afghanistan.

The next morning, I was shaving when the secure telephone jangled. My radio operator, Corporal Jacobek, picked it up, answered a few questions, and hung up.

"ARCENT," he said, "needed a little info about last night's ambush, sir."

I thought nothing further about it. Then it happened again after another successful but routine engagement. Jacobek was busy, so I answered the phone.

"About last night's action," a lieutenant colonel said, "we weren't informed beforehand. I need details. Someone's going to answer for this. Corporal, give me the name of the person responsible."

"Mattis," I said.

"Damn, he's the commanding general. . . . Who am I talking to?"

"Mattis."

A moment's pause.

"Shit, sorry, sir. It was a good kill. SecDef's happy. But we have no record of authorizing it."

We both laughed. Different folk, different systems. But it symbolized a culture of pre-briefs, orders, reports, and large staffs difficult to navigate.

TF 58 remained tied in place for reasons I still don't understand. Our mounted patrols occupied only a fraction of our fighting power. Plus, the center of the enemy's gravity lay in Kandahar, easily within our reach. Theoretically, our force did serve as a "threat-in-being." That is, by simply occupying Rhino, we affected the enemy's behavior. But I didn't want one thousand elite mobile troops ashore and thousands more on ships inhabiting a theoretical world; I wanted us turned loose to create chaos.

As was my habit, at night I'd walk the lines, hopping into fighting holes to chat with the shivering sentries. Under a spectacular array of stars, exhaling steam with every breath, it was easy to talk about the mission. Night after night, I got the same message.

"When do we get into the fight, sir?"

"Soon," I said. "Our turn will come soon. Don't let down your guard. Stay ready."

September 11 was fresh in our minds. We wanted to destroy Al Qaeda and the Taliban. Obliterate them, not sit on our cold asses, hocking up gobs of dust. The lads were chafing.

The unsettled Taliban were falling back in disorder toward Kandahar. An eleven-man Special Forces team was moving toward the city with Hamid Karzai, the political leader of the opposition. On the morning of December 5, our ops center informed me that a Cobra helicopter had crashed, with the crew safely recovered. A few hours later and 130 miles northeast of Rhino, due to a terrible error, a two-thousand-pound bomb exploded in the middle of the team that was supporting Karzai. The casualties, both killed and wounded, were severe. The coordinates for their location were uncertain, initially showing one location on the Pakistan border and, later, a different location closer to Kandahar. I didn't know which was correct. It was broad daylight, which meant that helicopters would be vulnerable if they were vectored to the wrong location, approaching a hot landing zone. Amid the confusion of the initial position reports, I declined to immediately launch the helicopters.

The Special Forces soldiers were furious, as I would have been in their place. They had suffered fatalities, and the wounded needed immediate help. But I had to weigh how many lives I placed at risk versus how many might be saved by instantaneous action. By around noon, the location had been confirmed and the helicopters went in, bringing back forty-one injured to Rhino.

One of the injured Afghan fighters died at Rhino, despite the efforts of our Navy surgeons. Had my delayed decision cost him— and his family—his life? Should I have sent the helos in earlier, as the Special Forces soldiers were urging? Or had I avoided more aircraft accidents and fatalities by not rushing to an unconfirmed location?

When you are in command, there is always the next decision waiting to be made. You don't have time to pace back and forth like Hamlet, zigzagging one way and the other. You do your best and live with the consequences. A commander has to compartmentalize his emotions and remain focused on the mission. You must decide, act, and move on.

Due to the gritty performance and selfless sacrifices of two Special Operations Forces teams, by the end of the first week in December, Karzai was approaching the outskirts of Kandahar. Hundreds of tribesmen, sensing the end of Taliban rule, cheered as he drove by. Bob Harward and I, accompanied by a Coalition Special Operations commander, helicoptered in to meet with him at a bombed-out villa on the edge of Kandahar, formerly occupied by Mullah Omar. Karzai was calm, confident, and content, and in league with our Special Forces. With occasional gunfire echoing in the background, we sat on rugs around a Coleman lantern, casting shadows on the wall. We discussed how my forces would seize the Kandahar airport. He assured us that Mullah Omar and the other Taliban leaders had fled.

During a break in the talks, Karzai and I went for a walk in the villa's garden.

At one point I said, "If I caused you any problems with my

statement about owning a piece of Afghanistan, I apologize. I didn't mean to."

Karzai stopped. "No," he said, "when I read that in the electronic edition of *The New York Times,* I went out and shouted at my troops, 'The Marines are in southern Afghanistan. We've won!'"

I had to laugh. What CENTCOM had seen as a disruption in the campaign was not even a tempest in a teapot. Quite the opposite, it had motivated Karzai's troops at a tough time.

Hundreds of Taliban were still in the city, sullen but powerless. In the days following the meeting, Task Force 58 and the Special Operations Forces met scant resistance in securing the airport, the main roads, and the government center in Kandahar. To the people's joy, the despised Taliban had been routed. I saw formerly prohibited kites flying, and men lined up in front of barbershops waiting to have their beards shaved off.

By mid-December, Kandahar airfield was secured and the battleground had shifted to the Tora Bora mountains, four hundred miles north of Rhino. Osama bin Laden had retreated there with two thousand of his most dedicated Al Qaeda fighters from a dozen nations. Years earlier, OBL had hired engineers with bulldozers to construct a network of caves outfitted with generators and electric power. His force was now holed up inside those fortifications.

Of course, I expected TF 58 to be employed in the final battle that would destroy Al Qaeda's high command. My brigade was the only American unit within reach that had the firepower, leadership, mobility, and shock troops to do the job and finish the fight. As a bonus, I was eager to use our helicopters to bring into the fight numerous commando teams under Harward's command. With a now well-honed team, we could bring a seamless conventional/special operations juggernaut into the hunt.

Our combined staffs and intelligence analysts were piecing together the reports of OBL's retreat. At a glance, there appeared to be several routes leading east out of Tora Bora into Pakistan, twenty miles away. But in snow and freezing temperatures among sixteen-thousand-foot peaks, few of the rocky and icy paths were accessible. We had high-resolution photomaps detailing every twist and turn on the high-altitude passes, and imagery revealed only a few dozen passable routes. All could be kept under observation and under fire from well-sited, interconnecting outposts on the high ground.

Again, history offered lessons. I had studied the Army's "Geronimo campaign." To track down the Apache leader in 1886, the Army had constructed twenty-three heliograph stations in southern Arizona and New Mexico to provide observation and communications. Whichever way the Apache turned, they were seen and cut off. Our own Marine intelligence staff back in the States had quickly provided computer-generated visibility diagrams. My staff plotted the locations where outposts on the high ground would have around-the-clock observation of all escape routes. The outposts were positioned so that each one could see another, thus providing interlocking fields of fire.

I was prepared to deploy Special Ops teams and Marine rifle platoons, all with forward observers who could direct air and artillery fire. At every pass, helicopters would insert overwatch teams equipped with cold-weather gear, forward air controllers, snipers, machine guns, and mortars. Attack aircraft would be on call. Our air could smash up the entrances, leaving the terrorists to die inside the caves. If they tried to escape, TF 58 would be waiting at the exits. Cutting off the escape passes was the anvil; I also had reinforced rifle companies waiting to swing the hammer and finish off the Al Qaeda forces. By December 14, we had helicopters on the Kandahar runway and tough, well-equipped troops ready to board.

We had sent our proposed scheme of maneuver back to ARCENT's staff in Kuwait (and to Admiral Moore, for his information). When we heard nothing back, I began making phone calls. At one point in early December, I was blunt; some described my presentation as highly obscene. I stated my concern that bin Laden could escape if we didn't quickly seal the valley exits. But I was shouting against the wind.

Having hit a stone wall with that option, I even offered to place myself and my troops under the operational control of Bob Harward, my junior in rank. This offer, too, fell on deaf ears. Over the next two maddening weeks, we were not called forward.

Instead, General Franks sent in Afghan tribal fighters loyal to warlords from the north. The thinking was that this would show

Afghans fighting their own war. But they were out of their tribal element in Tora Bora—poorly equipped and strangers among the locals. They proved incapable of closing with the tough, desperate Al Qaeda fighters. Many of the enemy leaders fled unscathed to Pakistan. By Christmas, the intel officers were informing me that they thought bin Laden had escaped. "That's a hell of a Christmas present," I commented.

In his memoir, General Franks explained why he chose not to employ my Marines. "We don't want to repeat the Soviets' mistakes," he wrote. "There's nothing to be gained by blundering around those mountains and gorges with armor battalions chasing a lightly armed enemy."

I didn't have armor; I had fast-moving light infantry and Bob Harward's Special Forces, all heliborne, reinforced by agile wheeled light armored vehicles. By closing off the mountain passes with overwatch teams and then attacking with well-supported infantry, we were ready to squeeze Al Qaeda in a vise. Here is how the White House correspondent for *The New York Times* described what happened: "Hank Crumpton, who was leading the CIA's operations in Afghanistan, brought his concerns to the White House, imploring Bush to send the marines to block escape routes. . . . Bush deferred to Franks. . . . In his desire to let the military call the shots, Bush had missed the best opportunity of his entire presidency to catch America's top enemy."

My view is a bit different. We in the military missed the opportunity, not the President, who properly deferred to his senior military commander on how to carry out the mission. Looking at myself, perhaps I hadn't invested the time to build understanding up the chain of command.

When I no longer worked for Admiral Moore for my ashore elements, I needed to adapt to a new Army commander with a different staff style. I should have paid more attention and gotten on the same wavelength as my higher headquarters if I wanted them to be my advocates.

Deploying teams with massive firepower to seal off the passes seemed patently compelling on the merits. I waited for the call to come. But I was in Afghanistan, and the decision-makers were continents away.

When you are engaged at the tactical level, you grasp your own reality so clearly it's tempting to assume that everyone above you sees it in the same light. Wrong. When you're the senior commander in a deployed force, time spent sharing your appreciation of the situation on the ground with your seniors is like time spent on reconnaissance: it's seldom wasted. If I had it to do over again, I would have called both the ARCENT commander and Admiral Moore and said, "Sir, I have a plan to accomplish the mission, kill Osama bin Laden, and hand you a victory. All I need is your permission."

In 2005, a *New York Times* correspondent wrote, "An American intelligence official told me that the Bush administration later concluded that the refusal of Centcom to dispatch the Marines . . . was the gravest error of the war."

PART II

EXECUTIVE LEADERSHIP

CHAPTER 6

The March Up

FOLLOWING TORA BORA, the Army's 101st Airborne flew a brigade into Kandahar, relieving my Marines and sailors. They went back aboard ship. I was ordered back to fleet headquarters in Bahrain, then flew to Camp Pendleton.

Returning to the States in late spring 2002, I reported in to the commander of I Marine Expeditionary Force, Lieutenant General Michael Hagee. "You're being promoted to two stars," he told me. "You will take command of the 1st Marine Division this summer and prepare them to go to war in Iraq."

The news both pleased and disoriented me. On the one hand, I was honored and humbled to take command of a division in which I'd served in peace and in combat. The 1st Marine Division had been the first American unit to seize the offensive in World War II, landing at Guadalcanal, in the Solomon Islands. The division patch, called the Blue Diamond, showed the five stars of the Southern Cross against the blue background of the evening sky. Since World War II, generations of Marines wearing that patch had answered the nation's call, in Korea, in Vietnam, and most recently in Kuwait. Assuming command was, for me, the culmination of thirty years of serving Corps and country.

On the other hand, invading Iraq stunned me. Why were we fighting them again? I was unaware of the discussions in Washington linking Al Qaeda to Saddam. There was broad consensus among international intelligence agencies that he possessed chemical weapons. The argument for invading and deposing him was based on preempting any future transfer of weapons of mass destruction to terrorists. Even assuming he had chemical weapons, I believed we had him boxed in with our daily combat air patrols and sanctions against his oil exports. Having served twenty years in the region, I knew that his hatred of Iran worked to our strategic advantage. When I questioned General Hagee, his response was straightforward. "The higher-level decisions are made in Washington by our civilian leaders, not us." He rightly pointed out that my job was to get the troops ready.

The night after my meeting with General Hagee, I dumped my gear in my quarters, pulled books off the shelves, and began studying campaigns in Mesopotamia, starting with Xenophon's *Anabasis* and books on Alexander the Great—working my way forward.

Taking command in early August, I called my senior officers and NCOs into a conference room. "Spend the weekend," I said, "putting your domestic affairs in order and make peace with your God. Starting Monday, we focus on destroying the Iraqi Army."

Over the weekend, I wrote a list of instructions to guide my staff. For me, the staff would be a warfighting instrument, shoring up my weaknesses and amplifying my vision.

In my division were 22,000 troops, some stationed a hundred miles away. In terms of numbers, geography, and demands upon my time, I had now fully transitioned from personal to executive leadership. I accepted the staff and commanders that the system had put in place. I made it clear that after ninety days, those who couldn't embrace my priorities were to move elsewhere for a fresh start.

The institutional excellence of the Corps ensured that I was inheriting varsity players. When Lieutenant General Jim Conway turned command of 1st Marine Division over to me, of forty-five key jobs, I personally selected only four. I placed Lieutenant Colonels Clarke Lethin in operations and John Broadmeadow in charge of logistics, because both had performed imaginatively with me in Afghanistan. Lieutenant Warren Cook remained my aide, and I chose Colonel John Toolan as my operations officer. John and I had worked well together in the past. He grasped my opportunistic style of warfighting, with its emphasis on on-the-spot adaptation to take advantage of each enemy misstep.

At this stage of executive leadership, I delegated routine chores of management—filling personnel gaps, requesting equipment, etc.—to my chief of staff. I reserved for myself and my subordinate commanders the designing of the plan for how we would fight. I focused the division on only two priorities: getting ready to deploy and how to fight under chemical attack. I canceled all division-level inspections that did not pertain to those two tasks. Attitudes are caught, not taught. I left it to the seasoned leaders to schedule the events they considered necessary for those two objectives. I wanted all training conducted as rehearsals for the coming fight. My aim was to create a restlessness in my commanders and make the learning environment contagious. I wanted them all to be asking, every day, *What have I overlooked?*

It was already my habit, at the close of staff meetings and even chance encounters, to push my Marines by insisting they put me on the spot with one hard question before we finished our conversation. I wanted to know what bothered them at night. I wanted all hands to pitch in, with the value of good ideas outweighing rank. In the infantry, I had learned early to listen to the young guys on point. Lieutenant Colonel Clarke Lethin provided a classic example.

Instead of landing from the sea, my fully mechanized division would be moving along a few roads in seven thousand vehicles, in the deepest major land assault in Marine Corps history. I needed a method to display this challenge without disrupting their urgent training. Having studied the initial American battle in World War I, where traffic jams delayed and undermined our own attack, I needed a method to prevent that from happening.

The Legoland theme park was near our California base. On his own, Clarke purchased seven thousand Lego blocks. The NCOs glued them to sheets of cardboard in numbers reflecting the varied composition of each unit and laid them out on our parade deck. Each commander then dragged his sheet of Legos across a map of Iraq marked out on the parade deck, in accord with our assault plan. We watched as dozens of sheets became entangled. Presto—we had identified the choke points from our Kuwait jumping-off positions to bridges deep inside Iraq, stacking up and resulting in massive traffic jams even without fighting an enemy. As a result of Clarke's display of the problem, commanders had a graphic understanding of what they had to fix, which we rehearsed in the Mojave Desert.

I assigned young intelligence officers to understudy the six enemy division commanders facing us. Were they aggressive or tentative? Where had they gone to military school? What had they studied? What did their subordinates gossip about them? I wanted to know their weaknesses and, most important, whether or not they would take the initiative. I kept pictures of those generals in my desk drawer so that I would focus on them and not on the number of tanks in their divisions. In any confrontation, you need to know your enemy.

On another front I was taken by surprise. In June 2002, General Hagee war-gamed the invasion. He identified the critical problem, one that had escaped me: it wasn't breaking through the Iraqi Army or seizing Baghdad and throwing Saddam out of power. Rather, it was what we would do after.

"General," I said, "can't we focus first on winning the war and then worry about what comes next?"

"No," he said. "What comes next after we depose Saddam will be the war. I'm getting no guidance about that. We have to do our own planning for post-hostilities."

What Hagee saw was what Xenophon faced when he marched deep into Mesopotamia 2,400 years ago. Xenophon's ten thousand soldiers were a tiny minority among the people. He recognized that they must quickly gain control or the countryside would rise up against them.

Hagee had taught me a lesson in generalship. Now I realized why he was reprising what our former Commandant, General Charles Krulak, looking to the future, had called the "three-block war." On one block you'd be fighting; on the next, bringing humanitarian aid to beleaguered civilians; and on the third, separating warring factions—all on the same day.

I heard the same refrain again in November. All the division's officers attended the Marine Corps Birthday Ball, celebrated with pomp and ceremony in every location and ship where two or more Marine veterans or those on active duty can gather to raise a glass or two. I invited retired General Tony Zinni, who had commanded CENTCOM, to speak. Prior to the ceremony, all my senior officers gathered in my hotel room, Zinni sitting on the edge of the bed. It was like sitting around a campfire listening to the wisdom of an elder. He bluntly told us what, in his view, lay ahead.

"The decision is made; you're going. I'll disown you if you don't go through the Iraqi Army in six weeks." Next he said, wagging his finger at us, "Then the hard work begins. Ripping out an authoritarian regime leaves you responsible for security, water, power, and everything else. Removing Saddam will unleash the majority Shiites, defanging the minority Sunnis, who won't take lightly their loss of domination."

The cautions of Xenophon, Hagee, and Zinni brought home to me a concern about postwar control. However, we were told that shortly after hostilities ended, Marines would depart for other missions. So whatever CENTCOM planned for the governance of Iraq, it did not come down to us. As the division commander, I planned for only short-term postwar administrative tasks. But I did take some precautions based on Hagee's war game. In particular, I augmented my artillery unit with a group of reserve officers who had civil affairs expertise.

After the Birthday Ball—a hundred days after I took command—my advance staff and I deployed to Kuwait. Back in California, my three infantry regiments were task-organized into the 1st, 5th, and 7th Regimental Combat Teams (RCT). These were the forces I would deploy, and each consisted of 5,000 to 6,500 troops, supported by tanks, artillery, and air. Back in the States, the units rehearsed incessantly.

In Kuwait, months of planning and rehearsals followed. As always, the war plan was forever in a state of change as assumptions about the enemy's intentions became clearer. This was iterative work, and planner fatigue was real. We kept our meetings short. Our intelligence officers would commence the update on enemy activities, often referencing overhead photos of enemy positions. Next, we all opined about enemy intentions. While I insisted on a sharp demarcation line between data-driven facts and speculative judgments, I wanted both, aware that you have to avoid the danger of accepting informed speculation as if it were fact. We then refined our fire and maneuver schemes. The logistics officer briefed next. The distances involved could tether us to slow progress, and his job was to push off the "culminating point" when we ran out of fuel, water, or ammo.

To the enjoyment of the staff, the most colorful briefing occurred when communications officer Colonel Nick Petronzio took the floor. In 2003, the Internet and chat rooms were coming into common usage. When Nick came into the Marine Corps, we thought it was a marvel to communicate ten miles over a ridgeline via radio. Now we had devices like Blue Force Tracker, a small digital screen in vehicles that displayed the location of all our elements. In our nightly roundups, Nick had to explain the reasons for the latest computer glitches to me in grunt's language. After his fourth or fifth unsuccessful effort, he would clutch his chest and say, "Sir, please do not throw another spear!" I am certain every chief information officer in the world would sympathize with Nick.

But Nick got off easy compared with John Toolan. We slept in small tents. Toolan had the misfortune of bunking in mine. After the evening brief, I'd eat an MRE and sack out. Toolan worked in the ops center until after midnight. As he staggered into the tent, I'd be getting up to go through a few hundred emails. I inadvertently reminded John why he had given me my call sign, Chaos—Colonel Has Another Outstanding Suggestion. Each night, I shared my latest suggestions until his mumbled replies became snores.

When John was asleep, I'd read books. *The Siege,* by Russell Braddon, described a British defeat in Iraq in World War I on the same ground I'd be fighting through. Of course, T. E. Lawrence's classic *Seven Pillars of Wisdom*: few Westerners in recent history had achieved his level of trust with Arabs on the battlefield. Biographies of Gertrude Bell, who helped create modern Iraq. I studied, again, Alexander the Great's campaign through Mesopotamia and Sherman's March to the Sea—I would adopt the latter's effort to always keep enemies on the horns of a dilemma, left or right, front or back. Marcus Aurelius's *Meditations* was my constant companion. His advice kept me dispassionate in some of the more infuriating planning conferences. I'm an opportunistic learner. I may not have come up with many new ideas, but I've adopted or integrated a lot from others.

By January of 2003, most of my division had arrived in their Kuwaiti desert bivouacs. Above me there were three separate commands. General Tommy Franks, who commanded U.S. Central

Command, led the entire military war effort. Beneath him, Lieutenant General David McKiernan, U.S. Army, commanded all land forces.

Beneath McKiernan was my immediate commander, Lieutenant General Jim Conway, leading I Marine Expeditionary Force. The I MEF was a combined Navy, Marine, and UK force consisting of air, logistics, and ground combat units. I commanded the 1st Marine Division, part of the ground force.

Overall, our ground forces were organized around three divisions—about sixty thousand troops—that would do the bulk of the fighting: the Army's 3rd Infantry Division (3ID), the British 1st Armoured Division (1UK), and my 1st Marine Division, divided into three regimental combat teams, one artillery regiment, and specialized battalions. These would be joined by contingents from other nations, a Marine brigade, and additional U.S. Army divisions. Special Operations Forces would infiltrate deep into western and northern Iraq.

The ground forces received vague guidance. That meant I was planning without knowing the answers to the most basic question: Were we going to go all the way to Baghdad? Or only deep enough into Iraq to force Saddam to allow UN inspectors back into the country? These and other gaps in our understanding required us to plan largely in a vacuum. We didn't know the ultimate political intent.

My division would advance in support of the coalition's main attack by the 3rd Infantry Division, commanded by Major General Buford Blount. "Buff" was a tall, tough warrior with a warm southern drawl, and he and I hit it off immediately. Higher headquarters had issued objectives that took us only into southern Iraq. That was clearly incomplete. Buff and I agreed to plan to keep going until we reached Baghdad, even though we had no orders to do so. Since we would attack side by side, we exchanged two personal liaisons—smart majors who knew our battle plans. Each served in the other's headquarters, with the authority to call either of us directly. It worked well, and I was kept current on Buff's plans and intent.

Buff's 3ID, on my left, and General Robin Brims's 1UK armored division, on my right, had excellent reputations. We three enjoyed a mutual confidence in one another's fighting spirit.

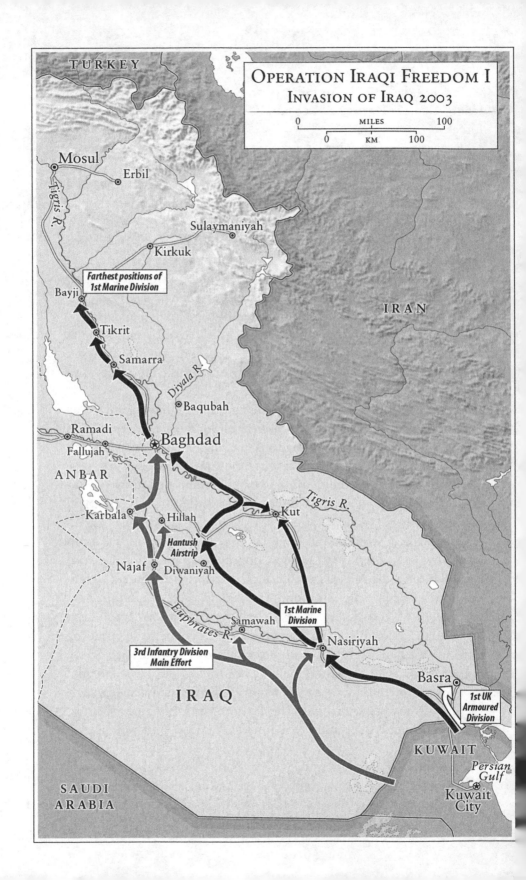

I don't care how operationally brilliant you are; if you can't create harmony—vicious harmony—on the battlefield, based on trust across different military services, foreign allied militaries, and diplomatic lines, you need to go home, because your leadership is obsolete.

Again, I emphasized brilliance in the basics. In my meetings with the troops, I had three Flat-Ass Rules, or "FARs": (1) Guardian Angel, where a hidden sentry is positioned to ambush the enemy; (2) Geometry of Fires, designed to reduce friendly fire casualties; and (3) Unity of Command, meaning that someone was in charge in any group. These rules were meant to emphasize the unrelenting level of attention that had to be paid to key operating principles. That level had to permeate every element of my forces.

I knew I needed an organizing principle, and to the commanders I made it clear that the success of the mission depended on speed: speed of operations and movement would be prefaced by speed of information-passing and decision-making. Armed with this intent, my troops would keep punching through before the enemy could react. Further, we believed that the Iraqis would use poison gas, and a moving target is harder to hit.

As the jumping-off day approached, I was confident in our division's fighting spirit and training, but I had to avoid complacency. I wasn't yet confident that all my commanders and the critical supporting elements fully appreciated our plan's complexity and its friction points. While I was discussing this problem with my chief of staff, my twenty-five-year-old aide, First Lieutenant Warren Cook, interrupted with a solution. He recommended that our combat leaders put on various-colored jerseys with their unit designations on the back and walk through the movement plan with everyone watching. I seized on his concept, and my chief of staff put the "mother of all sand tables" in motion.

Among the sand dunes, we found a natural amphitheater larger than a football field. Using rocks, tape, and cans of spray paint, our NCOs laid out a map of Iraq with enemy units highlighted. We invited all supporting and adjacent commanders and key staffs—Army, Air Force, Marine and Navy air, CIA, Marine logistics, Seabees, British, and other allies—to observe. We all watched as my commanders walked through the movements of their units, starting from Kuwait on D-Day and advancing deep into Iraq. Thanks to the Legos and the Mojave exercises, the units knew the order of attack and which had priority. Pilots and ground commanders had extensive discussions that continued following the formal sand table demonstration. Well-briefed aviators knew our scheme of maneuver and watched knowingly from the air as they aggressively supported what was coming next and the deception plan. Logistics officers were now alert to when we would be expending a lot of ammo or where we would need fuel, enabling them to anticipate how to keep us on the move. As far as I was concerned, young Warren Cook had come up with the most ingenious idea I'd heard in thirty years of war-gaming.

When the division attacked on D-Day (March 20, 2003), every unit leader knew his role and could visualize how the entire division intended to proceed according to my intent. When confronted with the inevitable combat challenges, junior leaders armed with my intent reacted swiftly. I could delegate decision authority to much lower levels, because now I knew that the junior leaders were set up for success. The Lego and colored-jersey drills had enabled us all to "image" what might occur. Note to all executives over the age of thirty: always keep close to you youngsters who are smarter than you.

War is all about reach and tempo. Logistics could easily prove to be my biggest constraint. Supply isn't the logistician's problem; it's the commander's problem. Only a commander has the authority to reduce extraneous demands on the logistics system. On his march to Vicksburg in 1863, General Grant specified that "one tent will be allowed each company for the protection of rations from rain; one wall tent for each regimental headquarters, one wall tent for each brigade headquarters, and one wall tent for each division headquarters." I admired Grant's parsimony, recognizing the freedom of maneuver it gained his army and the speed that resulted.

After I'd calculated the fuel requirements, my biggest problem was the amount and weight of artillery ammunition. To save weight and reduce the frequency of ammunition resupply once we were deep inside Iraq, I cut back on our artillery fire expectations. On my long airplane ride home from Afghanistan, I had recognized the revolutionary impact of precision in air-delivered bombs. In 1991, we had calculated how many aircraft sorties it took to destroy a target. In Afghanistan, we instead calculated how many targets one aircraft could take out. Going deep into Iraq on constantly length-ening supply lines, air support allowed us to husband our artillery ammunition, ensuring that our "cannon cockers" were fully loaded when we were deeper in enemy territory. Whenever possible, we would rely on Marine air to deliver the bulk of our fire support.

Taking a page from U. S. Grant, I told my assault elements to strip away all creature comforts. We carried only a few cots; these were for the sick or wounded. Everyone else slept on the ground, regardless of rank. I had Gypsy racks hung on each vehicle to carry cans of extra fuel. We had fuel-testing kits to take advantage of captured enemy stocks. Every Marine—from general to private—carried his home in his rucksack. No extras for anyone; all hands lived with the same level of discomfort as the lowest-ranking infan-tryman. We would eat two, not three, meals per day. We did, how-ever, store a case of humanitarian meals in every vehicle, to be passed out to the Iraqi people. We would demonstrate the Ameri-can tradition of liberating the people, not dominating them.

Logistics troops would be fighting their way past enemy rem-nants to keep us going. I wasn't going to risk their lives or our mis-sion with poor supply discipline. I told my Marines, "If you bounce a check at the post exchange, your first sergeant's gonna kick your ass. But if you waste gas by running a vehicle when you're not on the move or throw away half your MRE, I will court-martial you."

THE ENEMY'S DECISION LOOP

Just north of our jumping-off point in Kuwait, the Iraqis had one division defending the Rumaila oil fields and Basra. Four more divi-sions were posted along the northern and eastern banks of the Ti-gris, the historical invasion route to Baghdad, facing Iran. After seizing the southern oil fields, our plan was to advance north, stay-ing between the Euphrates and the Tigris, thus isolating and ren-dering irrelevant the four Iraqi divisions.

However, to bypass them I had to move across the Fertile Crescent—millions of acres of marshy farm fields interlaced by thousands of irrigation ditches. We would fight bad terrain while bypassing most of the enemy forces.

One night in the operations tent in Kuwait, dealing with the problems of putting my entire division on a single roadway, I had noticed a moving target indicator on an unfinished road not on our map. I asked the Army private monitoring the video screen, "How fast is that dude going?"

"Sixty-five kilometers an hour, sir," he said.

Sensing the opportunity, all eyes in the tent swung to me. I immediately made up my mind. I turned to Colonel Toolan: "Shift the Fifth and Seventh RCTs to that route." This became the main axis of our attack, and now we could proceed along two axes. A commander, given his own route, will be aggressive, however difficult the terrain. But tie him behind another unit and he has no option but to follow at the pace of the lead unit, stunting the initiative of troops who should be in the fight and rendering them idle. If we were temporarily blocked on one route, the other would continue to advance, turning the enemy's flank.

My mission was to guard Buff Blount's right flank. Now, with two routes—even though one was only two lanes wide and the other an unpaved, unfinished roadway—I was confident I could keep up with him, and, with the British pressing the Iraqis on my right flank, the Iraqis were on the horns of multiple dilemmas about where to mass their forces.

Our campaign's success was based on not giving the enemy time to react. We would turn inside the enemy's "OODA" loop, an acronym coined by the legendary maverick Air Force Colonel John Boyd. To win a dogfight, Boyd wrote, you have to *observe* what is going on, *orient* yourself, *decide* what to do, and *act* before your opponent has completed his version of that same process, repeating and repeating this loop faster than your foe. According to Boyd, a fighter pilot didn't win because he had faster reflexes; he won because his reflexes were connected to a brain that thought faster than his opponent's. Success in war requires seizing and maintaining the initiative—and the Marines had adopted Boyd's OODA loop as the intellectual framework for maneuver warfare. Used with decentralized decision-making, accelerating our OODA loops results in a cascading series of disasters confronting the enemy.

My intent to my regimental and battalion commanders was as follows.

COMMANDER'S INTENT: We will swiftly secure key oil nodes allowing the least possible opportunity for their destruction. We will shatter enemy forces south of the Euphrates, west of the Shatt al Basra and east of An Nasiriya, opening the MSR and gaining positions north of the river to facilitate operations in the vicinity of Kut via Routes 1, 7 or 6 as the situation dictates. In order to achieve tactical surprise we will first blind enemy reconnaissance, then close on the border. We will be prepared to accept enemy capitulation, but destroy the 51st Mech Division and its adjacent/supporting units if they fight. To the greatest extent possible, we will limit enemy or friendly damage to the oil infrastructure.

We must neutralize enemy artillery through shaping, preparatory, or responsive counter fires. I expect maximum use of air fires; assault support will be used if rapid linkup is achievable. Speed is the measure: speed coupled with harmony of information flow; rapidity in decision making; orders promulgation; counter fire; response to changing conditions; resupply; CASEVAC; identification of multiple routes; obstacle reduction; maneuver; relief in place; and hand off of EPWs. We will avoid all possible forward passages of lines and any other mingling of forces, and whenever possible create conditions of chaos for our enemies. Aggressive tempo and initiative are vital. Once we have seized the nodes, we will rapidly hand over the zone and EPWs to 1st UK Div and reposition north of Jalibah. Crossing the Euphrates and moving against Kut, 1st MarDiv supports 3ID's attack along our western flank denying the enemy the opportunity to mass against CFLCC's [the Coalition Forces Land Component Command's] main effort.

The end state will place the oil infrastructure safely in 1st UK Division's hands; 51st Mech and associated elements eliminated as a threat to Coalition Ops; our Division oriented against Kut; and the enemy's units facing absolute destruction if they choose to fight.

"No better friend, no worse enemy."

Supervision of the planning took me only an hour or two each day. The rest of my waking hours were spent coaching fighters—officers and enlisted. I spoke to the troops in groups, from thirteen-man squads to eight-hundred-man battalions. We went over our overall strategy and their unit's scheme of maneuver. My goal was to put a human face on the mission, answer every question, and build their confidence. I followed British Field Marshal Slim's advice that, in fairness to my troops, they had to know what their objective was and what my expectations of them were. Additionally, I needed to look the lads in the eye to get a sense of their levels of confidence and for them to directly feel the respect I had for those who would face our enemies. As Slim made clear, any general who isn't connected spiritually to his troops is not a combat leader.

To close the gap between me and my youngest Marines, I studied what others had said. Before leading his Marine Raiders ashore on Guadalcanal in 1942, Colonel Evans Carlson told his men that the mission was to "annihilate all enemy personnel and destroy as many military installations as they could." In the summer of 1944, General Eisenhower exhorted each of his soldiers "to go forward to his assigned objective with the determination that the enemy can survive only through surrender."

Now it was time for me to write a letter to my lads. It had to convey the nature and purpose of their mission. I needed every Marine to understand my two core principles:

First, don't stop. Don't slow down, don't create a traffic jam. Jab, feint, hit, and move, move, move.

Second, keep your honor clean. Thousands of homes, stores, stalls, and mud and concrete houses lined the roads. Terrified civilians would be in the line of fire. I made it clear that our division would do more than any unit in history to avoid civilian casualties.

While my commanders understood my operational design, I wanted to connect with every member of the Blue Diamond. I limited myself to one page they could carry with them, a message reconciling ferocity toward the foe with abiding concern for the innocents caught on the battlefield. Directly following is my letter.

March 2003

1ˢᵗ Marine Division (REIN)

Commanding General's Message to All Hands

For decades, Saddam Hussein has tortured, imprisoned, raped and murdered the Iraqi people; invaded neighboring countries without provocation; and threatened the world with weapons of mass destruction. The time has come to end his reign of terror. On your young shoulders rest the hopes of mankind.

When I give you the word, together we will cross the Line of Departure, close with those forces that choose to fight, and destroy them. Our fight is not with the Iraqi people, nor is it with members of the Iraqi army who choose to surrender. While we will move swiftly and aggressively against those who resist, we will treat all others with decency, demonstrating chivalry and soldierly compassion for people who have endured a lifetime under Saddam's oppression.

Chemical attack, treachery, and use of the innocent as human shields can be expected, as can other unethical tactics. Take it all in stride. Be the hunter, not the hunted: never allow your unit to be caught with its guard down. Use good judgement and act in best interests of our Nation.

You are part of the world's most feared and trusted force. Engage your brain before you engage your weapon. Share your courage with each other as we enter the uncertain terrain north of the Line of Departure. Keep faith in your comrades on your left and right and Marine Air overhead. Fight with a happy heart and strong spirit.

For the mission's sake, our country's sake, and the sake of the men who carried the Division's colors in past battles-*who fought for life and never lost their nerve*-carry out your mission and *keep your honor clean*. Demonstrate to the world there is "No Better Friend, No Worse Enemy" than a U.S. Marine.

J.N. Mattis
Major General, U.S. Marines
Commanding

My letter was distributed to all hands on the day before the attack. Over the years since, many have taken that letter out of their wallets and shown it to me. In an age when cynicism too often passes for critical thinking, it's worthwhile to remember that young men and women who sign up for the military still fight for ideals.

My meetings with the troops weren't quite so highbrow. They enjoyed prodding me, and I enjoyed giving it right back. After 9/11, everyone who signed on knew he'd go into battle, and the vast majority actually looked forward to the test. I did my best to keep the young lads primed and cocky. On one occasion, a lance corporal referred to a World War I painting of Marines attacking in gas masks: "That looked like rough stuff."

"The press will shove cameras in your faces," I said. "If you suck your thumb and say you're worried about poison gas, then you're emboldening the enemy. If you are not tough enough and need to talk about your midlife crisis, stand aside and let a tougher Marine represent us."

My grunts burst out laughing, and "thumb-suckers" became a running joke.

Operation Iraqi Freedom was set to begin with a massive air and ground assault on March 21, 2003. Due to late-breaking intelligence, however, my division was sent across the line of departure in the early evening of March 20. My regimental combat teams adapted smoothly to this change. Just north of the Kuwaiti border, Iraqi soldiers manned an observation post atop a steep rise called Safwan Hill, the sole high ground in all southern Iraq, overlooking Kuwait.

"When we kick off," I had told my staff, "I want that hill a foot shorter."

The CIA was sending a message to the enemy commanders: *Don't fight us and we won't kill you.* By bombing the hill, I would be sending my own message to all the Iraqi soldiers who could see Safwan from a great distance: *Go home while you still can walk.*

By the afternoon of March 21, we had advanced thirty miles into Iraq, ahead of our pre-attack estimates. As we had rehearsed, the units communicated with one another, shifted accordingly, and kept driving forward, knocking aside the flimsy resistance encountered. British units embedded with us and on our right flank smoothly orchestrated our combined operations. As the commander, I didn't have to urge on any unit or adjust any movement.

Initiative and decentralized decision authority were paying off. Let me give an example.

A critical goal was to prevent Saddam from torching the southern oil fields, as he had done in Kuwait a decade earlier, causing an environmental disaster. A key objective was the pumping station called Zubayr, which facilitated the flow of two million barrels of oil each day. If the station was sabotaged, all that thick black liquid would gush out, creating a widespread oily swamp and oozing into the Gulf. In our planning, we nicknamed this critical objective the Crown Jewel.

Getting to the station and preventing that disaster was the job assigned to "Suicide Charlie" Company of the 1st Battalion, 7th Marines. Having led that battalion in Operation Desert Storm, I kept a fond eye on its movement. When company commander Captain Tom Lacroix got to the wall surrounding the station, he halted to check his "go/no-go" list. Months before in California, Lacroix's lieutenants and NCOs had visited an Exxon refinery. Engineers had walked them through the maze of high-pressure pipes and control valves, stressing where not to shoot, lest sparks set off a massive explosion. On Lacroix's list were the conditions that would make the station unsafe to enter. One key tipoff was to look for the pyramids of flame spurting harmlessly in the air from the tops of the vertical pipes. If there were no flames, that meant the natural gas pressure was building up. Lacroix saw no flames, and no workers moving anywhere inside the station.

Was he now facing a bomb waiting to be touched off once a hundred or more Marines were inside? Acting on instinct, he ordered all his drivers to turn off their engines. Then the Marines listened. They heard a few random shouts and some half-hearted bursts of fire from a few AKs, but nothing more. It was the lack of sound that tipped Lacroix off. Three massive 1,500-horsepower engines generated the power to pump those millions of barrels. Obviously, they made quite a racket. But now there was silence. Lacroix decided that meant the station had been shut down, and any buildup of natural gas had dissipated. He ordered his Marines to break through the wall and take control of the station.

That was a good, on-the-spot call far down the chain of command.

That small incident illustrates a larger principle. Lacroix consulted with no one. When a key indicator flashed a danger signal, he didn't pull back to call headquarters for guidance. That was decentralized execution. Based on understanding his commander's intent, Lacroix decided on his own course of action, and the Crown Jewel was firmly in our hands.

Suppose gas pressure had built up, resulting in a severe explosion? In that tragic case, I still would have fully supported Captain Lacroix. Why? Because he had reviewed the situation smartly, weighed the risk factors against what he knew—and acted swiftly in accord with my intent. To expect success every time is wishful thinking, but we should default to supporting commanders who move boldly against the enemy. This time things worked out— thanks to Lacroix and his men. When things go wrong, a leader must stand by those who made the decision under extreme pressure and with incomplete information. Initiative and audacity must be supported, whether or not successful.

During the afternoon of March 21, while we were in contact with the enemy, the British division smoothly relieved us and turned northeast toward the city of Basra. A relief under fire seems easy on paper, but only to those who have never done it. The well-led British allowed the 7th Marines to turn west and rejoin my division's main effort to protect the 3rd Infantry Division's right flank. So far, so good.

Battlefields are unforgiving of mistakes. On the third day of the attack, the 1st Regimental Combat Team (RCT 1) was to turn directly north across the Euphrates River at the city of Nasiriyah, while RCTs 5 and 7 bypassed the city to the west and then turned north. I MEF had dispatched a brigade from the 2nd Marine Division, called Task Force Tarawa, to lead the way and hold open the two bridges at Nasiriyah. RCT 1 would pass through Tarawa's lines across both bridges before proceeding north. This meant that thousands of military vehicles under two chains of command—TF Tarawa and Blue Diamond—would converge on this choke point where the enemy intended to fight.

I had learned that passing one unit through another when in contact with the enemy is a supremely difficult job. It is a tactic to be avoided whenever possible, especially in channelized terrain, such as congested city streets and where you are confined to bridges.

Units get jumbled, the enemy often takes advantage, and there is usually hell to pay.

In the early-morning hours of March 23, an Army logistics convoy got lost, wandered into Nasiriyah, and was torn apart by Iraqi forces. Pushing forward to help, Marines from Tarawa briefly seized both bridges. In the ensuing fight, a misdirected A-10 aircraft accidentally destroyed friendly vehicles, killing Marines. Amid the confused melee, the Marines in TF Tarawa pulled back. This forced the thousand vehicles of RCT 1 to stop and wait in a two-mile column behind Tarawa's lines.

While RCTs 5 and 7 had continued on their separate route up the unfinished highway, I sent my Boston Irish deputy, Brigadier General John Kelly, to urge the RCT 1 commander to pass through Tarawa and press forward. We couldn't allow the enemy to dig in and gain confidence, as my right flank was increasingly exposed. John reached the city at night, passing the smoldering Army trucks.

The commander of RCT 1 was hesitant to press forward into Tarawa's zone while their troops were in contact with the enemy. Estimating we had suffered ten to eighteen killed, Kelly cut through the anxieties.

"Get moving," he told the RCT commander. "I'll help in any way. But it's your regiment, and you have to push through."

Over the next several hours, John reiterated my order in increasingly strong terms. Still more delays. After a sixteen-hour halt, RCT 1 finally moved through Nasiriyah, sustaining only one man wounded. On one level, I empathized with the RCT commander. A passage of lines, with one unit moving through another while under fire, was a tough challenge. Adding to that, because of Tarawa's late arrival in theater, the passage had to be undertaken without a rehearsal. Anticipatory leadership at the senior level had failed to grasp the challenge of mixing units in urban terrain.

On another level, I was disturbed that RCT 1 had not accelerated through. The core of my commander's intent had made speed the driving force for the division. As Rommel once wrote, "A commander must accustom his staff to a high tempo from the outset, and continually keep them up to it." While RCT 1 was delayed, Buff's division and mine had received orders to attack all the way to Baghdad. The combined operations of the British division's attack into Basra and the 3rd Marine Aircraft Wing were currently holding in place four bypassed Iraqi divisions. But RCT 1 had to keep moving in order to cover our right flank, in case those divisions chose to move against our advance on Baghdad.

By March 25, RCT 1 had picked up speed and the whole force was surging forward. Then a massive sandstorm swept in. Thunder and lightning were followed by seventy-mile-per-hour winds that swept up the sand, mixed it with rain and hail, and dumped tons of this blinding mess on our invasion force. The world turned a strange orange color. Wet and filthy, the Blue Diamond pressed on.

Now more than 130 miles inside Iraq, the enemy was starting to fight harder. A leading light armored reconnaissance battalion was engaged in a sharp fight, to which I directed every element of our air support. We continued to advance.

Every Marine lived and fought alongside others in his small team. For months, showers would be a distant memory. From general to private, we had no privacy, swapped for our favorite MREs and slept in holes next to our vehicles. Job, not rank, determined every Marine's family. I was reminded of a pithy sentiment Field Marshal Slim wrote in World War II:

"As officers," he wrote, "you will neither eat, nor drink, nor sleep, nor smoke, nor even sit down until you have personally seen that your men have done those things. If you will do this for them, they will follow you to the end of the world. And, if you do not, I will break you."

With my small team of two dozen, I was always on the move. My communicator, Sergeant Ryan Woolwort, ensured that I was never out of touch, which was no small matter with the division spread out. Corporal Yaniv Newman, my driver and map reader par excellence, stayed in constant touch with our headquarters, ensuring that I knew the real-time locations of my RCTs and of the enemy. My aide from Afghanistan, Lieutenant Warren Cook, knew me so well that he could convey my intent when I was busy checking another unit. Having learned a lesson during Operation Desert Storm, where, because I was dead tired, I allowed my own battalion to drive into an ambush in the open desert, I would not allow a unit duty officer to awaken a commander who was catching some rest.

Lying in the dust, breathing it, and constantly cleaning out weapons and radios became second nature to every Marine. Some of the men were suffering through "the crud," the result of dust particles clogging the membranes of the lungs, causing them to cough and hack up wads of yellow mucus. Many Marines wrapped bandannas around their faces. It did little good. Because stubble prevented a gas mask from sealing, and we believed the Iraqis possessed chemical weapons, the troops shaved daily. It was odd to see all those clean-shaven faces caked with dirt around their eyes.

Every day during the attack, my fast-moving staff would turn my hurried updates from the leading edge of our units into succinct mission orders to the assault unit commanders. Halfway to Baghdad, I began seeing words like "whilst RCT 5 engages . . ." When I asked, "Where did this 'whilst' stuff come from?" Clarke Lethin explained that the UK liaison officer embedded in our operations shop wrote the best orders, and he was the author.

This was an outgrowth of my policy of embedding outside liaison officers in my staff. I didn't want them listening in and reporting back to their units. Rather, by being inside our staffs and our processes, they would necessarily have a better look at our intentions and tempo, and thus be able to keep the units they represented better informed than they would if they were simply sitting, odd man out, in the back of the briefing room, removed from the give-and-take of sorting out how we were assessing and reacting to situations.

I knew that foreign units send some of their best officers when given the opportunity and that outside liaison officers, employed well, brought further strength to our operations. So "whilst" I continued to spend my time forward to sense how operations were trending at the front, my now multinational operations staff transmitted my intent more clearly to my tens of thousands of U.S. Marines.

On March 27, as part of our deception plan, we executed a major feint. Colonel Joe Dunford's RCT 5 drove ahead and seized the Hantush airfield, a smooth, well-paved strip of Highway 1. From there, the highway ran straight toward the city, so it was heavily defended. One glance at a map would convince the Iraqi high command that my division was seeking to link up with Buff Buford's division. This made military sense. Our combined force would then fall on Baghdad from the south like a sledgehammer.

Actually, our intent was the opposite. My intelligence officers had identified a flaw in the enemy's artillery coverage. RCT 5 would advance only a few dozen miles. When the Iraqis responded to block us, RCT 5 would pivot back to the northeast, crossing the Tigris through a gap left uncovered by Iraqi artillery. My division would then turn, assaulting Baghdad from the west while Buff's division attacked from the south. My maneuver required all three of my RCTs attacking in concert.

Out of the blue, I was ordered to halt my division dead in its tracks. I was stunned. We were strung out with fifteen thousand of my men directly downwind of any chemical attacks. General Franks, CENTCOM commander, later wrote that his operations director had told him that "the Marines are tangling with more Fedayeen on Highways 1 and 7. The log [logistic] tails just aren't catching up to the maneuver units."

Nothing could have been further from the truth. And I knew my boss, General Conway, held no such concerns. Beginning at Nasiriyah, fervent civilian supporters of Saddam, called fedayeen, had joined the fight. But their effect was minimal. Our biggest challenge was avoiding civilian casualties, because the fedayeen were firing at us from among the populace. We dealt with them as irritants—fire practice, nothing more. When a fighter popped out firing wildly, a Marine turret gunner would take him out and the troops would roll on. In my division's wake, the logistics convoys— *every Marine a rifleman*—kept pace.

A reporter asked me about the fedayeen threat. I gave a straight answer.

"They lack manhood," I said. "Fighting from among women and children, they're as worthless an example of men as we've ever fought."

Secretary of Defense Donald Rumsfeld later wrote, "General James Conway, commanding general of I MEF, and General William Wallace of the Army's V Corps ordered a seventy-two-hour pause to resupply their troops. I understood the reason for the pause, given the logistical challenges."

The secretary had received bad information. My boss, General Conway, was first perplexed, then furious, when ordered to halt. Neither General Conway nor I had any concerns about running out of supplies. He had insisted to higher headquarters, "The Marines are ready for the push to Baghdad." There was no reason to pause across the whole front. You never know an enemy until you fight him, but by now we knew we faced an enemy unable to mount a serious defense. This was our opportunity to exploit and charge on, increasing mental and physical pressure on the enemy. We should accelerate the tempo, confounding our foe with cascading disasters and utterly shattering his cohesion.

Conway's arguments were of no avail. Somehow at higher head-quarters the fedayeen had been elevated to an operational threat. To this day, I do not know how such an exaggerated perception gained enough traction to stop us.

Uncertainty runs riot if you don't keep cool. From my liaison officers and my talks with Buff, I knew that his division was moving swiftly abreast of mine. I'd seen this before, the disconnect between frontline thinking and higher staffs' more remote assessments. I'd always found first reports to be half wrong and half incorrect. That's a bit of an exaggeration, but digital technologies can falsely encourage remote staffs to believe they possess a God's-eye view of combat. Digital technologies do not dissipate confusion; the fog of war can actually thicken when misinformation is instantly ampli-fied.

The order to halt the entire ground attack came at the worst possible moment. Two-thirds of my division was strung out, un-able to disperse into the soft marshland on either side.

I could not leave the 5th Marines forward at Hantush. The Iraqis knew we had taken the runway. Even a cursory glance showed the road behind them leading northeast across the Tigris. The risk that the Iraqis would deduce my feint and recognize the gap in their artillery coverage increased by the hour. I called Joe Dunford.

"Joe, we've been ordered to halt," I said. "If you stay out in front, the Iraqis will figure out our plan. I have to pull you back."

Joe could see that as well as I. He had the gift of synthesis; he could coolly evaluate the larger picture. Joe reminded me of Em-peror Justinian, consistently reaching fair conclusions and able to summarize a complex situation in a few words.

"Yes, sir," he said. "I'll turn my Marines around."

Trust. That's what held us together. I knew General Conway had argued as hard as he could against stopping our offensive. Joe knew I had considered every option before deciding he had to pull back. Similarly, Joe's battalion commanders knew he was compe-tent. Whatever the cause of the retreat, the Marines from top to bottom knew it wasn't due to unsound reasoning by their immediate leaders. The more trust there is inside a unit, the more strain that unit can withstand without a lot of discussion.

To throw off the enemy, Joe issued some unencrypted and jittery radio instructions, indicating that his troops had encountered too much opposition. We intended the enemy to intercept and be deceived by these messages. Then RCT 5 pulled back.

It was the hardest decision I made on the march to Baghdad. You sharpen your Marines to a razor's edge. You commit them, knowing some will die. The enemy couldn't stop us, but I had to pull my troops back. Then I remembered that in the Korean War, this division had been surrounded six to one and fought its way through freezing mountains. I thought to myself, *This isn't that tough. If they could get through that, I would figure a way out of this.* I was determined that this operational mistake wouldn't cost my men their lives. Never think that you're impotent. Choose how you respond.

CHAPTER 7

A Division
in Its Prime

WE HAD CAPTURED SEVERAL Iraqi Army generals on the first day of fighting outside Basra, and they warned that Saddam would attack us with chemical weapons as we approached the Tigris River, just as he had threatened to do to his own army, were it ever to turn on him. Stuck in this maddeningly vulnerable position, I considered designating RCT 5 as a "reconnaissance regiment" in order to send Colonel Joe Dunford's Marines on a "reconnaissance" to seize the critical bridges across the Saddam Canal and the Tigris River before the enemy could destroy them. My boss, Jim Conway, chuckled and observed that it was stretching even poetic license to imagine that CENTCOM would accept a "reconnaissance" that comprised a third of my entire division.

Instead of stewing, Conway told us to "throw elbows" to keep the enemy off-balance. We did so with probing attacks all along our forty-five-mile front. When I was touring RCT 1's zone, I came upon an engineer reading a book when his platoon should have been hard at work. I took him aside—praise in public, criticize in private—before ripping into him. I told him to get off his ass and do his job. I had repeatedly emphasized speed—information passing, response to orders, movement, and resupply. But leadership can't depend on emails or written words. Leaders are not potted plants, and at all levels they must be constantly out at the critical points doing whatever is required to keep their teams energized, especially when everyone is exhausted.

Operational tempo is a state of mind. I've always tried to be hard on issues but not on spirits. Yet I needed unity of commitment, from every commander down through the youngest sailor and Marine. Once across the Tigris, my spread-out division could face two Republican Guard divisions. I needed the entire division on the same tempo. We had to be all in, all the time.

At one point during the pause, I was sitting with a squad that was understandably uneasy about remaining in one place for so long. One Marine asked what we'd do if hit by chemicals. For these assault troops, there was something uniquely malicious about fighting on a battlefield where the very air is poisoned.

"Just like we've trained," I said. "Fight for twenty-four hours 'dirty' in your suits and kill those sons of bitches. Then we'll get you decontaminated, with fresh gear, and you'll go back into the fight." I wanted them to know they would live to fight another day and should press the fight, chemicals or no chemicals. They got it. As we prepared to cross the Tigris, they zipped tight their chemical suits. Their quiet individual determination will always stay with me.

On the third day, the imposed halt was finally lifted and we eagerly resumed the attack. My troops were smiling and flashing thumbs-up as they rolled by. I was relieved we were on the move. RCT 5 swiftly seized the Hantush highway strip again. Our air wing commander, General Jim Amos, flew in to cut through the time-consuming process of declaring the strip operational. Within hours, KC-130s began landing, off-loading bladders filled with 88,000 gallons of fuel. Water and ammo flowed in and the wounded were flown out.

Unleashed, RCT 5 stormed over the Saddam Canal. The Marines overran the dug-in Iraqi troops hastily sent forward. Because of our feint, the Iraqi generals had recognized too late the gap in their artillery fans that my intel guys had found. Seizing the Tigris River Bridge intact, Joe Dunford turned his RCT west. Destination: Baghdad. Now the enemy could see our attack route.

The next day, I hustled to catch up with Dunford. Corporal Newman hastily parked us in a culvert adjacent to the regimental commander, and I hopped out. Iraqi military trucks were burning alongside the road. Marines, sweating in their chemical suits, were bounding forward. To the front, mortar shells were dropping around a redbrick building held by a rear guard fighting to hold us back.

Dunford and I were joined by his lead battalion commander, Lieutenant Colonel Sam Mundy. Setting up a map board next to my Humvee, I popped open a Coke and gauged the distances separating my three RCTs. Rounds were zipping high over our heads, machine guns were barking, shells were exploding to the front, and several buildings were on fire, the flames leaping high.

A squad of Marines, half walking and half trotting, brushed by us. Just another normal day for our young grunts. When the squad leader paused to survey the surroundings, I offered him water from a jerry can on my Humvee's gypsy rack. He guzzled down a few swallows without taking his eyes off the enemy positions ahead. He wiped his mouth, patted me on the shoulder, and continued on. Absorbed in the fight, he had no idea that I was the division commander. Or if he did, it made no impression. He had a job to do.

We had the momentum. It was now a straight forty-five-mile shot to Baghdad. But Sam Mundy's battalion needed a break. An infantry fight is like a marathon. Marines can push themselves without rest for eight or ten hours under fire. But then the fatigue factor, both mental and physical, will impact even the fittest troops and the unit will eventually start breaking down. That's when the worst tactical and ethical mistakes can occur.

To exploit the opening we had found, I had to bring up reinforcements. Now within striking distance of Baghdad, I needed all hands fully in the fray. I called Kelly at division headquarters and told him to have RCTs 1 and 7 move up to our forward position. I knew it would take the RCTs a day to break contact and catch up. Ahead of us lay an intact Republican Guard armored division. I wanted to continue the attack before they could adapt their defense to our now clear attack vector.

"Overnight I'll bring up my tank battalion to take the lead," Dunford told me. "We'll resume the attack at dawn."

Classic Dunford. He assessed the pros and cons, reached a decision, and in two succinct sentences conveyed his plan.

I had my own hard decision to make. My deputy, John Kelly, was waiting for me when I got back to my headquarters that afternoon. RCT 7 was, as instructed, swiftly moving forward. John then explained that RCT 1 was again not pressing forward aggressively enough. Following the delay at Nasiriyah, I was already concerned. Now the overly cautious pace was persisting. Fighting was getting harder, and a third of my division was lagging. My mission to support 3ID, which was closing on Baghdad, was in jeopardy.

Because it is so hard to write about, relief of command is rarely mentioned. You know how hard dedicated officers have worked, and you know what the effect of relief will be, upon them, their families, and their troops. Often they are friends in every sense of the word. But I would be remiss if I did not address the necessity to relieve someone of command, because it is so fundamental to leadership. We learn most about ourselves when things go wrong.

While RCT 5 was crossing the Tigris, RCT 1 was to feint an assault against the Republican Guard division holding the city of Kut, farther to the east. With that division frozen, we would bypass it. Kelly saw that some Iraqi artillery pieces had been abandoned in place, soldiers were discarding their uniforms, and bands of males in civilian clothes and without weapons were streaming out of the city. The enemy appeared to have fallen apart. Yet RCT 1 hadn't delivered a few short, hard jabs to hasten that disintegration and then swiftly shifted to join my main attack. I don't have the words to describe the level of fatigue that engulfs any commander in combat; it is beyond anything I've experienced elsewhere. I wondered if the RCT 1 commander was exhausted past his limit.

I dispatched a helicopter, and a few hours later the RCT 1 commander entered my tent. He looked worn out and nervous.

"What's going on?" I asked him. "Nasiriyah, Kut . . . Why aren't you pressing harder? Why the hesitation?"

I wanted to see a flash of fire and ferocity of tone. I hoped he'd say something like "We're just hitting our stride. In one more day, we'll be there."

Instead he expressed his heartfelt reluctance to lose any of his men by pushing at what might seem to be a reckless pace.

I was torn by his answer. I want officers to nurture a deep affection for their men, as I do—in my view, it's fundamental to building the trust that glues an organization together. Your troops must be confident about how much you care about them before they can commit fully to a mission that could cost them their lives. I also understood how difficult it is to order men you've come to love into a fight that some won't survive. But the mission must come first. Once you're committed, hesitancy in battle can expose other units to failure. I needed all hands in the fight, sharing the burden equally.

On the spot, I relieved the RCT commander, a noble and capable officer who in past posts had performed superbly. But when the zeal of a commander flags, you must make a change. Sometimes you order them into their sleeping bag, and rest restores them. In this case I believed that rest alone would not work. In good conscience, he was reluctant to follow my intent, which involved speed as the top priority. You cannot order someone to abandon a spiritual burden they're wrestling with. Fear of losing his Marines, coupled with his tremendous fatigue, cost the division an officer I admire greatly to this day.

This was the first relief in combat of a regimental commander in this fight, and it was front-page news the next day. You can imagine what it felt like to be that colonel, his family, or his admirers. While I was criticized by some whom I respect, their disapproval didn't make me question my decision.

To take command of RCT 1, I gave up my operations officer, Colonel John Toolan. In the midst of this campaign, he had the leadership savvy to swiftly earn the respect of five thousand troops who didn't know him, bringing their power fully into the fight. Lieutenant Colonel Clarke Lethin stepped up as operations officer and my division staff didn't miss a beat.

On April 4, RCT 5 attacked toward Baghdad. Elements of an Iraqi division, dug in on both sides of the narrow road, fired Sagger missiles, rocket-propelled grenades, PKM machine guns, and AKs. Hidden in culverts, Iraqi soldiers disabled a tank just as Colonel Dunford was driving by. Stopping to help, he and his crew engaged in a furious exchange of fire with Iraqi soldiers. When an ambulance sped up, the driver was shot in the hand. With the enemy routed, Dunford proceeded toward Baghdad, his driver steering with his head out the window because bullets had shattered the windshield. Over the radio, Dunford heard that First Lieutenant Brian McPhillips, a graduate of his own high school, had just been killed a few hundred yards to his front.

A few hours later, energetic First Sergeant Edward Smith was killed. Two days earlier, while I was talking with Dunford, Sergeant Smith had been standing a few feet away, smiling at us as he puffed on a cigar. I had joked that he wasn't supposed to deploy with us. He had put in his retirement papers and was about to start a second career on the Anaheim police force. But he put off his retirement to stay with his rifle company, where he knew his experience was needed. Such were the men I served alongside.

The last obstacle between us and Baghdad was the steep-banked Diyala River. I sent RCT 5 to the north, looking for a fording point. Moving to the front was RCT 7, commanded by Colonel Steve Hummer. We had served together in the 1980s, and I knew he was a deliberate planner who was both an aggressive battle leader and a father figure to his men. To get into Baghdad, his RCT had to get across the half-demolished Diyala Bridge, which led directly into the city. When I drove up on the morning of April 6, I passed a line of Abrams tanks and hundreds of Marines, engineers, and assault infantry crouching along the side of the road, ready to sprint forward into Baghdad. The approach to the bridge was unnaturally quiet, all eyes and guns trained on the many apartment buildings and a copse of palm trees on the far shore.

A steady wind and explosions had scattered the detritus of war—torn awnings, wrecked cars, dead cats, overturned chairs, slinking dogs, a few stiff corpses, rattling tin cans, odd bits of clothing and papers swirling about, mud and filth underfoot. At the edge of the bridge, Steve was crouched beside a wrecked one-room brick building with sagging sandbags.

The bridge had a gaping hole in the middle. Again I saw the Marine Corps watchwords—*improvise, adapt, and overcome*—in action as Marines dragged up lumber. We would break into a city of seven million by sending Marines in single file across a plank.

A short artillery barrage was called on the far bank. At the same time, our intelligence assets warned us that an Iraqi general was calling a fire mission against us. Seconds later, the ground shuddered slightly, followed by the thunderclap of a heavy shell exploding nearby. Several yards behind us, Corporal Jesus Martin Antonio Medellin and Lance Corporal Andrew Aviles lay dead. Aviles was eighteen and the youngest Marine to die in the invasion, a patriot who had given up an academic scholarship in order to serve. My teenage grunts were more men than some guys I've met who were twice their age.

As I drove away, Marines were running in single file across that construction plank into Baghdad. Farther downstream, Dunford's RCT 5 searched for another crossing of the Diyala so we could cut off Baghdad from the north and link up with 3ID. Colonel John Toolan was bringing a reenergized RCT 1 into the fight. Without pause, his troops swiftly crossed the Diyala in hard-used amphibious vehicles, an incongruous sight hundreds of miles from the nearest ocean.

Within five hours, we had battalions from two regiments inside the city. On his side of the city, Buff Blount's "thunder runs" of armored columns were wreaking havoc on the Iraqi defenses. To our amusement, Iraqi commanders sent out panicky warnings that American tanks were "swimming across the river."

Inside the city, I caught up with one of John Toolan's battalions and watched a squad attacking the enemy.

The squad leader shouted to his men, "Don't fire at the second-story apartment on the right. The bastard's got women and children in there. Keep moving. We'll come back and kill him."

I turned around and walked away. I knew my touchstone of "No better friend, no worse enemy" was in play, and I sent a smile of thanks to General Lucius Cornelius Sulla, the Roman soldier who, two thousand years ago, had those words inscribed on his tombstone and passed it on to me.

Packed in among civilian evacuees fleeing the city were the remnants of Saddam's Special Republican Guard, many now wearing civilian clothes. Our aircraft didn't attack the entangled columns. Against light resistance at a few strongpoints, our regiments were moving swiftly across eastern Baghdad. General Jim Amos, hearing that we were running short of food, gathered the air wing's MREs into helicopters, which then flew low over Marines in the city, kicking out boxes of chow. The infantry was dashing forward, knowing the Iraqi Army had given up the fight. In Firdos Square, at the request of rejoicing Iraqis, my Marines tore down a large statue of Saddam.

Lieutenant McPhillips, First Sergeant Smith, Corporal Medellin, Lance Corporal Aviles . . . Death doesn't care about your age or rank. At the front, we're all together, shoulder to shoulder. We nod or grin at one another. As the commanding general, you concentrate on outsmarting and outmaneuvering the enemy. But you cannot outmaneuver the odds. No matter how ferociously you study, plot, and attack, some of your brave young troops will die. You try your best to make that number as small as possible. But you can never drive it to zero.

"It is not the young man who misses the days he does not know," Marcus Aurelius wrote. "It is the living who bear the pain of those missed days."

Of course, few of us are as stoic as Aurelius. We seek a reason for their sacrifice and live with our sorrow, knowing they did not die without accomplishment. They knew I had confidence in them, and they never failed to carry out their mission, ethically and efficiently. I would happily storm hell in the company of those troops.

By the time we set up my headquarters in Baghdad, Joe Dunford had encircled the city from the north, linking up with Buff Blount's 3rd Infantry Division.

There was still rough fighting; at a mosque in the center of town, one of our battalions took eighty-one casualties in one night. When I drove to the scene, the Marines were still in the fight, and I could see reporters holding plasma bags over wounded Marines being treated by our corpsmen. But we had toppled the Saddam regime. Baghdad was the only objective the high command had given to 3ID and the 1st Marine Division. We could have gotten there faster but for the unfortunate pause we could not prevent. Due to the terrain and our maneuvering, the Blue Diamond had already covered more than four hundred miles over seventeen days, and it wasn't over yet.

From the very start, the Iraqi Army was a tall, dead tree. On the outside, its thick bark appeared tough. Once we cut into it, it was clear that the tree had been hollowed out by a lack of morale, leadership, and belief in itself.

Saddam had fled Baghdad. Washington and CENTCOM wanted a swift search of his hometown of Tikrit. I was asked how long it would take to dispatch a force over a hundred miles north and seize the city. "Tomorrow," I said. Less than twenty-four hours later, John Kelly was on his way with a 3,500-man task force.

On the way to Tikrit, a local policeman told Lieutenant Nathan Boaz, a platoon commander, that American prisoners were being held in a nearby house. Boaz handed him a GPS, instructing him to click the button as he walked past the house. Half an hour later, the policeman returned the GPS, with the location marked. Boaz took his Marines, burst into the house, and freed seven American soldiers who'd been taken prisoner at Nasiriyah. This demonstrated the initiative I expected of my Marine small-unit leaders.

Kelly's task force did not find Saddam as it advanced to Tikrit and beyond. After Tikrit was in John's hands, I flew up to see him, and together we went for a swim in the muddy waters of the Tigris. After weeks on the move without a shower, both of us thought we could see the water turning an even darker brown as we scrubbed off layers of grime.

The march up was over, with my division spread over half of Baghdad and my forward elements 150 miles north, closer to the Mediterranean than to the Persian Gulf, where we had started.

In Baghdad, the people were pouring into the streets. Complete nonviolent chaos reigned. Government buildings were ransacked, stripped clean of everything of value, down to the last copper wire. In a sprawling metropolis of more than seven million, there were no police, no services, and no local authority. We hadn't enough troops to prevent widespread looting, other than at some government buildings, but even those had largely been overrun before our arrival on the scene and stripped bare.

Reinforced, the 3rd Infantry Division now held the western half of Baghdad, and the Blue Diamond held the east. We received no clear orders, but thanks to General Hagee's post-combat plan, my artillery units were ready to step in and swiftly provide or start repairing city services, augmented by the Marine reserve specialists I had embedded with them.

In June, the Blue Diamond was ordered into Shiite southern Iraq. I sent home the tanks, artillery tubes, and my four regimental headquarters, flattening my organization to ten battalions, all answering directly to division. Within a month, the battalion commanders were acting as de facto mayors, working with local officials, restoring electric power and water, opening schools, recruiting police, paying government salaries, and settling disputes.

In the holy city of Najaf, Lieutenant Colonel Chris Conlin established a working relationship with the Shiite mullahs by restoring electricity and removing the mayor, who was stealing contractor funds. The anti-American cleric Moqtada al-Sadr conspired with Shiite elements to build his political influence there. Each Friday, he bused in from Baghdad thousands of his militia to listen to his fiery sermons. He then unleashed them into the streets to protest our presence. One day, with the temperature near 115 degrees and Marines holding the crowd in check with fixed bayonets, Conlin patiently listened to the angry crowd, hurling invective. In the sweltering heat, our division chaplain, Father Bill Devine, gathered several sailors and Marines. They waded into the surly crowd, handing out bottles of cold water. It's hard on a blistering hot day to attack someone giving you water. Once they had shared their complaints, the crowd dispersed. Through such efforts, we kept a shaky peace across our zone.

Alerted that Sadr intended to hold a huge Friday demonstration in Najaf, I told my logistics officers to go to Baghdad and contract with every bus company we could find, to take their buses out of town for a few days. As a result, Sadr's sermon had few Baghdad attendees, and again we kept the peace without using bayonets. Conlin's popularity soared. When it was time for him to leave, as a gesture of thanks, the leading mullahs invited him to a prominent mosque for afternoon tea. In the city of Karbala, fifty miles to the north, the town council tried to elect Lieutenant Colonel Matt Lopez as the mayor, so that he and his Marines, contractors, and funds could not leave. I watched as our troops adapted. My purpose was to find common cause, work to keep the peace, and avoid antagonisms for one more month, one more week, one more day. Don't let it go wrong.

From British officers I learned a lot during this time. I adopted their approach of showing no triumphalism—we had come to liberate, not dominate. We did not push our way around.

I believed the environment in my zone provided a basis for building sound local governance structure. Still, we received no helpful guidance from above. President Bush had appointed former ambassador Paul Bremer as his presidential envoy and director of what came to be called the Coalition Provisional Authority, making him the most powerful American in Iraq. Bremer and his large CPA staff worked in a palace alongside Army Lieutenant General Ricardo Sanchez and his staff. Sanchez commanded Joint Task Force 7, which included all coalition military units in Iraq. JTF 7 was responsible for security. However, the CPA retained the authority and funding to design and organize a new democratic government. In this complex managerial environment, Bremer and his CPA played a key role in all dimensions.

At the same time, we Marines were working with the remnants of the Iraqi Army, excluding only those openly hostile to us or with innocent Iraqi blood on their hands. Over coffee, I hosted former Iraqi generals and elicited their views about reestablishing their army alongside us.

One sweltering afternoon, I dropped in to see Lieutenant Colonel Pat Malay, my battalion commander in the city of Diwaniyah. He had commandeered a soccer field and nailed together a string of plywood booths, staffed by Iraqi women counting out stacks of dinars. Outside the booths, thousands of dismissed soldiers were lined up, waiting to be paid their stipend to return to their unit's barracks. The payment was the idea of my Army civil affairs officer. I concurred. They had no money and no job prospects, and I certainly did not want them taking up arms against us. Pat escorted me along the line.

"Take your pick, sir," Pat said. "Military police, engineers, infantry, even a commando company—you name it and I can have it ready to deploy in three days. Every soldier here wants to be put back to work."

It was not to be. Without consulting our military commanders in the field, Bremer disbanded the Iraqi Army and banned most members of the Baath Party from government positions. Under Saddam, technocrats had kept their jobs by belonging to the party. We could have weeded out the oppressors and die-hard Baathists without slicing off the sinews of governance, public services, and security. Demobilizing the Iraqi Army instead of depoliticizing it set the most capable group of men in the country on an adversarial course against us.

As an example of the disarray, we were methodically building the process for local elections when, against our advice, CPA told me to press for immediate elections. Swallowing our misgivings, we publicly engaged with tribal and local leaders to urge rapid elections, and then CPA suddenly reversed course, leaving us with egg on our face as we had to explain why we were now delaying elections we had been extolling.

In accord with CENTCOM planning, the U.S. Army was remaining, but we Marines were leaving Iraq, our positions taken over by Polish, Spanish, and Ukrainian units.

At the end of that long, hot summer, I took my division home. We had deposed Saddam and bought time for a new order to take shape. The British strategist B. H. Liddell Hart wrote that the object of war is to produce a "better state of peace." I left having no confidence that we had done that.

As a battalion commander in Desert Storm, 1991
(CHRIS WOODBRIDGE)

*As Naval Task Force 58 commander at
Rhino, Afghanistan, 2001*
(MARIO TAMA/GETTY IMAGES)

Arriving at Kandahar airfield, 2001
(REUTERS/POOL/DAVE MARTIN)

Bob Harward, my alter ego over many years
(BOB HARWARD)

With Joe Dunford, RCT 5 commander, a leader for all seasons, March 2003
(GUNNERY SGT. M. M. SMITH, USMC)

The world turning orange in a dust storm, March 2003
(BING WEST)

Lunging at Baghdad,
April 3, 2003
(BING WEST)

Last push to Baghdad, April 2003
(BING WEST)

Marine tanks close on Baghdad, April 4, 2003
(BING WEST)

*Crossing the Diyala River into Baghdad with
battalion commander Bryan McCoy (center) and
RCT7 commander Steve Hummer (right)*
(BING WEST)

Marines topple Saddam statue, Firdos Square, April 2003
(GETTY IMAGES)

A squad in Baghdad, April 2003
(BING WEST)

John Kelly, my right arm
(JOHN KELLY)

Probing into Fallujah, April 2004
(BING WEST)

The terrorist puppet Janabi
(BING WEST)

Ordering Fallujah assault with ops officer and battalion commanders, 2004
(BING WEST)

IED hidden on Ramadi street, 2004
(BING WEST)

CHAPTER 8

Incoherence

BY THE FALL OF 2003, my 1st Marine Division was back in Camp Pendleton, and ships were at sea returning our equipment to California ports. I thought we were finished with Iraq and that we Marines would return to our traditional role of being a naval force in readiness. I focused on refurbishing our hard-used equipment and kicking training schedules into high gear. I was focused on North Korea. I always choose the toughest threat to train against.

Meanwhile in Iraq, mob protests were erupting, initially in the Sunni areas. Our soldiers were being engaged by hit-and-run attacks. From Baghdad to Basra, violence was also growing in Shiite areas.

Two months later, in November, as I was dressing for the Marine Corps Birthday Ball, a televised Pentagon briefing announced that the Marines were going back to Iraq. Shortly after, we received an official warning order: prepare to relieve the 82nd Airborne Division in Anbar Province, the heart of what was called the "Sunni Triangle."

I immediately called John Kelly and said, "Get over there and find out what we're getting into."

I had to read the newspapers to understand the end state desired by President Bush. It was called the "Freedom Agenda."

"America will take the side of brave men and women who advocate these values around the world," the President said, "including the Islamic world, because we have a greater objective than eliminating threats and containing resentment. We seek a just and peaceful world beyond the war on terror."

Now we were going back, and again I had no specific policy guidance. I knew that we would have to provide security for the population, because in these "wars among the people," the Iraqi people, not the nation's capital, were the prize. That meant we would also be training Iraqi forces to take over security.

I was also certain that, within days of our taking over, sheiks, elders, and an assortment of local characters would expect my Marines' take on civil matters. I wanted to know whether CPA had an economic blueprint for fostering recovery. Would we restart state-run industries or try to jump-start free enterprise? Would we focus on large-scale projects or microloans? Were elections in the offing, or should we support the traditional tribal sheiks?

In the U.S. military, we ride for the brand. If a civilian leader tells me to fight rustlers, that's what I do. If he tells me to round up wild horses, I do that. And if he tells me my job is to help a new settler plow his cornfield, I'll get off my horse, cinch my holster around my saddle horn, and get behind the plow. But again, in this case guidance was not forthcoming. My requests for clarity up the chain of command went largely unanswered.

John Kelly returned from his reconnaissance to Anbar. More than a million Sunnis lived there, split among a dozen major and more minor tribes. Most lived in a string of cities and farming communities running two hundred miles northwest from Baghdad along the Euphrates, all the way to the Syrian border. John explained that there was a difference of opinion about what was happening in Anbar.

"Corps headquarters in Baghdad," Kelly said, "claims we're fighting robbers and a few disgruntled former soldiers. The 82nd showed me coordinated patterns of attacks, especially in Fallujah."

This struck me as odd, given that General John Abizaid, our new CENTCOM commander, had said months earlier that we faced a "classical guerrilla-type campaign." Apparently the fedayeen, of little consequence the year before, had grown in capability.

"I've checked all our intel sources," added Joe Dunford, who

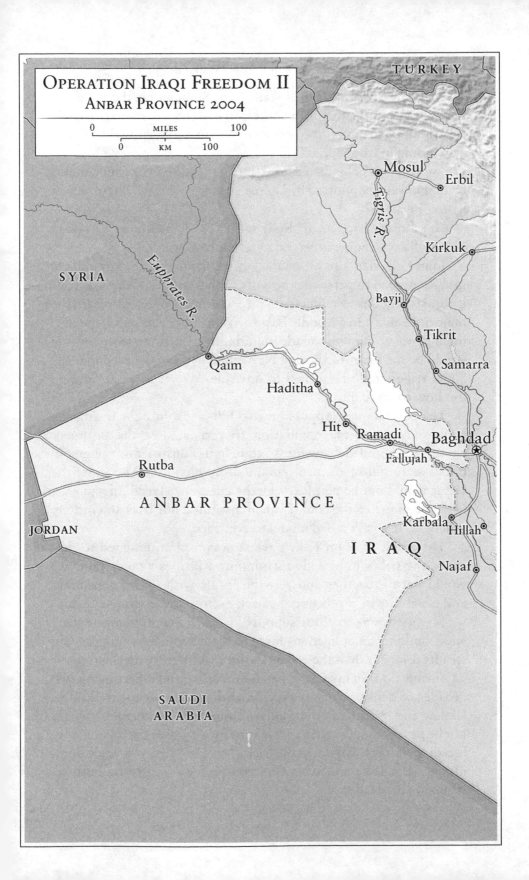

OPERATION IRAQI FREEDOM II
ANBAR PROVINCE 2004

0   MILES   100
0   KM   100

TURKEY

Mosul   Erbil

Tigris R.

Kirkuk

SYRIA

Euphrates R.

Bayji

Tikrit

Samarra

Qaim

Haditha

Hit   Ramadi   Baghdad

Rutba   Fallujah

ANBAR PROVINCE

Karbala   Hillah

JORDAN   I R A Q

Najaf

SAUDI
ARABIA

was now my division chief of staff. "The Sunnis were the top dogs. Now we've put the majority Shiites on top. The Sunni Salafists are preaching jihad across the province. About 150 terrorists a month are coming in from Syria."

"So you two believe," I said, "that we face an insurgency fueled by religion and supported by Sunnis who were thrown out of power by our invasion?"

"It's already happened," Kelly said. "The 82nd knows it's facing a guerrilla war. Some in Baghdad refuse to admit it."

John Kelly had also hit on the key to turning things around. He said we needed to persuade the Sunni tribes to accept the new reality and to organize a counterweight to compete politically with the majority Shiites. In a Middle East torn apart by sectarian strife, our intelligence community made abundantly clear that score settling would be the order of the day. Nevertheless, John believed that the Sunni tribes could be turned to our side. We set to work figuring out how to do that.

The central question was how to kill or capture the insurgents while persuading the population to turn against the insurgent cause. If we needed "new ideas" to help us construct our plan, old books were full of them. I reminded my men that Alexander the Great would not be perplexed by the enemy we faced. In 330 B.C., he first conquered the country, then instituted fair laws and orderly practices. It wasn't a bad model to consider.

The result of John Kelly's recon was a plan designed to persuade the tribes to provide recruits my Marines would train. We would patrol together and vest the locals with the responsibility and capability of protecting themselves from our common enemy.

My intent was to erode support for the Sunni extremist enemy while building an indigenous force to replace us. We would remain steadfast longer than the enemy could sustain their mayhem.

Sitting alone in my Camp Pendleton office and reflecting on two decades of deployments to a region with no democratic traditions, I knew the transition to a Shiite-dominated "democracy" would not be peaceful. I had to make clear to my Marines the dilemma we faced: We had to dial down the overall cycle of violence while dominating it at the point of enemy contact. We had to be both restrained and deadly.

· · ·

On the march to Baghdad, my refrain had been "speed and chivalry." Now I had to persuade those same Marines to slow down, work with the locals, and think. Engage your brain before your trigger finger. As I had done before, I composed a one-page letter to describe my intent to all hands.

COMMANDING GENERAL
1ST MARINE DIVISION (REIN), FMF
CAMP PENDLETON, CALIFORNIA 92055-5380

February 2004

Letter to All Hands,

We are going back in to the brawl. We will be relieving the magnificent soldiers fighting under the 82nd Airborne Division, whose hard won successes in the Sunni Triangle have opened opportunities for us to exploit. For the last year, the 82nd Airborne has been operating against the heart of the enemy's resistance. It's appropriate that we relieve them: When it's time to move a piano, Marines don't pick up the piano bench - we move the piano. So this is the right place for Marines in this fight, where we can carry on the legacy of Chesty Puller in the Banana Wars in the same sort of complex environment that he knew in his early years. Shoulder to shoulder with our comrades in the Army, Coalition Forces and maturing Iraqi Security Forces, we are going to destroy the enemy with precise firepower while diminishing the conditions that create adversarial relationships between us and the Iraqi people.

This is going to be hard, dangerous work. It is going to require patient, persistent presence. Using our individual initiative, courage, moral judgment and battle skills, we will build on the 82nd Airborne's victories. Our country is counting on us even as our enemies watch and calculate, hoping that America does not have warriors strong enough to withstand discomfort and danger. You, my fine young men, are going to prove the enemy wrong - dead wrong. You will demonstrate the same uncompromising spirit that has always caused the enemy to fear America's Marines.

The enemy will try to manipulate you into hating all Iraqis. Do not allow the enemy that victory. With strong discipline, solid faith, unwavering alertness, and undiminished chivalry to the innocent, we will carry out this mission. Remember, I have added, "First, do no harm" to our passwords of "No Better Friend, No Worse Enemy." Keep your honor clean as we gain information about the enemy from the Iraqi people. Then, armed with that information and working in conjunction with fledgling Iraqi Security Forces, we will move precisely against the enemy elements and crush them without harming the innocent.

This is our test - our Guadalcanal, our Chosin Reservoir, our Hue City. Fight with a happy heart and keep faith in your comrades and your unit. We must be under no illusions about the nature of the enemy and the dangers that lie ahead. Stay alert, take it all in stride, remain sturdy, and share your courage with each other and the world. You are going to write history, my fine young sailors and Marines, so write it well.

Semper Fidelis,

J.N. MATTIS
Major General, U. S. Marines

A senior leader in any organization must recognize when his environment has changed. I adapted my touchstones accordingly. In my letter, I stressed that the fight would be long and we could not slack off as the months dragged on. I turned to the past to make my central point. In 300 B.C., Hippocrates, the father of medicine, wrote the oath taken by all doctors: "First, do no harm." That fit our approach: We would perform our profession with discipline, rigor, and care. Finally, I stressed our heritage: Marines do not fail.

When I visited with each of my battalions, I stressed the same principles over and over. *Behave with the same politeness you show at home. Remove your sunglasses when talking, and ask permission to enter a house; don't kick the door down. If a man shoots at you on a crowded street, don't fire back. Hunt him down another day and kill him.*

I rapidly established "pre-deployment training" at an abandoned Air Force base near Camp Pendleton. It included rudimentary Arabic language training, a revised reading list on counterinsurgency operations, Vietnam Marine vets from the Combined Action Platoons on their techniques, and Los Angeles Police Department officers sharing community and barrio policing techniques.

Knowing that this would be a hard fight, I also sent a letter to the families (see Appendix D), assuring them that together we could overcome any challenge, sharing our courage and steadfastness. I next prepared and distributed my commander's intent, as follows.

COMMANDER'S INTENT: My aim is to make common cause with the Iraqis, providing security until Iraqi forces are fully manned, trained, and equipped to assume the mission in order to restore civil administration.

Exploiting the 82d ABN's successes and creating a model of stability in our zone for all Iraq, we will act swiftly to diminish frustrations and conditions that cause any Iraqis to support anti-coalition efforts. Rewarding those Iraqi areas that turn against former regime elements, we use their example to turn the population against the enemy. Concurrently we will defeat noncompliant elements through interdiction, elimination of sanctuary, and building trust with Iraqis to gain actionable intelligence. These two lines of operations—diminishing the causes for anti-coalition efforts and destroying non-compliant forces—will facilitate transition to political, administrative, and social conditions for a free Iraq in our zone. Wrapping all our actions in a blanket of information operations, we will do no harm to innocent Iraqis, using focused and discriminate force by sturdy Marines who will remain unfazed by enemy actions.

Through presence, persistence, and patience, our end state is a functioning Iraqi civil administration with Iraqi security forces replacing USMC security elements.

ANBAR

I knew from the British experience in Malaysia and our experience in Vietnam that we needed one soldier per twenty inhabitants to succeed in a counterinsurgency. In Anbar, our ratio would be closer to one per forty civilians.

As the CIA and military intelligence officers briefed me, it became obvious that the densely packed cities of Fallujah and Ramadi, thirty miles apart, represented the most violent area in all of Iraq. I set up my division headquarters on the outskirts of Ramadi, the provincial capital. The MEF headquarters was located adjacent to Fallujah, the most hostile city in the country.

When General John Abizaid arrived to talk with the sheiks, insurgents attacked the meeting place and tried to kill him.

In Fallujah, a month before we took charge from the 82nd Airborne, Al Qaeda in Iraq (AQI) stormed the city jail, killing twenty-three policemen. The murders went unavenged, leeching power from the sheiks. AQI's most notorious leader, Abu Musab al-Zarqawi, a cunning thug with a lust for killing, was hiding in the city. Zarqawi directed suicide bombers against Westerners, Shiites, and those Sunnis he deemed apostate. Even the Al Qaeda leadership, hiding in Pakistan, told him to restrain his wanton killing.

Abdullah al-Janabi, the highest-ranking mullah in Fallujah and a sly, excitable zealot, was Zarqawi's patron. Following his example, hundreds of clerics were preaching anti-American sentiment with increasing venom. Among the sheiks and city elders, it was hard to distinguish the ones who were keeping their mouths shut to stay alive from those who were the true jihadists.

By the time my small leadership team and I arrived in late January 2004 to start coordination for my inbound troops arriving in

February, attacks inside Fallujah were becoming more and more common. The on-scene U.S. Army battalion commander, Lieutenant Colonel Brian Drinkwine, speaking from six months' experience, warned that my Marines would "be bloodied." I could sense that the window of opportunity to avoid a full-blown fight was closing rapidly. The highways and ratlines from Syria were wide open for foreign fighters. We had very few reliable local Iraqi forces, and we were still developing informant networks. The terrorists were coming together for attacks and then falling back into safe houses in the city. Very few civilians would dare inform against them, and even if someone wanted to inform, they didn't know which Iraqi officials could be trusted not to betray them, and we Americans hadn't proved that we would stick around.

In late March 2004, the transfer of U.S. military authority for Fallujah passed from a battalion of the 82nd Airborne Division to one of my Marine battalions. During the low-key ceremony at City Hall, insurgents snuck up and let loose a fusillade of rocket-propelled grenades and mortar shells in an attempt to kill their own town council members.

Less than a week after my division had taken charge of Anbar, I was on the highway approaching Saqlawiyah, a small village near Fallujah. The local sheiks had semi-agreed to expel a gang of insurgents in return for electric power. If we sealed the deal, I'd provide the generators. I heard over the radio that John Kelly and his team had been in a scrape several miles away and were returning to base with the wounded. The op center also reported that two hundred miles to the northwest, on the Syrian border, a Marine company was heavily engaged. At the same time, Army Colonel Buck Connor, commanding an Army/Marine brigade in the Ramadi zone, came up on the radio, asking me to drop by to talk about a big fight he had on his hands. Already, these were the normal reports coming in from across fifty thousand square miles of battle space.

One item relayed to me was that four civilian contractors had driven into Fallujah without checking in with the Marines. This was a frequent frustration for me, because they didn't understand the danger. Joe Dunford called me.

"CNN is showing the burnt bodies of the contractors hanging from a bridge," he said. "The whole world is seeing this."

When I walked into our operations center about an hour later, I saw pictures of a gleeful mob dancing below the blackened bodies dangling on the bridge. Knowing this enemy, I was not surprised by the barbarity, and I was already thinking about how to get the bodies back and kill those responsible. Among the competing tribes in the city, we had contacts who would help us.

John Kelly and Joe Dunford joined me in my office to assess the situation. The lynching had been seen on television sets across Iraq. If we charged in, many innocent people would die, uniting the city behind the killers.

"The best we can hope for in Fallujah," Joe said, "is not to lose ground with the people. Not to have an emotional jihad uprising because of something we do, or let Fallujah fester as an insurgent base."

I didn't want to provoke an already aroused population further. If we rolled in with tanks, excited teenagers would hurl rocks and bottles of gasoline with flaming wicks. One errant round from a tank gun could have tragic consequences. It didn't take us more than fifteen minutes to decide on a low-key, three-step approach.

First, we would avoid sparking further outbursts. Working with certain sheiks, after the mob dispersed, John Toolan would arrange to bring out the bodies. Second, we had to hold to a steady course. Across Anbar, our commanders would continue their patrols to provide security. Third, we would deliver justice by the discriminate use of force. We would learn the identities and locations of the ringleaders, using pictures of the murderers who had posed among the bodies and overhead photos of their homes. We would respond with raids at times of our choosing. I would employ, to quote Napoleon, "an iron fist in a velvet glove."

The defilement of the human body affronts our sense of dignity. Homer, in describing how Achilles had dragged Hector's body behind his chariot during the Trojan War, condemned Achilles, regardless of his warrior fame. Civilization progresses, Homer taught us, only when the strongest nations and armies respect the dignity of the weakest. In Fallujah, our military strength would be guided by moral power, just as it has been since George Washington first commanded our Continental Army. By killing those who had violated our common humanity while maintaining our moral compass, I intended to demonstrate that there is no better friend and no worse enemy than a United States Marine.

As the ground commander on-scene, I knew what to do and how to do it. The generals above me agreed with my plan.

But we were all overruled. I was unaware that Ambassador Bremer, in a teleconference with the White House, had argued that strong military action must be taken. General Sanchez, also on the line, described President Bush as angry and as having said that we had to be "tougher than hell." Secretary of Defense Rumsfeld later explained that he thought the United States had "to send a message that anyone who engaged in acts of terror would face the might of the U.S. military."

A battle inside a city would inflict horrendous damage on noncombatants. I had studied the 1968 Marine battle in Hue City, Vietnam, and didn't want to go down that road. Plus, an all-out assault would unify the residents against us. In World War II, despite horrendous casualties in German cities, the more we bombed, the more unified the German population became. This was the most critical objection I and the generals above me raised, but to no avail. Our perspective was lost in the cacophony of intense emotions evoked by the grotesque front-page picture of a mob dancing around dangling corpses.

General Conway reluctantly told me that I had to attack in force. I was to assault a city of twelve square miles, comprising hundreds of blocks of concrete houses containing 300,000 increasingly resentful residents and a dispersed host of armed enemy.

Great nations don't get angry; military action should be undertaken only to achieve specific strategic effects. In this case, we were in an extremely violent political campaign over ideas, and we were trying to treat the problem of Fallujah like a conventional war. I believed we had a more effective, sustainable approach for the situation we faced.

But that was the order: *Attack*.

I had made my objections clear. While some might urge a senior officer to resign his post in this circumstance, your troops cannot resign and go home. They will carry out that specific order regardless of whether you are still with them.

Loyalty to your troops, to your superiors, and to your oath to obey orders from civilian authority matters most, even when there are a hundred reasons to disagree.

"Right, let's get on with it," I said to my network of commanders.

While normally a commander would have received a detailed order, in this case the assault order was only verbal. We had to attack and drive out the terrorists, gaining control of the city. We'd start by shepherding out of danger hundreds of thousands of recalcitrant civilians. We broadcast repeated warnings for all civilians to leave the city. As a quarter of a million people poured out, insurgents with freedom of movement were coming into the city.

I made one strong statement up the chain of command: *Once we assault, don't stop us.* Inside the city, we would be engaged in a full-scale brawl. When the battle was over, the city and the adjacent major highway would be open, and the terrorists would be dead.

Again I had to reorient my Marines going in. I did so by reversing my standard "capture or kill" guidance to "kill or capture" those who fight you. I deliberately placed the verb *kill* before *capture* to make clear that this was close-quarters combat against a foe with the home-court advantage.

Having only scant intelligence, we estimated the enemy force at somewhere between six hundred and two thousand hard-core fighters, reinforced by perhaps a thousand resentful locals, along with about twenty key leaders.

I had no reserve and had to pull forces from other cities and the border posts, leaving only small detachments behind. Major General Marty Dempsey's 1st Armored Division, which had been rotating back to Germany, was stopped in mid-stride, its units returned to Iraq to relieve pressure in my southern sector.

I was fortunate to have Colonel John Toolan in command of the assault, a man who kept cool in the worst circumstances and responded to adversity with roguish irony.

"You're assaulting with only two battalions at the start," I said.

This meant he was initially attacking with only two thousand grunts to root out terrorists from among tens of thousands of concrete buildings, without knowing where the enemy was hiding.

"Well, we don't want to overdo it, sir," he said.

Seizing Fallujah was John's fight. I focused on coordinating the activities of fourteen thousand American soldiers and Marines while meeting with dozens of tribal sheiks and carrying out CPA's political and developmental programs. As for my responsibilities in the battle for Fallujah, I intended to stay close to the action without interfering in John's fight.

. . .

John attacked on April 4, sending one battalion in from the north and another from the south. The intent was to keep the insurgents off-balance and confused, jabbing from different directions to assess their fighting style and then moving quickly to overwhelm them. After our first pitched battle, I wanted the enemy to be convinced that they should never again seek to fight American Marines in close combat.

Early that morning, Lieutenant Colonel Gregg Olson led his battalion into the city's northern outskirts. He was astonished to see a dozen men, mostly unarmed, pushing a trailer truck across the highway to block the Marines while other insurgents opened fire from the flanks. To Olson, it seemed senseless. The Marines made short work of the enemy.

The battle for Fallujah had begun.

All day, the battle seesawed up and down the streets. Every few hours a group of five to ten young insurgents ran forward, eager to close on the Marines, meeting only death. At dusk, as the dogs began their nightly howling, bands of insurgents began slipping forward, groping for the Marine lines. The muezzins exhorted the remaining population to take to the streets in support of the "brave martyrs."

At the same time, a second battalion, under Lieutenant Colonel Giles Kyser, was attacking from the south. Methodically, the squads advanced. From the rooftops, company commanders ensured that their platoons and squads stayed abreast, supporting one another. The Marines picked their way among rows of shabby repair shops, heaps of broken pipes, and junked cars. Visiting the assault units, my feet crunched on the broken shards of drug vials.

By the fourth day of the assault, I had one more battalion to give John. Together we visited a battalion ops center a block back from the front lines. The fighting spirit of the troops was infectious. Seizing rooftops, we held the high ground. Our snipers, joined by every SEAL sniper who had heard there was a fight, turned the streets into kill zones beyond a distance of 700 yards. The enemy was being driven back, block by block, street by street.

. . .

Fallujah quickly became a spark in a keg of gunpowder. Heavier fighting was exploding across Iraq. Adjacent to my headquarters, fighting broke out in Ramadi.

At one point in Ramadi, I walked up behind a squad in a furious firefight with insurgents farther down the street. When I inanely asked, "Hey, guys, what's going on?" the squad leader dropped his rifle from his shoulder and smiled.

"We're taking the fun out of fundamentalism, sir!"

I laughed. When you have tightly knit squads, fire superiority, and troops keeping their sense of humor, the fight is in good hands.

Each day, I drove back and forth between Ramadi and Fallujah, and I often flew by helicopter hundreds of miles across my far-flung command. The fighting in Fallujah raged, with piles of insurgent bodies heaped at intersections because there wasn't enough room at the city morgue. Toolan and I understood the insurgents' style. They had no formal, hierarchical military structure, with a commander and sub-commanders. Rather, they were gangs organized around mosques, neighborhoods, and local leaders. Knowing the streets and alleys as they did, they were able to engage in a running battle, but not a mutually supporting, coordinated fight. They could bloody us, but they could not hold out against the Marine assault.

In the second week of the fight, I brought in a fourth battalion to reinforce John Toolan's attack from the south. We were losing Marines, but John had the insurgents in a vise and was squeezing hard. Our intelligence assets identified desperate insurgent leaders who didn't know which way to turn, their demands for ammo resupply growing increasingly strident.

I was now confident that the fight would be over within a few days. Having learned from Tora Bora to overreport if necessary, I was keeping my seniors abreast. My aim was for a speedy recovery, removing rubble, reestablishing sewage disposal, increasing electric power, and restoring a sense of normalcy as swiftly as possible. I was contracting for garbage trucks and bulldozers to come in from Baghdad.

The reporters embedded with our platoons had freedom to report what they were seeing, and they were accurate. However, inside enemy lines, there were Al Jazeera reporters and local stringers for international media sympathetic to the terrorists. A stringer would leave the city and drive the forty miles to Baghdad. From there, the "news" from Fallujah, plus video and still pictures, was picked up by news bureaus around the globe. The vast majority of news organizations did not have reporters on the ground, so the enemy's propaganda dominated the news cycle.

The coalition had no effective response to the propaganda. Images of dead babies that would cause a rock to cry and assertions of agonizing civilian losses caused even our allies to voice strong objections.

By constant repetition, the false allegations acquired plausibility. Although damage and death in the city were real, that damage was not difficult for policymakers to anticipate when ordering us to attack the city. Most noncombatants had fled the area, but not all. I was reporting our increasing progress, but that truth was submerged beneath enemy propaganda. In Baghdad, London, and Washington, the battle seemed endlessly destructive. I had lance corporals who could better express the nobility of our methods than U.S. government spokespeople in Washington.

The UN envoy in Baghdad expressed dismay. "You have also seen on the television screens," he told *The Guardian* of London, "images of yet another mosque which had taken a direct hit. Reports today of attacks from and on a mosque are a source of shock." I later learned that he was threatening to pull the UN out of Iraq if the assault continued. The Iraqi Governing Council, composed of Sunni and Shiite politicians, insisted to Ambassador Bremer that he stop the attack or they would resign. "Continuing military operations in Fallujah," Bremer wrote in his memoir, "would result in the collapse of the entire political process." Bremer called Generals Abizaid and Sanchez into his office. He had decided to halt the offensive.

After a heated discussion, General Sanchez called Jim Conway, telling him to stop offensive operations by noon on April 9. Bremer intended to announce his decision over Iraqi radio and television before the end of the Friday services in the mosques. We had lost the information war.

The President's envoy had argued first for an assault I believed was reckless, and now, with my troops in house-to-house fighting and close to victory, he had succeeded in halting the assault. I didn't see the order to halt coming. At the top level, there was loose, uninformed speculation that the attack might take weeks. My judgment, that we were close to crushing an enemy now in disarray, was not solicited.

General Abizaid flew to MEF headquarters, outside Fallujah, to convey the order. I immediately headed for the meeting to find out what they were thinking. But on my way, we encountered a Marine patrol under fire. Working together with helicopter gunships and the patrol, we took out the enemy position. But I had lost time and arrived at the meeting late, sweaty and disheveled, passing a few journalists in the corridor. General Abizaid interrupted the meeting, courteously asking for my input as the division commander.

"First we're ordered to attack, and now we're ordered to halt," I said. "If you're going to take Vienna, take fucking Vienna."

I was repeating Napoleon's outburst to his field marshal who had hesitated to seize that city. I expected my frontline commanders to speak frankly to me, and I did the same to my seniors.

Silence followed. The several dozen officers and NCOs in the room were looking at the floor or gazing into middle space. All recognized that no one in that room, regardless of rank, could change the political decision. There wasn't anything more to say. Although we were on the brink of at least a tactical success, we were stopped dead in our tracks.

I had launched the assault emphasizing only one point: that I not be stopped. You don't order your men to attack and risk death, and then go wobbly, stopping the attack and allowing the enemy to resupply and to recover his fighting spirit. He will be tougher when he next fights you, and your troops could understandably lose confidence in your leadership.

On April 10, Iraqi politicians from Baghdad drove into Fallujah to negotiate with the insurgents, who slapped one dignitary, jerked the tie of a second, and kicked a third in the ass. When the official party scurried back to the capital, I hoped that was the end of that harebrained idea. We had only agreed to a twenty-four-hour pause, and it was expiring without anything to show for it.

I tried to think of how to persuade the policymakers to my point of view about what we had to do. My political liaison was Stuart E. "Stu" Jones, a shrewd diplomat as calm under fire as a Marine, who reported to Ambassador Bremer. He, too, knew the insurgents were playing for time. But after the twenty-four-hour deadline passed, it was extended by Bremer. I knew that the underlying motivations of the policymakers were not malicious. Indeed, they wanted to do the best thing. But they had no grasp of the tactical opportunity or peril that their decision to assault the city now presented. They were spinning in a circle, without a strategic compass to keep them pointed in a consistent direction.

The next day—Easter Sunday—I secured permission to straighten out our lines. The resultant movements of our battalions caused the insurgents to come unglued. Our intelligence assets identified frantic communications. Overhead surveillance showed trucks and taxis scurrying around, but no signs of a coherent defense. A battalion commander, Bryan McCoy, immediately grasped that we had an opening and called the operations center.

"We're prepared to continue the attack," he said. "I'll have the Hidra mosque inside an hour."

Between informants and other intelligence, we had identified Hidra as the enemy's command-and-control center in the core of the city, from which they tried to organize their defense. Once our troops seized Hidra, organized resistance would be impossible. The terrorists would be forced to try to get out of the now surrounded city if they didn't want to die there. Once again, though, word came down: *Do not advance.*

For the next several weeks, we traded shots across fixed lines. The insurgents, now reassured that the Marines were not on the attack, were shooting at them from immediately adjacent concrete houses. During the day, no one on either side moved in the open.

Zarqawi was directing his terrorists while producing video pieces to give to Al Jazeera. We had intelligence placing him in the Jolan market, west of the Hidra mosque. That mosque was controlled by the mullah Abdullah al-Janabi. Fearing a popular backlash, the Iraqi Governing Council tried through CPA to prevent us from capturing or killing Janabi. He set the tone for dozens of other mullahs. The longer we were stopped, the more resistance became a community obligation.

Every day, John Toolan and I separately made the rounds, checking in with the platoons. By mid-April, whenever a corporal, captain, or colonel asked me when we would attack, I just said, "Hold the line. Our time will come." I knew that a policy of keeping us frozen in place was not a strategy; the status quo could not last forever. Believing that the assault would eventually resume, we were quietly reinforcing the barbed wire and earthen berms fully cutting off the city. I was determined that there would be no escape for the terrorists. Fallujah would be their graveyard.

The stiff backbone of our senior NCOs and the animating energy of junior officers and NCOs helped our teams stick together, focused on the mission.

After being halted on Easter Sunday, I was directed to negotiate at a neutral site a half-mile east of the city, with safe passage guaranteed for the opposition. There, I met with a revolving cast of characters—cunning Iraqi politicians from Baghdad, bewildered civil servants from Fallujah, self-important imams, and fearful sheiks. The true terrorist leaders never appeared. I was shuttling back and forth from Ramadi in my light armored vehicle. On the way, my detail was, like everyone else, hit by IEDs and small arms. There were reports that Janabi was trying to knock me off. I didn't blame him for trying, given that I was trying to do the same to him.

I was issued no written terms of reference for the negotiations. At night, I discussed with my boss, Jim Conway, different ideas about what I might propose the next day. We held firmly to the principle that our Marines must be given access to the entire city. On the civilian side, the unflappable diplomat Stu Jones counseled me well, but he had no authority to propose negotiating terms.

The negotiations proved fruitless. The front men would arrive and turn over a few rusty old weapons, as if that proved their sincerity. They would sip tea, talk sonorously for hours, claim that more weapons would be collected, promise us access to the city, and leave. We were being played. Every night, I went over the growing list of our casualties. John Toolan wanted to throw down the gauntlet and say, "That's the end; we're coming for you tomorrow."

In one of the more contentious discussions, a sheik demanded to know when we were leaving.

"I'm not," I replied. "I bought a little piece of property on the Euphrates. I'm going to marry one of your daughters and retire there."

Reporters came in from Baghdad, so my words would sometimes make news. Language is a weapon. In formal circumstances, I'm calculating but I speak pointedly. There's nothing to be gained by speaking obliquely about important matters. Brought up in the American West, I don't hide behind euphemisms. As the negotiations turned into a kabuki dance, I warned my interlocutors:

"I come in peace. I didn't bring artillery. But I'm pleading with you, with tears in my eyes: If you fuck with me, I'll kill you all."

The sheiks did not act on my warning. They were allowing their sons to be recruited by the insurgents while they were talking to me—unwittingly abrogating their own authority.

Every day, our position was becoming increasingly untenable. Ramadi, the provincial capital, saw frequent fighting; we had to protect the governor, who was under siege in his own office. Convoys from Kuwait coming through my southern sector were ambushed regularly, and supplies were running low in Baghdad. I heard talk about evacuating the diplomatic quarter known as the Green Zone.

In my nightly conversations with Jim Conway, we suppressed our frustrations and dealt with the situation. We had few options. I had to maneuver and reposition those of my troops least engaged against the enemy to the most dangerous locations. But there was no denying the increased danger for the Iraqi population we left unprotected. Whenever a member of Congress, a Washington staffer, or any other visitor from the States or Baghdad paid a courtesy call or asked for a briefing, I made the same point: *I can't win on the defense, and I can't prevail while chained in place. So release my Marines to swiftly finish Fallujah. And then I can redistribute them across the zone.*

The military staffs in Baghdad were as frustrated as I was with the fruitless negotiations and sensed that we would be allowed to continue the attack. I was verbally told by the higher military staffs to be prepared, and that I would soon be unleashed. So, on April 23, I again told John Toolan to prepare to resume the offensive. The next day, he called his assault battalion commanders into the briefing room in his ops center, one mile outside Fallujah. The assault plan was straightforward: Battalions would attack from the north, south, and east and drive toward the Euphrates River, where an Army battalion was waiting. In classic hammer-and-anvil fashion, we would smash the Islamist force, killing it physically and destroying its psychological appeal. No way out.

But then policy disarray reared its head. I had to call John out of his briefing to give him the bad news.

General Sanchez had just called Jim Conway. We were not to resume the attack.

"Our orders changed," Conway later explained to the press.

"Orders from higher, like Washington?" a *New York Times* reporter asked.

"I don't ask those questions," Conway said. "We were probably going to mount up and those [orders] simply changed and that's not uncommon."

The impact of such incoherence at the theater and national command levels cannot be overstated. *Dizzying* is the appropriate word. My division was given orders about what not to do—*Do not attack*—but we weren't given any orders about what *to* do.

It was *Groundhog Day*. In continued urban fighting, over the next few days, my division lost eighteen killed and wounded.

Conway had had enough. Through the CIA, the MEF was in contact with several former Iraqi generals. They wanted the Marines pulled out so they could form an Iraqi "home guard" inside the city—a "Fallujah Brigade." After eighteen days of negotiation that went nowhere, General Conway agreed to pull back the Marines and let the former Iraqi generals try to evict the terrorists. I thought it was a forlorn hope. We had no way of vetting these Fallujah Brigade recruits. Because Zarqawi and Janabi dominated the city, those who joined this unit would likely become our enemy. Once they were armed, they would be under Zarqawi's thumb, and the only way I could retire them would be to kill them.

From the very start, the ad hoc arrangement was fraught. A few days later, I drove to our negotiation site. John Toolan was there, talking with Lieutenant Colonel Suleiman, the commander of the Iraqi National Guardsmen working with us. A Fallujah native, Suleiman was a tough, fair man who viewed Janabi and the Islamists as the real threat. Shortly after I arrived, an Iraqi "brigadier general" named Saleh unexpectedly arrived, wearing his best Saddam-era green uniform. This caught me by surprise.

When he saw Saleh, Lieutenant Colonel Suleiman clenched his jaw, his face turning scarlet with rage. John hastily steered him into another room, where Suleiman emphatically protested that he had worked with us. But now this so-called Fallujah Brigade would be controlled by the terrorists and Saddam-era generals like Saleh. "You've been duped," he told John.

As Saleh was leaving, Tony Perry, a reporter for the *Los Angeles Times,* asked him if he had come to take over. In fractured English, a smiling Saleh indicated that he was indeed taking command of the Fallujah Brigade. Tony had snared a scoop. To soften the impact of the story I knew Tony was about to write, I interrupted to say, "We'll make it work."

Over the next seventy-two hours, in response to our emboldened enemy's attacks, we launched three dozen strikes at targets in the city. In Baghdad, the same Iraqi politicians who had opposed the use of military force in Fallujah now reversed field. The Iraqi Governing Council warned against the "appeasement" of terrorists. Shiite politicians argued that the creation of a Sunni brigade was a double cross. Arguing against the handover, Bremer objected strongly to the White House.

It was at this difficult moment that CBS's *60 Minutes* broke the story of abuses at Abu Ghraib prison, twenty miles east of Fallujah. Pictures taken by American guards showed Iraqi men lying naked in piles and standing blindfolded on stools, with wires attached to their arms. These graphic images repulsed us all and ignited a worldwide firestorm of political and press condemnation. Combined with the inability to sustain the attack on Fallujah, this did grave damage to the entire coalition campaign. The imposed tactical halt in Fallujah and the egregious behavior of rogue guards at Abu Ghraib had cost us the moral high ground.

John Toolan sent me a terse note saying the Fallujah Brigade was a cover for the terrorists. "This," he wrote, "is a deal with the devil." I wholeheartedly agreed. But in a gesture of political theater, in early May I was to meet with the Iraqi generals and turn over control of the city. The negotiators insisted that I be accompanied by only a handful of Marines. Suspecting an ambush, Toolan had a battalion in armored vehicles standing by outside the city.

"Remember, Bryan," I told the battalion commander, "if shooting starts, your mission is to break through and pull us out, not charge to the Euphrates. We'll come back later and finish the job."

The morning of the meeting, a brave CIA officer and two

Iraqis—all three bearded and dressed as insurgents—drove a non-descript car into town on the route I was to take. When they saw several men emplacing a large bomb, they marked down the GPS coordinates. Once several blocks away, they transmitted the data via cellphone. In this case, we exploded the bomb remotely, killing those who were preparing it.

An hour later, my small Marine retinue drove into the center of the city, linking up with Suleiman's nervous soldiers at the conference site. A Cobra gunship pilot overhead radioed sightings of insurgents hiding around street corners adjacent to my route. Were we driving into a shootout? We had no way of knowing, but we were fully prepared to shoot our way out if necessary.

Inside City Hall, two dozen sheiks and clerics—including Janabi—sat rigidly along the square walls. I said a few words to a Japanese TV crew. (I had no idea how they got there.) I also wished good luck to a newly assigned "brigade commander," a small, tentative Iraqi general in a business suit. In the fraught atmosphere, I sat down next to Janabi.

In exchange for the pause, I explained that all heavy weapons had to be collected and turned over to us, and that government and coalition forces had to have full access to the city. The Fallujah Brigade would patrol the streets, and government services would be restored.

Janabi smugly agreed to the conditions, knowing that our attack had been stalled by political restraints on my force. I doubted his sincere intention to do one bit of what he promised, and walked out.

The insurgents, knowing they had won politically, held their fire as we drove out of town, past dozens of grim men with their arms folded. Some held up fingers in the V-for-victory sign. Others turned their backs and gestured as if defecating.

Our troops pulled out of their positions deep inside the city, gained at the cost of their buddies. A freckle-faced, filthy Marine, his machine gun over his shoulder, was asked by a reporter how he felt about losing his buddies and then being ordered to pull out. He looked into the camera and, in a slow southern drawl, said, "Doesn't matter. We'll hunt 'em down somewhere else and kill 'em."

Reflecting back on the weeks of brutal urban fighting, I thought of a Kipling line: "For the strength of the pack is the wolf, and the strength of the wolf is the pack." For all the dysfunction of the on-again, off-again attack, I was proud beyond words that our Marines kept the faith when they'd had every reason to give it up.

The day after we pulled out of Fallujah, Al Qaeda posted on the Internet a video of the gruesome beheading of twenty-six-year-old American Nicholas Berg. The executioner, dressed in black and wielding a sword, was a hooded Zarqawi. The location was somewhere in the Jolan market.

Our invasion had unleashed impulses, historical and current, that were sweeping across the Middle East. Zarqawi was out to tear apart Iraq and make it an Islamist terrorist caliphate. We had entered a twilight zone of directionless policy that defied strategic logic. Zarqawi and his terrorists were killing thousands, and they weren't hiding their intent from us. One of Zarqawi's deputies, who was reported to be in Fallujah as early as February 2004, was Abu Bakr al-Baghdadi, who would emerge as the leader of ISIS a decade later.

The Fallujah Brigade seemed to provide a political off-ramp from a situation my seniors deemed unresolvable. In execution, it provided no solution, political or military. Instead it sent a message of defeat. The fig leaf of the Fallujah Brigade did not hide the fact that we had been stopped, and the consequences would be felt for years.

I believed I had let my men down, having failed to prevent the attack in the first place and subsequently failing to prevent a stop order once we were deep inside the city. It was a tough time for me, because higher-level decisions had cost us lives, but now was not the time to go inward. You must always keep fighting for those who are still with you.

CHAPTER 9

Cascading Consequences

BECAUSE ANBAR'S SUNNIS were seen by central authorities in Baghdad as the most recalcitrant in Iraq, the province was assigned as a secondary priority for pacification, an "economy of force" zone, in military parlance. It was 2004, and the insurgency was morphing into a civil war, not least because we had erred in handling Fallujah.

On long nighttime helicopter flights, I watched the arcs of green and red tracers and the bright flashes of explosions flaring up in a dozen towns and cities. The tribal sheiks, whether they liked Marines or not, were now complaining to me about their young men joining Zarqawi's terrorists. In undiplomatic language, I replied that they had to stand up to stop the destruction they had brought upon themselves.

From their point of view, the sheiks now saw us as unreliable. The fight for Fallujah had put us on our back foot. We were going to have to work long and hard to find trustworthy Iraqi partners.

In the last week of May, President Bush gave a speech at the Army War College, announcing a change in policy. Going forward, security would be a "shared responsibility in Fallujah. . . . Coalition commanders have worked with local leaders to create an all-Iraqi security force. . . . I sent American troops to Iraq to make its people free, not to make them American. Iraqis will write their own history, and find their own way."

I believed the President's goal was idealistic and tragically misplaced, based on misguided assessments that appeared impervious to my reporting. Of all places in Iraq, Fallujah was certainly the wrong example for the President to cite. I had no idea who told him that responsibility for security was being "shared." Not one American was left inside the city.

Zarqawi, safe in his Fallujah sanctuary, had a plan that was working. By targeting Shiites, he provoked Shiite militias into exacting indiscriminate revenge upon hapless Sunnis. The President envisioned Iraqis left to "find their own way" coming together. The reality, tragically, was that they were forced to choose sides in a rapidly developing civil war.

Washington was focused on the transfer of political power from Ambassador Bremer to Iraqi leaders who had no conception of democracy and the power sharing it requires. Joe Dunford, John Kelly, and I conveyed our blunt assessments to Washington visitors. But we were out in Anbar, far removed from the political conversations taking place in Baghdad and Washington.

At the end of June, Bremer departed after turning over control to Iraqi officials. He wrote to President Bush, "As a result of the President's courage and the Coalition's efforts, Iraq has before it a path to a better future." In reality, nascent Iraqi leaders jockeyed for power amid ever-shifting alliances, with the Shiite factions maneuvering to consolidate power, some with Iranian financial and weaponry support. Anbar received no help from the Shiite-controlled government in Baghdad. The province was remote, restive, and impoverished—and all hell was breaking loose.

Al Qaeda's approach was to recruit unemployed youths, mostly from the lower rungs of society. Then, by intimidation, they took over towns and farmlands. This should surprise no one. Think of any Hollywood western. Tough guys with guns move in. The townsfolk do not rebel; instead, they accommodate. Not one man in a hundred will stand up alone to a bad man with a gun. The more fanatical the killers, the more intimidated the community.

There were no resolute sheriffs here. Tribal insurgent bands sprouted up, manned by disenfranchised, enthusiastic young men, bored and unemployed. Most fought in the vague hope of restoring Sunni primacy and for the excitement of shooting at an American and later bragging about it. When the Marines killed them, their friends grew bitter. It was now a matter of revenge, and the cycle of violence spun faster.

Having studied the British occupation of Iraq after World War I, I saw that much of what was happening to us could have been predicted. I also studied the 1956–57 French battle for Algiers. In neighborhoods where French troops employed targeted operations and kept up better relationships with the Arab population, they met with more success than in areas where they were more heavy-handed. Hence, I returned to my dictum "First, do no harm" and re-prescribed strict rules. We were uninvited guests seeking friendship, not resentment.

Writing after his command in the Balkans in the 1990s, British general Rupert Smith had observed, "War amongst the people is conducted best as an intelligence and information operation, not as one of manoeuvre and attrition in the manner of industrial war." This was how the British troops dealt with Northern Ireland. In that war, the antagonists shared much the same culture. But we were American troops from a largely Christian nation, in the heart of the Islamic Middle East. To overcome cultural barriers, we had to all work together until we created a common purpose. I knew it would take years of patient, persistent presence before we had adequate nets of informants, interpreters, and tribal leaders who understood that their interests were aligned with ours.

Few officials from the Saddam era were left in Anbar. In Ramadi, the provincial governor stayed alive because we posted a twenty-four-hour guard around him, with a tank on his front lawn. But after Al Qaeda kidnapped his son, the governor apologized on TV for supporting the coalition, tearfully embraced his released son, gathered his family, shook hands with the battalion commander, and left for Jordan.

As in Chicago in the early thirties, the local sheiks knew by sight the local gangsters and terrorists. They understood what was going on in their communities. But they didn't share that with my battalion commanders. In many heated exchanges, I told them they were aligning with the wrong team. The fundamentalists would eventually kill them and rule their tribes in their place, using their young men as cannon fodder. Having seen us fall back from Fallujah, the terrified sheiks had no way of knowing what they could expect from us, and took pains not to antagonize Zarqawi's terrorists.

In the hot summer of 2004, Green Beret Major Adam Such, working with the poor Albu Nimr tribe, numbering fewer than twenty thousand, found the first flicker of determination among the tribes to stand up to Al Qaeda. Adam nourished the relationship, reinforcing the tribal sheiks' standing, and violence ebbed in their western Euphrates villages.

While that small tribe proved the exception at the time, I mulled things over with John Toolan, Joe Dunford, John Kelly, Stu Jones, and our staffs, plus the CIA. We agreed that bringing over the tribes remained the key to a successful counterinsurgency campaign in Anbar. But we also saw that it would be a long, long road.

At midnight one night in late May, an officer from the ops center awakened me to report that an Al Qaeda team we had been tracking for weeks had crossed from Syria into Iraq. Immediately I gave the order to attack. A short time later, F-18s and Cobra gunships struck the target, while recon Marines moved to cut off any escape. A Special Forces team helo-assaulted into the shattered campsite, scooping up papers, passports, and computers. The team reported twenty-six men killed, recovering weapons and satellite phones.

However, a British newspaper published a sharply different account: "US soldiers started to shoot us, one by one . . . Survivors describe wedding massacre as generals refuse to apologise." The story alleged that women and children had been the ones killed, because the gathering was actually a wedding party.

When reporters asked for my response, I replied, "We'd tracked these guys when they crossed the Syrian border and caught them sixty-five miles from the nearest town. More than two dozen military-age males just happened to pick a campsite with no women? That's a heck of a wedding party. Let's not be naive."

The press rightly plays a devil's advocate role and doesn't have to be right or accurate in that capacity. But whether you're a general or a CEO, win or lose, you have to fight a false narrative or it will assuredly be accepted as fact. In the information age, you can't retreat to your office and let your public affairs officer take the tough questions.

My directive was to let reporters go where they wanted. Assign them an NCO so they don't walk into a helicopter's rotor blade, but let them see reality. I didn't want a repeat of the "five o'clock follies" of the 1960s, when overly positive and often mischaracterized information from Vietnam was fed by the senior military ranks to an increasingly skeptical, then cynical press. If there's something you don't want people to see, you ought to reconsider what you're doing. The most compelling story for us should be the naked truth about the reality of our operations.

"I wanted to tell the stories of the grunts," Tony Perry of the *Los Angeles Times* wrote. "I was allowed into [General Mattis's] ops centers. Keeping a few secrets was a small price to pay for the open access the Marine brass gave me to the enlisted troops."

Giving reporters free rein with the troops works only if the commander's intent is embraced by the troops and genuinely reflected in the operations the reporters witness. Any inconsistency between word and deed would become the story. But seldom was I disappointed.

As a consequence of the "wedding" story, a U.S. military investigation team arrived in my zone from Baghdad to determine whether I or others should be charged with murder. A military lawyer asked me a list of questions, one of which caused a stir.

"General, how much time did you consider before authorizing the strike?"

He knew from the record that the time from when I was awakened until I authorized a strike had been less than thirty seconds.

"About thirty years," I replied.

I may have sounded nonchalant or dismissive, but my point was that a thirty-second decision rested upon thirty years of experience and study. At Midway, for instance, Rear Admiral Raymond Spruance pondered for two minutes before launching his carrier aircraft at extreme range against the Japanese fleet. Two minutes to turn the tide of war in the Pacific. That's how battles are won or lost.

The investigative report, issued weeks later, found no evidence that we had struck anything other than an enemy-occupied desert camp. But by then it was too late. The initial false reports had become ground truth; correcting it was not considered news. We had once again lost the battle of the narrative. As Churchill noted, "A lie gets halfway around the world before truth gets its pants on." In our age, a lie can get a thousand times around the world before the truth gets its pants on.

.   .   .

After we had pulled out of Fallujah, now the epicenter of kidnappings, bombings, and beheadings, Janabi appeared anew, this time as the head of the "moderate" Mujahideen Council.

In June, after we ambushed a gang of terrorists on the city's outskirts, he appeared on television to bemoan their "martyrdom."

"This leads," he declared, "to nothing but more confrontation with the enemy."

If he was calling me the enemy, then it was time to confront him in his own lair. In our last meeting, he'd agreed that if we withdrew from the city, the Fallujah Brigade would seize all heavy weapons and Marines would have access to the city. He hadn't delivered on anything. By June, that gave me all the reason I needed to confront him.

I would tell him to cut loose from Zarqawi now. And that if he didn't deliver on his promises, it was inevitable that Marines would attack again and the terrorists would lose. Janabi and his family would lose everything. *Cut a deal now,* I would say. If that led to a fight on the spot, so be it, and game on.

I promised not to arrest him. He agreed to talk deep inside insurgent-controlled Fallujah. John Toolan asked Army Staff Sergeant Rashed Qawasimi to run a check with his sources. Fluent in Arabic, "Qwas" served as Toolan's interpreter and more. Qwas was so uneasy about what he heard that John was convinced the meeting would in fact be a trap to kill me.

"Killing my general," John joked, "would be a coup for the terrorists, and hurt my career."

With a few Marines and some of Suleiman's National Guardsmen, I drove to the City Hall. John was observing the meeting site from a helicopter, with a battalion on full alert at the edge of town. We were meeting in the sector where we believed Zarqawi was located. I decided that only four of us would go into the meeting room, with the others tactically dispersed outside to ward off any assault. Qwas, two Marines, and I walked inside.

"If a fight breaks out," I told them, "I'll kill Janabi. You keep firing and empty your magazines until the others break in."

Janabi was seated at the room's far end, showing off his influence, with forty-odd sheiks seated along the walls, many armed. The atmosphere was tense as I sat down next to Janabi, with my carbine casually lying across my thighs, pointed at him.

The words between Janabi and me, with Qwas translating, quickly became blunt. Janabi was acting earnest, playing to the crowd.

"There are no foreigners here," Janabi lied. "You bomb innocent people. We only protect our homes you come to destroy."

He protested that my Marines were the ones causing the city's problems.

At one point he asked, "Do I look like a terrorist?"

I cocked my head, halfway smiling, and examined him closely. "Why, as a matter of fact, you do," I said. "And from reading your sermons, you sound like one, too."

I dropped my hand and double-clicked the carbine selector to automatic. He heard the click. If this escalated, I was killing him first. In May, he had tried to blow me up. There was no way he had walked into this meeting without a similar plan.

We sat there for several long seconds without speaking, staring at each other. He broke my stare and was visibly uncomfortable. As Qwas shifted to look alertly around the room, the *whump-whump* of John's helicopter could be heard. Whatever Janabi had up his sleeve, he didn't have the courage to carry it out.

"One way or another, we Marines are coming back into Fallujah," I said as the meeting ended.

As we left, I nodded to several sheiks whom I knew, and John breathed a sigh of relief when we reentered Marine lines about ten minutes later.

While we could not bring any Marines into the city, John met routinely with Lieutenant Colonel Suleiman, who was glumly watching the radical jihadists grow bolder. Suleiman was a relatively junior officer without a real Iraqi chain of command. By dint of duty and personality, he was trying to protect his city. He quietly informed John where IEDs were being emplaced and which neighborhoods were falling under control of the terrorists. He wanted to take action but was not strong enough to do so with his outnumbered men.

Then, one torrid day in early August, Suleiman called John to say that his second-in-command had been kidnapped by Janabi. Suleiman said he was driving to the mosque to get him released.

John urged him to wait until we received permission to go with him. Suleiman refused; he believed he had to move immediately.

When he arrived at the mosque, Janabi had him seized and dragged inside. That night, he was beaten, scalding water was poured over him, and he "confessed" to betraying Islam. His decapitated body was dumped outside our lines, and recordings of his "confession" were distributed in the marketplaces. John was furious and wanted to take tanks to the mosque and seize Janabi. But our orders from Baghdad remained firm: *No.*

Each day, somewhere in Anbar, Marine patrols were killing insurgents, and each day, a U.S. soldier, sailor, or Marine lost his life or a limb. It was a morally bruising fight, in most instances ceding the first shot to an enemy in civilian clothes. I was out every day, driving hundreds of miles a week to meet with the squads, village elders, and company commanders. My biggest concern was that somewhere in the chain of command, a commander was not keeping up the spirits of his men or was losing touch with the reality faced by his grunts. Nothing was more important to me than maintaining the fighting spirit of our troops and their confidence in their leaders on the battlefield.

You can't fool the troops. Our young men had to harden their hearts to kill proficiently, without allowing indifference to noncombatant suffering to form a callus on their souls. I had to understand the light and the dark competing in their hearts, because we needed lads who could do grim, violent work without becoming evil in the process, lads who could do harsh things yet not lose their humanity.

By dropping in and getting face-to-face with the grunts, I could get a feel for what the squads were thinking, what frustrated them. Was there anything I could do spiritually or physically to help?

My command challenge was to convey to my troops a seemingly contradictory message: "Be polite, be professional—but have a plan to kill everyone you meet." A twenty-year-old corporal is in command of nineteen-year-olds and speaks only a few Arabic phrases. In an atavistic environment, his squad has to act ethically and without lashing out at the fearful and the innocent.

But when someone shoots at a Marine, he becomes fair game. I wanted my lads to keep an offensive mindset. If fired upon, their job was to hunt down the enemy and take him out; I wanted no passivity or ceding of initiative to the enemy.

"There are some jerks in the world," I said, "that need to be shot. There are hunters and there are victims. No complacency! Keep your discipline and you will be the hunter. I feel sorry for every son of a bitch that doesn't get to serve alongside you fine young men."

Each morning, I'd wake up around four, sort through emails, check in at the ops center, and put on my combat gear. By seven I'd be ready to hit the road. Outside the headquarters, my communicators, drivers, and aide staged my five vehicles. No matter how worn down, they had already rehearsed the day's mission. Often during our ten to twelve hours on the roads and dirt paths, someone would shoot at us or detonate an IED, or we'd come across a unit that needed a hand. When that happened, we were all equally engaged. Across Iraq, this was the norm for the battalion and regimental commanders.

At the end of each day, I told my team what I'd learned and asked what they had picked up at the outposts we visited. They often came back with information I hadn't heard. We kept one another informed.

Staying in close contact with the troops came at a cost. Of the twenty-nine sailors and Marines in my detail, two were killed and fifteen wounded (some more than once) in five months. In late May, an IED killed Staff Sergeant Jorge Molina, thirty-seven, who had changed his last name to Molina Bautista to honor his mother, Maria Bautista. Jorge, who was born in Chihuahua, Mexico, left behind his wife, Dina, and three sons. He was even-keeled, occasionally breaking into a broad grin during our post-patrol debriefs. In June, we lost twenty-one-year-old Lance Corporal Jeremy Lee Bohlman. Always alert when we were on the road, he was high-spirited off-duty, a lot of fun for the team to have around. I still see them standing in front of me today, and I miss them and so many others lost in that long, hot tour of duty.

I visited a half dozen units each day, evaluating the mood of each: Were the troops comfortable speaking in my presence? Did they nudge one another in appreciation of a wisecrack or incorrect remark? Did they feel at ease with their immediate superiors? It was refreshing to listen to a gunnery sergeant or lieutenant verbally spar with his men in the casual but respectful manner that reflected mutual fondness. That told me the lads' hearts were still in the game.

Building trust and affection in units is not the same as chasing popularity, which relies on favoritism, nor does it replace the priority of accomplishing the mission. For this reason I came down hard on anyone who said, "Sir, my mission is to bring all my men home safely." That's a laudable and necessary goal, but the primary mission was to defeat the enemy, even as we did everything possible to keep our young men and women alive.

In late summer, I was nearing the end of two years commanding the 1st Marine Division and would soon be reassigned. I wanted to finish the fight, and I repeatedly said we had to clean out the enemy's safe haven in Fallujah. I was fed up with the dithering. I wanted to surround the Jolan market and search every building until we found and killed Zarqawi, Janabi, and the other terrorists who were spreading mayhem.

My higher command reiterated that we were not to go into Fallujah. My efforts to influence American policy decisions had fallen short.

I had never before left a job unfinished, yet I was leaving my troops facing a maddening situation: we were playing defense. American policymakers were still restricting necessary tactical actions. I had been raised by Vietnam-era Marines who drummed into me the importance of making sure the policymakers grasped the nature of the war they were responsible for. Don't get trapped into using halfway measures or leaving safe havens for the enemy. I believed I had spoken clearly. But I hadn't gotten through.

When it came time to relinquish command, in late August 2004, I had to think of what to say to the troops. I couldn't congratulate them for a hard-fought success; victory had been snatched from them. What they did have was one another, and their abiding sense of duty.

I remembered a poem written by French lieutenant André Zirnheld in 1942, as German Field Marshal Erwin Rommel was sweeping across North Africa. Knowing the odds against him were overwhelming, Zirnheld volunteered to parachute in behind German lines near the British-held port of Tobruk. He was killed. Zirnheld had remained loyal to his sense of duty. He had chosen to be a soldier. That didn't change because the Battle of Tobruk was lost. His poem was discovered when his body was recovered. Today it is known as "The Paratrooper's Prayer."

The war was lengthening. But that wouldn't change who we were or sap our fighting spirit. The Marine motto is "Semper Fidelis"—always faithful, not just when things go your way. Nobody had forced us to be where we were; we had all volunteered to fight. My troops had kept the faith, thanks to their will and discipline, and I said good-bye to my rambunctious and undaunted Marines by reading the French "Paratrooper's Prayer":

> *I bring this prayer to you, Lord,*
> *For you alone can give*
> *What one cannot demand from oneself.*
> *Give me, Lord, what you have left over,*
> *Give me what no one ever asks of you.*
>
> *I don't ask you for rest or quiet,*
> *Whether of soul or body;*
> *I don't ask you for wealth,*
> *Nor for success, nor even health perhaps.*
>
> *That sort of thing you get asked for so much*
> *That you can't have any of it left.*
> *Give me, Lord, what you have left over,*
> *Give me what no one wants from you.*
>
> *I want insecurity, strife,*
> *And I want you to give me these*
> *Once and for all.*
> *So that I can be sure of having them always,*
> *Since I shall not always have the courage*
> *To ask you for them.*

CHAPTER 10

Fighting While Transforming

R ETURNING TO THE STATES IN THE FALL OF 2004, my first priority was to visit Gold Star families. I know that nothing can assuage the grief of losing a loved one. I could not offer the solace of victory. All I could do was share with them the feeling of loss. Sitting in their living rooms, I doubted that I or anyone outside their families could ever feel the enormity of their sacrifice. But I tried to convey the love that we comrades in arms shared for one another. The fallen, volunteers all, had rallied to the flag and stood guard over our beloved nation, never quitting their posts. Our nation will always need such steadfast guardians, as every American generation has learned.

Between Afghanistan and Iraq, I'd been fighting for three years, never thinking about a follow-on assignment in the States. But the Commandant, General Michael Hagee, assigned me to be his three-star deputy for "combat development." Headquartered in Quantico, Virginia, the Marine Corps Combat Development Command (MCCDC) is responsible for education, training, doctrine development, and establishing requirements for equipment and weapon systems. Because of my recent experience, General Hagee said he wanted my perceptions to permeate the Corps. Returning from fighting, I was determined to use what I had learned to help sharpen our spears. First we had to have our troops at the top of their game for the fighting in the Middle East. At the same time, our other adversaries were not taking a holiday, and we had to be prepared for fights in the future.

General Hagee and I agreed that my first priority would be to prepare the troops for the kind of combat awaiting them in the Middle East. Emphasis would have to be on the lower-level leaders: Lieutenants, sergeants, and corporals were now of strategic importance. We needed to adapt our doctrine to reenergize counterinsurgency techniques, with an emphasis on the key small-unit leaders charged with winning the trust and support of the local people.

Anyone who has studied history knows that an enemy always moves against your perceived weakness, and this enemy had chosen irregular warfare. Now we had to adapt faster than they could, getting inside their OODA loop. Having watched how swiftly Islamist terrorism was spreading, I believed we would be fighting for years. Accordingly, irregular warfare had to be a core competency, but without the Marine Corps's developing tunnel vision and ignoring other kinds of threats. My approach in adapting our warfighting to this enemy was to insist on the pervasive implementation of decentralized decision-making, drawing from the well of ideas I had developed and honed in previous wars.

General George Marshall, the Chief of Staff of the Army during World War II, was faced with a similar challenge. In World War I, Marshall had seen too many soldiers die due to a lack of training in fundamental tactics. When he served in the 1930s at the Army Infantry School, he instituted an iron rule: Establish a base of fire before maneuvering against the enemy. "Fire and Flank" became the elemental tactic for thousands of novice platoon leaders rapidly trained in World War II.

I placed renewed emphasis on elementary tactics. I recalled "brilliance in the basics." Watch a basketball team passing the ball back and forth, each player knowing who is being set up to take the shot. They've rehearsed their plays so often that they don't have to think about it or wait for instructions. Similarly, every squad, platoon, and company needed a repertoire of plays, with everyone fully capable of executing a mix of well-drilled tactics, and few commands needed when engaging the enemy.

Close-quarters combat demands hard practice. But honing the skills to shoot and move was only the first step. Equally important was improving cognitive skills. A corporal from Des Moines would be patrolling in a totally foreign environment. How would he sense what was going on? In Iraq, for example, insurgents would often shoot first, hidden among the people. As the situation developed, the squad leader had to read the cues, so that we could be the ones to initiate contact, not the enemy. This had to be accomplished without hurting the innocents.

I took as a model the example of a chess master at a tournament who, after taking a single glance at the board, predicts the winner three moves hence. How could he do that? The economist Herbert Simon explained, "The situation [on the chessboard] provided a cue; this cue has given the chess master access to information stored in his memory; and the information provides the answer. Intuition is nothing more and nothing less than recognition."

Anticipation was critical, so my goal became to teach our young squad leaders how to pick up on the slightest cue like a chess master and sense what it meant. I searched for tools that could help develop this skill, settling on two approaches: tactical simulators and a training program to sharpen the cunning of our small-unit leaders.

Computerized flight simulators had long provided a valuable cognitive training tool for aviators. Behind the controls in a simulator, the novice pilot crashes into a mountain or is taken out by a missile. He dies, comes back to life, reviews his technique, takes off again, and avoids the mountain or the missile. As a result, our pilots don't repeat in actual flight the deadly mistakes drilled out of them in the simulators. So valuable is simulator training that we will not buy a new airplane without buying a simulator that mimics its flight. Yet, despite our country's having suffered 85 percent of its post–World War II casualties in infantry units, we had no simulators for those at the tip of the spear.

I knew that if we kept a Marine alive through his first three firefights, his chances of survival improved. We needed a simulator to train and sharpen cognitive skills until a young leader could swiftly appraise a situation and not hesitate before taking action. He had to develop the cognitive equivalent of muscle memory in order to instinctively seize the initiative. Let him get killed a few times in simulated ambushes to learn the consequences of his mistakes.

Situational recognition isn't unique to battle. Notice how often a college quarterback calls out the wrong signal, resulting in a broken play. To cut down on those mental mistakes, former Ohio State coach Urban Meyer devoted team meetings to hands-on simulation exercises, demanding that his players respond to confused situations. The goal was the assimilation of knowledge to take with them into the next game so that they would recognize the same situation when it occurred.

Regardless of rank or occupation, I believe that all leaders should be coaches at heart. For me, "player-coach" aptly describes the role of a combat leader, or any real leader.

I employed dozens of techniques. For instance, I recalled from Desert Storm how my NCOs threw rocks at our vehicles to simulate shrapnel from explosives. Talk about a rudimentary simulator! We built simulators complete with smoke, flash-bang detonations, sewage smells, foreign background actors playing the roles of villagers and insurgents, fluids that looked like blood—any setting, any scenario, any artifact that immersed the troops in as realistic a semblance as possible of the chaos of combat they would encounter.

At Camp Pendleton, we constructed a simulator by converting an abandoned tomato-packing plant into a Middle Eastern town. We set up an indoor simulation where the noise, smells, temperature, screams, detonations, casualties, scenery, and situations allowed a squad leader to confront tactical and ethical decisions, screw up and see his men die, or kill an innocent. Thus would they image their way through combat situations, envisioning what was going to happen before it happened, better imprinting immediate action drills and calculated decision-making into their squad's DNA. We detonated small explosives and flash-bang grenades, piped in smoke and putrid smells and casualties with horrible wounds gushing fake blood, and hired Arab Americans who screamed invective in Arabic. We threw in anything and everything—even holograms of enemies mysteriously appearing and disappearing—to rattle and disorient the squads. Repeated bouts in the simulator began to build swifter-acting squads, their confidence growing as their skills sharpened.

Both veteran NCOs and fresh recruits lauded their time in the simulator. It also became the best tool we had to build communications—through mutual understanding—among all the members of a squad. We called it the Infantry Immersion Simulator, because everyone was thrown into the combat scenario together—immersed in it. After someone "drowned" a few times, he learned how to swim.

Related to the simulator, but distinct from it, was another program aimed at enhancing tactical cunning. We called it Combat Hunter. The inputs came from an eclectic group. A Los Angeles police detective explained counter-IED and counter-sniper techniques in urban settings. An African big-game hunter demonstrated how to pick out telltale signs of an ambush. A football coach stressed how to build a book of plays, so that one word from a point man would cause each squad member to take up a set position. A former officer of the Rhodesian Selous Scouts showed how to detect even the smallest depressions in an open field where an enemy sniper might lurk and how to track an enemy's path. Instructors from the Marine Sniper School added the "Keep-in-Mind" (KIM) game, giving each Marine thirty seconds to look around a farmyard or alleyway and then turn around and describe how many objects he had seen and what was out of place. Or how to watch a marketplace for an hour in order to pick out the newcomer in the crowd.

By 2003 our military was fully at war, and our military families had fallen into the fraught routine of repeat deployments, fearful their loved ones might not return. The brutality and intensity of combat are impossible to grasp for those without skin in the game. The result has been a growing divide in understanding between the 1 percent in the fight and the 99 percent who are not. The families abreast that divide live in America yet have their hearts and minds half a world away.

One event in particular drove that disconnect home to me. I was speaking at a San Diego conference, to a mixed audience of sailors and civilian contractors, including dozens of Marines. I knew they had seen hard fighting and were deploying again shortly. When asked about fighting the enemy, I spoke candidly.

"You go into Afghanistan, you got guys who slap women around for five years because they didn't wear a veil," I said. "You know, guys like that ain't got no manhood left anyway. So it's a hell of a lot of fun to shoot them. Actually it's quite fun to fight them, you know. It's a hell of a hoot. It's fun to shoot some people. I'll be right up there with you. I like brawling."

As I spoke, I was looking right at those young grunts. As S. L. A. Marshall, the noted Army historian, wrote, "It is by virtue of the spoken word rather than by the sight or any other medium that men in combat gather courage from the knowledge that they are being supported by others. . . . Speech galvanizes the desire to work together. It is the beginning of the urge to get something done." By my words, I wanted them to know I was with them in spirit and expected them to act as warriors. They deserved to know that I respected and supported them.

My remarks made national news and I was soundly criticized, many pundits and some members of Congress outraged by my apparent lack of sensitivity. Frankly, I was surprised and found their comments bizarre. Our Commandant, Mike Hagee, publicly stood up for me, saying, "Lt. Gen. Mattis often speaks with a great deal of candor. . . . While I understand that some people may take issue with the comments made by him, I also know he intended to reflect the unfortunate and harsh realities of war." Further, I never moderated my words or apologized. Knowing our enemies also read my words, I wanted them to know that America had troops who were not tormented about fighting people who murder in the name of religion or deny human rights to others. In an age when so many think they must guard their every word for fear of career-ending repercussions, the Marine Corps stood with me.

Three months after I left Iraq, the Marines and the Army fought a second battle to seize Fallujah. The terrorists had taken full advantage of the delay to stockpile ammunition, and we lost hundreds killed and wounded while the top terrorists escaped. The centrifugal forces tearing Iraq apart were accelerating. Concurrently, inside the U.S. military, a debate was raging: Should we pull back to bases to avoid increasingly angering the Iraqis, or should we redouble our efforts to be on patrol among the people?

At Quantico, I received a call from Army Lieutenant General David Petraeus, who had taken over at the Combined Arms Center at Fort Leavenworth, Kansas. We had met as colonels in the Pentagon, and both of us had commanded divisions in Iraq. Essentially, we now had the same jobs in our respective services. Our views about the wars were aligned: we had to adapt, and quickly. Dave proposed that we jointly produce an Army/Marine counterinsurgency (COIN) doctrine. We needed our two services on the same sheet of music. If we did it right, the allies would follow.

"Dave, you and I can do this," I said. "But let's keep it between our two commands. If we take this to the Pentagon, it'll take forever. We need to move fast."

Dave was already in that mindset. We split up the work and moved out smartly.

What is war doctrine? Basically, it's a written guide, based on historical precedents, of the best fighting practices for commanders and troops to follow. Doctrine lays out principles that have worked in the past and establishes guidelines for how an organization fights, based on lessons learned in experiments or at great cost in bloody battles. Every corporation and government agency follows a doctrine, whether written or unwritten.

We assembled first-rate teams of writers, who produced a document based on enduring lessons from past insurgencies as well as what we were learning in Iraq and Afghanistan. I met with wounded Marines at Bethesda Naval Hospital and asked them what we could do better, and I made numerous changes as a result. We had no birthright to victory; we had to outthink this enemy.

One of the eight chapters was of special interest to me, and the Marines took the lead in writing it. Never again did I want to invade a country, pull down a statue, and then ask, *What do I do now?* We called this chapter "Campaign Design," meaning we would define the military problem to be solved inside its political context. This would ensure that the military solution we subsequently planned to execute would be fit for its political purpose.

Also in the manual were touchstones to help young officers come to grips with the esoteric nature of irregular warfare among the people: *Always try to partner on patrol with the local forces you are training. Conduct a census and issue identification cards. Get to know the local leaders, sheiks, and imams in your area of operations. Conduct yourself as a guest. In today's insurgent wars, the vital ground is not a mountaintop or a key road—it's the people.*

I also published a guide for small-unit leaders, stressing that doctrine was not prescriptive.

"There is no magic bullet," I wrote, "nor technological breakthrough that will win this fight for us. . . . Empathy may be as important a weapon as an assault rifle." The guide's tactics "provide methods for reference and are not prescriptive. . . . This type of warfare defies 'templates' or rigid adherence to techniques. Rather it is a test of our imagination and ability to improvise."

To provide the background needed to permeate our thinking and training, I established a center for "operational" cultural learning. Staffed with specialists who understood the warfighting requirement for cultural awareness, it contributed immediately, institutionalizing cultural training across our schools and training centers. I was delighted to see Staff Sergeant Qwas, my interpreter in my Fallujah meetings with Janabi, joining the faculty. With his immigrant background, he was the right fit.

As critical as it was to institutionalize the lessons of the current war, I had to look to the future as well. Eventually the anti-jihadist wars would end. They were not yet existential threats to America. But other nations were rising that could soon pose such a threat. There will come another big war, as there will come another big hurricane, and if we want to deter it, we can do so only from strength.

I had to ask: Was the Marine Corps on the right track to fight future wars? Was a complete transformation necessary? The essential nature of the Marine Corps was to launch forces from the sea. We use the water as an avenue of approach, unlike some armies that see water as an obstacle.

Every decade since the end of World War II, critics had come forward to declare that landing from the sea was now impossible. As far back as 1949, Secretary of Defense Louis Johnson had said, "We'll never have any more amphibious operations. That does away with the Marine Corps." That prophecy proved wrong the very next year. As American forces were on the brink of being driven from South Korea by the invasion of the North Korean army, General MacArthur ordered an amphibious landing deep behind enemy lines. This reversed the Korean War virtually overnight. Perennially, the refrain of amphibious assault obsolescence has been repeated. A half century later, my Marines launched from ships in the North Arabian Sea, flew over the mountains of Pakistan, and seized a lodgment in landlocked Afghanistan, four hundred miles from the sea. As the only nation with the capability of forcible entry from the sea, the question was: Does America's survival still require this capability?

I concluded that the answer was yes. While we are reducing our forces overseas, we must retain the ability to reassure our friends that we can quickly get to them when trouble looms. We also need this capability to temper our adversaries' designs. Without credible military force, our diplomacy is toothless. So, as I viewed it, the Marines could not abandon their core business even while adapting how we fought as new technology changed the character of the fight. It's a national capability and cannot be re-created overnight. The sea is an unforgiving environment, and dabblers die.

I also knew that our Achilles' heel was overconfidence in uninterrupted communications. In a future war, these communications are certain to be broken. Therefore, we had to know how to continue fighting when (not if) our networks fail. Because opportunities and catastrophes on the battlefield appear and disappear rapidly, only a decentralized command system can unleash a unit's full potential. We couldn't become reliant on communication networks that will not be there when most needed.

In my judgment, Admiral Nelson's instruction before the 1805 Battle of Trafalgar remains the standard for all senior commanders. "In case signals can neither be seen nor perfectly understood," he said, "no captain can do very wrong if he places his ship alongside that of the enemy." In countless coaching sessions and fleet exercises, Nelson had trained the captains of his ships. Once the battle was joined, he trusted them to execute aggressively. In future battles, outcomes will depend on the aligned independence of subordinate units.

Operations occur at the speed of trust. If, unlike Nelson, senior commanders don't sufficiently train their subordinates so they can trust their initiative, then those commanders have failed before combat begins. Commanders don't drive from the back seat. Credit those below you with the same level of commitment and ability with which you credit yourself. Make your intent clear, and then encourage your subordinates to employ a bias for action. The result will be faster decisions, stronger unity of effort, and unleashed audacity throughout the force, enabling us to out-turn and outfight the enemy.

As always, I did not rely on the chain of command to bring all important issues to my attention. I let it be known that every Friday afternoon I would be at the club for happy hour. As one man explained, when asked why Robert Burns wrote his poetry in taverns, it was in those places that one could hear "the elemental passions, the open heart and the bold tongue, and no masks."

For two years, I'd played my part in a military sea change. Side by side with the Army, we had modified our doctrine to fit the fight. We had stressed the critical role of the squad leader who was actually engaging the elusive enemy. I concluded that transforming the Marine Corps away from its amphibious roots and away from attacking from the sea would be a grave error. America needed its Navy/Marine expeditionary force precisely in order not to build more bases overseas. I had done my best to advocate decentralization of decision-making, emphasizing a return to command and feedback rather than embracing the illusion of command and control down to the lowest capable level.

Three-star positions being scarce, I was prepared and ready to go home. But in the spring of 2006, Commandant Mike Hagee surprised me with the best possible news.

CHAPTER 11

Hold the Line

"Jim," general hagee said, "it's time you got back into the fight."

Like an old cavalry horse whose ears perk up when he hears the Boots and Saddles bugle call, I stood a little straighter that day. Iraq was looking bad, and the American public was losing patience. But a leader's role is problem solving. If you don't like problems, stay out of leadership. Smooth sailing teaches nothing, and there was nothing smooth about the Middle East. Plus, I'd be back with the troops.

In the summer of 2006, I took command of the forty thousand troops of I Marine Expeditionary Force (I MEF) on the West Coast as well as operational command of twenty-five thousand Marines in the Middle East, prominently including thirteen thousand in Iraq and four thousand in Afghanistan. I was sure this would be my final job, and, having served so long in the region, I could not have chosen any duty I was better prepared to carry out.

As the commander of I MEF, I was also double-hatted as commander of Marine Corps Forces Central Command (MARCENT), one of five operational commanders (Army, Navy, Air Force, Marine, and Special Operations Forces) who dispatched and supported the tactical units in the CENTCOM region. Although my home base was Camp Pendleton, I would spend considerable time in the Middle East and at my operational headquarters in Tampa, Florida.

My boss, Army General John Abizaid, was now in his third year as commander of CENTCOM. He was a wise mentor, and we shared a common outlook. He had long impressed me with his grasp of history and his penetrating way of getting to the essence of any issue. He rightly considered service doctrine to be only a starting point. As with any war or complex situation, there was no cookie-cutter model that would lead to success in Iraq. The country was like looking into a kaleidoscope: change one element and a wholly different, unexpected pattern emerges. The Shiites, Sunnis, Kurds, Iranians, Syrians, United Nations, European politics, American politics—all the parts shaken together and poured out across the Middle East and onto the desks at CENTCOM. On one occasion, we were caught off guard by an unanticipated political decision from the Baghdad government. "We're too old to be surprised," Abizaid said. "Adjust to it."

Adjusting was certainly necessary. In the summer and early fall of 2006, the mood was souring—in the press, in Washington policymaking circles, and even at operational headquarters in Iraq. Some in Congress and in the press were declaring that the war was lost. As the senior Marine in the operational chain of command, I spoke out strongly against that mood. Attitudes are caught, not taught. The morale of a fighting force, from corporal to four-star general, must be positive. With the press and in my visits, I seized every opportunity to repeat my touchstones. *No better friend*: To the one million Sunnis in Anbar, we offered friendship and protection. *No worse enemy*: To the terrorists, we offered a grave.

As long as the population lived in fear and kept silent about the insurgents among them, the war would go on. We had been at this for more than three years in Anbar, with little observable success in connecting the Sunni tribes to the Shiite-heavy government in Baghdad. We were still building a new Iraqi Army, while the tens of thousands who had belonged to the purged Baath Party remained beyond the pale and marginalized. After interminable meetings, policy papers, plans, and pontification, I still couldn't detect a coherent model for jump-starting the moribund economy or improving the standard of living. By now, Iraq faced both an insurgency and an incipient civil war—basically it was a free-for-all, with the Iraqi people paying the price.

The press reported that we were stalemated. Having been there in 2003 and 2004, I took a longer view. On my visits in 2006, I noticed that the sheiks who in 2004 had resented us now came forward to harangue me with a litany of complaints. I took these discussions as a sign of progress. Edging closer, the tribes were no longer holding us at arm's length.

But that wasn't enough. The Sunnis themselves would have to fight for their freedom. Yet Al Qaeda in Iraq (AQI) was now so strong that only by allying with the U.S. troops could the Anbari tribes overthrow the terrorists. They had to gamble that we'd remain steadfast—or they'd be dead men walking.

"Hold firm," I told my Marines. "These tribes have centuries of tradition. If we hold the line, they will eventually fight for themselves, but it can only happen with our presence."

Throughout the fall of 2006, I delivered the same message. *Keep training and encouraging local forces. Stay professional and polite. Whenever you show anger or disgust toward civilians, it's a victory for the insurgents. Victory is not an abstraction. We will train Iraqi forces and patrol until the last terrorist is dead.*

In Ramadi, our Army brigade commander, Colonel Sean Mac-Farland, and his savvy Special Forces adviser, Captain Travis Patriquin, were impressed with a young sheik named Abdul Sattar, also known as Abu Risha. In September, Sean had rescued Sattar from an ambush. A few weeks later, Sattar proclaimed the formation of the Sahwa—the Awakening. The sheiks would no longer sleep while Al Qaeda took control of their tribes. He contacted the Iraqi press, proclaiming that he had the support of twenty-five of the thirty-one tribes in Anbar, which meant thirty thousand armed tribesmen. An inspirational leader, Sattar was expressing a hope, not a reality. At this point, possibly six mostly minor tribes stood firmly with him. The others waited to see what would happen. In my meetings with MacFarland, he was adamant that Sattar was the man. Things were changing. And as I moved around in November, I heard story after story along the same lines.

"We should help all the tribes," I repeated at every meeting in Iraq, "kill every last one of those AQI bastards. You're making a snowball. You pack the snow, it gets harder. Keep pressing and it fractures and falls apart."

The Sunni tribes were concluding—having exhausted all other alternatives—that we were their last, best hope for survival. We didn't need formal agreements. As a gesture of friendship, we presented some of the sheiks with Marine officer dress swords when they came over to our side.

One day on a back road in the middle of nowhere, my vehicle had a flat. While the tire was being changed, I wandered out into a field, where an old farmer was shoveling away in his irrigation ditch. We sat down and talked in passable English. He was a Sunni who had been run out of his home in Baghdad by Shiite death squads. I gave him a pack of cigarettes as we spoke. When I started to say good-bye, he stopped me and fumbled for words.

Pointing to his heart, the farmer said, "Here, I want you gone now." Then he pointed to his head. "Here, I know we need you to stay."

I joined Sheik Sattar at a large outdoor tribal sheik meeting soon after. He was stronger than ever. As he walked around introducing me to the other sheiks, the warmth and deference he was shown were unmistakable. Having spent enough time in the Middle East and lost too many allies, I warned him, "You be careful. You're a bigger threat to Al Qaeda right now than I am. They will try to kill you."

He smiled knowingly and nodded.

When the Anbar Awakening flowered in the second half of 2006, the key to it was the bottom-up relationship between local leaders and the U.S. battalions. Without fear, a sheik could argue with Colonel MacFarland, disagree and pound his fist on the table. If the sheik did that with his erstwhile Al Qaeda partners, he would be shot. In fact, I'll wager that at one time or another, every grunt platoon sergeant, platoon commander, and company commander was chewed out by a tribal leader pissed off about something.

Encouraged by the American forces, the Iraqi government forces, on the one hand, and the sheiks and armed tribal members, on the other, achieved a satisfactory sharing of power. John Kelly had identified this as part of the solution when he briefed John Toolan, Joe Dunford, and me in early 2004, pointing out the key role the tribes played. I found it galling that it had taken years of bitter fighting for all sides to arrive at the only sensible conclusion.

At the end of 2006, I gave the press my assessment of Anbar.

"When you see the amount of violence and criminal activity," I said, "it is easy to say this just isn't working or at best we are just going sideways, when in fact a lot of progress has been made. . . . I don't want to put lipstick on a pig, but the one point I would make very strongly is this: Violence and progress can and do coexist. . . . I think it will take five years. Over that period, we will see a declining level of U.S. forces and casualties and a corresponding decline in enemy effectiveness."

When I made those remarks, I didn't realize how out of step I was with the gloom inside Washington. The reason for the disconnect was that we had two different battlegrounds in the Iraqi theater, each going in a different direction. Anbar was now improving, while Baghdad was teetering out of control. Naturally, the focus was on Iraq's capital. The President did not mention the Anbar Awakening, which had already occurred, and may have known nothing about it. At the highest level, the ramifications stemming from the ongoing shift of the Sunnis had not yet been grasped. But in Anbar, we had turned the corner and conclusively seized the offensive.

Visiting Ramadi in February 2007, I said, "The war in Anbar is being won." Wherever I went, the atmosphere of victory was pervasive. I shucked my armor and helmet when walking the streets of Ramadi. I ate chicken kebabs in downtown Fallujah. I felt the shared camaraderie when our grunts, Iraqi soldiers, police, and armed tribesmen gathered around to tell me their war stories, some of which included the Marines retaking Fallujah back in late 2004.

I flew to Baghdad, where Dave Petraeus was assuming command. I agreed with him that in order to consolidate our gains in Anbar, one fresh "surge" Marine battalion would suffice. Dave immediately grasped the idea and extended the concept of the Awakening all the way across Iraq. He offered the Sunnis modest pay and close association with American troops to act as home guards for their villages and city neighborhoods.

The cost was high. Both the heroic Sheik Sattar and his sturdy supporter, Army Captain Travis Patriquin, died in the fight to retake Ramadi. But by the fall of 2007, the winning trend seemed undeniable. Our strategy, first identified by John Kelly three years before, of working with—not against—the tribes was finally paying off.

What did I take away from this? We had to play the ball where it lay in Iraq. There are no do-overs, and we had to make the best of it. The cost had been high over years of heartbreaking violence to innocent Iraqis and in grievous losses to our troops. Despair was understandable. Staring failure in the face, we had to hold the line. By standing strong with our persistent presence, the innate strength of John Kelly's initial assessment—that we had to break the tribes from Al Qaeda—won out in the end.

However, the mood in the States had turned even more negative. In September, when Ambassador Ryan Crocker and General Dave Petraeus testified before the Senate, an anti-war group took out a full-page ad in *The New York Times,* entitled "General Betray Us." A senator declared, "This war is lost." It was an acrimonious debate, with no consensus inside the Senate that our soldiers and Marines were achieving our national objectives. Defeatism was the soup du jour: poorly articulated policy goals, a wavering and initially under-resourced plan that lacked a coherent strategic approach, and our inability to define progress meant that the timing for testimony was unfortunate. Despite the cards stacked against them, Crocker and Petraeus were persuasive enough to gain congressional support for continuing the surge.

The operational successes and strategic opportunities had come at a cost. Prior to my arrival as MARCENT commander, a tragic incident occurred that would demand much of my attention. In November 2005, a Marine squad traveling in four Humvees had turned a corner in the restive town of Haditha, seventy miles northwest of Ramadi. One Humvee was suddenly torn apart by an IED. A well-liked and respected Marine, Lance Corporal Miguel Terrazas, was killed, and two other Marines were badly burned. Amid the shouts and commands, in the ensuing action the squad shot five men who had stepped out of a car. They also assaulted two suspect houses, firing and throwing grenades. In less than an hour, fourteen Iraqi men, four women, and six children were killed.

As initially reported by the battalion, the deaths at Haditha did not gain the command attention they deserved. In fact, the initial report was erroneous, implying that most of the casualties were insurgents or civilians caught in crossfire.

Four months later, Iraqi officials gave *Time* magazine photographs and names of the victims, including the women and children. Haditha immediately captured worldwide attention as a symbol of an-out-of-control war corrupting the soul of America. The publisher of *Harper's* magazine, John MacArthur, epitomized that reaction. "Marines are, if anything," he wrote, "more dangerous to civilians than the Army, because of the way they're juiced up in basic training. Now the Marines seem to have their own My Lai, and I'll bargain that the murders in Haditha were unexceptional events in the dirty war we're fighting in Iraq—an unjustifiable and unwinnable war created by venal politicians." A prominent politician said that "the Marine squad had killed innocent civilians in cold blood. They actually went into the houses and killed women and children."

Even as Marines were depicted as "juiced up" and "cold-blooded killers," daily I read press stories, couched in a passive voice, about "bombs detonating in a marketplace," or, "research shows that 27,000 civilian deaths from violence were reported in 2006."

Note the neutral wordings: "bombs detonating" and "deaths from violence." It sounds as if a hurricane or other force of nature caused the "incidents." This agent-less reporting granted a moral bye to an enemy that had murdered hundreds of women and children. Conversely, mistakes by our forces were reported in the active voice, putting them in the worst possible light, as if these acts defined the customary performance of our units.

AQI's narrative was tyranny dressed up in false religious garb, and these reports played directly into that corrupt narrative. In the United States, we had no counter-narrative. During my time at Quantico, I had sat down with reporters and expressed my concerns.

I said, "This enemy has decided that the war will be fought in the narrative, in the media. If we don't have people like you [reporters] committed [to factual reporting], trying to figure out the complexities of this war and . . . put it in terms their audience can understand, then we lose the moral high ground with the global audience."

I wasn't asking that immoral action on our part be excused; rather, I was arguing for journalists to practice their profession with the same integrity they expected of us. Intentionally attacking noncombatants, otherwise known as innocent women and children, or endangering them by firing from among the innocent was never our style; but it was our enemy's modus operandi. There was no moral equivalency between jihadist terrorists and our troops. In the morally bruising environment of war, we still hold our Marines to the highest moral standards. Discipline is our protective fabric. I took career-ending actions, including some up the chain of command above the tactical unit. We will maintain America's ethical high ground.

Our approach was not new, or an outgrowth of political correctness. In 1863, President Lincoln approved a general order to all Union soldiers: "Men who take up arms against one another in public war do not cease in this account to be moral beings, responsible for one another and to God."

In 2003–2004, thirty-five thousand troops rotated through the 1st Marine Division under my command. I had convened twenty-three general courts-martial—less than one per one thousand Marines serving in a most brutal environment. The charges in most cases were for abusing, but never killing, prisoners. Some of those few abuses were minor, like putting a gunnysack blindfold over a prisoner's head in the extreme summer heat. But I made clear that I would not tolerate any such conduct. In the Naval Service you are held to account for breaches in discipline.

As the commander, it was my responsibility to determine whether to court-martial Marines responsible for the deaths of civilians in Haditha. I received several boxes of investigative materials about the shootings. I sat alone night after night, reading every word, more than nine thousand pages—the equivalent of two dozen books. Were the congressman and the magazine publisher correct in judging that Marines had killed innocent civilians in cold blood? This is not easy analysis: the world of an infantryman is unlike any other, and a soldier's motivations in battle are hard to judge from the outside looking in. Yet empathy must never cloud a commander's judgment or excuse wrongdoing.

I had to determine what had caused the deaths of the civilians. Who should be judged culpable? Were these criminal acts, deserving of court-martial? The grunt makes instant, difficult choices in the heat of battle. He may open a door and hesitate, and a week later be buried six thousand miles away. Or he may open a door, perceive an immediate threat, and open fire, only to kill a noncombatant.

I examined the maps and photos, read the interrogations and witness statements. I took notes on what each Marine had said, and how he had reacted. I went to Haditha and walked the neighborhood. On a schematic, I followed the squad's actions after one was killed and two others wounded. Believing they were under fire from high ground, they assaulted one house and then another, firing and hurling grenades.

They were trained in urban combat, where one must take immediate action. When under fire from a building, you must attempt to close with the enemy. You can't remain exposed on the street. That's how we had trained these Marines to respond, staying inside their rules of engagement. At Haditha, the sergeant leading the squad had no battle experience. It was his first combat deployment, although a number of his men were veterans. In the chaos, they developed mental tunnel vision, and some were unable to distinguish genuine threats amid the chaos of the fight.

The most important six inches on the battlefield are between your ears. I concluded that several Marines forgot that and made serious mistakes in the moment of crisis. In each case, a young Marine was reacting to what he thought was the continuation of the attack initiated by the IED blast that had killed and maimed his brothers. This enemy routinely hid among the civilians. In the moments they had to react, several Marines had failed, or had tried but were unable, to distinguish who was a threat and who was an innocent. I concluded that several had made tragic mistakes, but others had lost their discipline. So I recommended courts-martial for some members of the squad but not for others.

There's a profound difference between a mistake and a lack of discipline. Mistakes are made when you're trying to carry out a commander's intent and you screw up in the pressure of the moment. I'm a walking example of the Marine Corps giving second chances to those who make mistakes—I've made many—recognizing that my mistakes served as a bridge to learning how to do things right.

But the Naval Service is the varsity, and a lack of discipline is not a mistake. In the Naval Service, consistent with the enormous authority granted to a commander, and the wide latitude and deference they're given to exercise their judgment, if a ship strikes a shoal, the captain is relieved, even if he was asleep at the time and his subordinates were at the helm. Similarly, if lance corporals are not trained properly, their superiors must be held to account for their lack of leadership competence and professional supervision.

The local commander—in this case, the battalion commander at Haditha—should have known the details the same day it happened. The killings were brought to light only months later, thanks to the diligence of a reporter for *Time*. The commander was then relieved because the number of civilian deaths and the lack of detailed reporting should have alerted him that something very out of the ordinary, even in a chaotic firefight, had occurred. He ignored what his training, seniority, and leadership role demanded that he notice.

That was not the end of it. The lack of discipline extended to higher ranks. Specifically, it was a gross oversight not to notice and critically examine a tragic event so far out of the norm. I recommended letters of censure for the division commander—a major general—and two senior colonels. "By their actions or inactions," I wrote, "they demonstrated lack of due diligence." These officers were forced to leave active service, an abrupt end to decades of honorable service.

In dismissing charges for courts-martial against several of the junior squad members at the bottom rank (see Appendix E), I wrote:

> The experience of combat is difficult to understand intellectually and very difficult to appreciate emotionally. One of our Nation's most articulate Supreme Court Justices, Oliver Wendell Holmes, Jr., served as an infantryman during the Civil War and described war as an "incommunicable experience." He has also noted elsewhere that "Detached reflection cannot be demanded in the face of an uplifted knife." Marines have a well-earned reputation for remaining cool in the face of enemies brandishing much more than knives. The brutal reality that Justice Holmes described is experienced each day in Iraq, where you willingly put yourself at great risk to protect innocent civilians. Where the enemy disregards any attempt to comply with ethical norms of warfare,

we exercise discipline and restraint to protect the innocent caught on the battlefield. Our way is right, but it is also difficult.

You have served as a Marine infantryman in Iraq where our Nation is fighting a shadowy enemy who hides among the innocent people, does not comply with any aspect of the law of war, and routinely targets and intentionally draws fire toward civilians. As you well know, the challenges of this combat environment put extreme pressures on you and your fellow Marines. Operational, moral, and legal imperatives demand that we Marines stay true to our own standards and maintain compliance with the law of war in this morally bruising environment. With the dismissal of these charges you may fairly conclude that you did your best to live up to the standards, followed by U.S. fighting men throughout our many wars, in the face of life or death decisions made by you in a matter of seconds in combat. And as you have always remained cloaked in the presumption of innocence, with this dismissal of charges, you remain in the eyes of the law—and in my eyes—innocent.

CHAPTER 12

Essential NATO

As the fighting in Anbar was winding down in the spring of 2007, Secretary of Defense Robert Gates summoned me to the Pentagon. Several months earlier, he had called me to Washington to interview for the top command job in Iraq. "We've already decided to send Dave Petraeus," he had said when we met. I assured him that I knew Dave well and he was the best possible choice. After we talked about the challenges of our two wars, I flew back to California wondering what that was all about. Looking back, it seems the secretary may have wanted to size me up in case some other job opened up.

Before flying to Washington this time, I had received phone calls from Jim Conway, now Commandant, and Jaap de Hoop Scheffer, the Secretary-General of NATO. Both told me that Secretary Gates intended to recommend me for a fourth star. I was to take command of the U.S. Joint Forces Command (JFCOM) and concurrently serve as NATO's Supreme Allied Commander for Transformation (SACT), two jobs traditionally linked together. Of course, it was an honor to be selected for four stars, but I was already in the best three-star job I could have imagined. I was not eager to leave. But the American people had paid my tuition going on thirty-five years, and if this was where my seniors wanted me, I would go. (See Appendix F.)

For those who had forecast that I'd never receive the Senate's consent for another promotion in light of some well-publicized remarks: my past statements never came up, and I was confirmed by a non-contentious voice vote.

Given my job at MCCDC, I had experience in the "transformation" business, but I had no background in NATO. By now, however, I had learned in the field the value of allies and of America's leadership role. The sense of purpose that would guide me was taking shape even before I arrived at my headquarters, in Norfolk, Virginia, to commence my duties. NATO, not Joint Forces Command, would be my main effort. Why? History is compelling; nations with allies thrive; those without them die.

I sized up my readiness for the job. I had never served in the European theater. But I had great familiarity with NATO and NATO partner troops in combat in Afghanistan. Commanding at Quantico, I had learned how to transform my own service. However, trying to persuade twenty-six sovereign nations to align the transformation of their militaries was a much bigger challenge.

Like the Marshall Plan, the United Nations, and Bretton Woods, the North Atlantic Treaty Organization was part of the organizational cement binding the security of North America with that of Europe. Created as part of the Greatest Generation's vision for how to prevent catastrophic wars such as had occurred twice in the first half of the twentieth century, NATO was founded after World War II to deter an attack by the Soviet Union on Western European democracies. The founding nations pledged solidarity: an attack on one would be an attack on all.

The Soviet threat had faded when the Berlin Wall came down and the Soviet Union collapsed. But Western Europe wanted the security assurance NATO provided to continue, with American might remaining its core. Moreover, a succession of newly independent Eastern European nations formerly in the Soviet orbit quickly asked to join NATO, and were accepted. By 2007 NATO had expanded from its original twelve nations to twenty-six.

Over a lunch in Washington, the Australian ambassador, Kim Beazley, remarked that, following World War II, our nation's willingness to commit a hundred million dead Americans in a thermonuclear war to defend Europe was the single most self-sacrificial pledge in history. For me, that cut right through the criticisms of NATO that I continually heard in Washington, D.C. Whether we liked it or not, we were part of the world and needed allies, for our benefit as much as theirs. I was determined to leave the alliance in better shape than it had been in when I started the job.

I had to consider how to prepare for a job that required a new skill set. As the saying goes, the military does not accept "difficult" as an excuse for failing at anything. I recalled also how hard Secretaries Perry and Cohen had worked to keep the alliance effective. I had reached a break point in my military frame of reference. I was no longer a military operator; instead I was now at a place where policy and military factors intersected. I had to understand the politics and motivations shaping member nations' militaries and defining the unwritten rules by which they operated. These rules were as much cultural as martial, stemming from each individual nation's history. I had to determine what future threats could be out there so that we'd have the fewest regrets when crises struck. Transformation meant getting everyone together to adapt their militaries to confront those future threats.

I turned to first-rate minds on military transformation: Professor Colin Gray, Dr. Williamson Murray, Dr. Frank Hoffman, and Australian Lieutenant Colonel David Kilcullen. I consumed their writings and asked for their guidance. Eventually I settled on twenty-two books to guide me. I expanded my contacts with practitioners of strategic leadership. Most important among them were Generals Colin Powell, Tony Zinni, John Abizaid, Gary Luck, and George Joulwan, as well as others; statesmen like Henry Kissinger, George Shultz, and Newt Gingrich; and former Secretaries of Defense. They gave freely of their time. These three lines of effort allowed me to build a framework within which I could operate in the years to come as I dealt with transformation.

At one point, it struck me as odd that the generals and statesmen I focused on were all retired. In a country that, outside of a few universities, no longer teaches military history, it should have come as no surprise. I was having to come to grips with a lack of strategic thinking in active diplomatic, military, and political circles—and the need for a renaissance in this domain.

SACT's headquarters in Norfolk was the only NATO headquarters in America. There, I inherited a staff of fine officers from across the NATO nations, plus forty other nations partnered with NATO around the world. SACT's task was to facilitate the adaptation and integration of military forces among nations—each with its own distinct military culture and doctrine. The goal was to be able to fight together seamlessly in the future.

Reviewing my self-assigned reading, one fact stood out repeatedly about militaries that successfully transformed to stay at the top of their game: they had all identified and defined to a Jesuit's level of satisfaction a specific problem they had to solve. The effort to define the military problems we had to solve in our time would consume a lot of my attention.

History shows that wars don't wait until you're ready, so it was unsettling, coming from a culture that considers every week of peace your last opportunity to prepare for war, to experience the exasperatingly slow decision cycles required to get twenty-six independent democracies aligned.

Any coalition has two parts: political and military. Political agreement on the purpose must be the first priority. Trust permits coalition militaries to work harmoniously together. On the battlefield, strength comes with unity of effort and a strong spirit of collaboration. I often reminded my American officers, with their hard-won pride in combat leadership and tremendous capabilities, that not all good ideas come from the nation with the most aircraft carriers. Additionally, the various NATO headquarters, my own included, had to maintain an atmosphere of respect that nurtured team readiness. That wasn't always easy.

In NATO service, when an American senior officer failed to perform well, with a few phone calls and a word in private I could send him back to a job in his own service. It was a bit trickier with foreign officers, because they represent their nations and have a political role that you have to grasp. I had a brilliant admiral from a European nation. He looked and acted every inch the leader, always crisp, intellectually fit, and forceful. Too forceful. He yelled, dressing officers down in front of others, and publicly mocked reports that he considered shallow instead of clarifying what he wanted. He was harsh and inconsiderate toward officers from half a dozen countries. My NATO sergeant major was Czech; my deputies were British and Italian. My personal staff was largely German. All were disturbed by his conduct, and his subordinates were fearful. I called in the admiral and carefully explained why I disapproved of his leadership.

"Your staff resents you," I said. "You're disappointed in their input. Okay. But your criticism makes that input worse, not better. You're going the wrong way. You cannot allow your passion for excellence to destroy your compassion for them as human beings."

This was a point I had always driven home to my subordinates.

"Change your leadership style." I continued. "Coach and encourage, don't berate, least of all in public."

He was one of my finest operational thinkers and I didn't want to lose him. After our talk, there was no doubt he understood my message, and things were all right for a time. But he soon reverted to demeaning his subordinates. I shouldn't have been surprised. When for decades you have been rewarded and promoted within your own nation's service, it's difficult to break the habits you've acquired, regardless of how they may have worked in another setting. Now collaboration had become brittle, and officers were complaining of ill treatment to their home countries. Finally, I told him to go home. He was the senior officer from his country serving in the States, and my action did not play well in the news back there. But my decision stood.

The underlying problem with NATO transformation was not individual personalities, though; it was, rather, a lack of energy and initiative, resulting from a process-driven culture. Entropy prevailed; process had replaced output. They had many papers about what NATO needed to do, but, reviewing them, I could detect no steps taken as the outcome of what looked like good thinking. Why was that? Part of the reason was that fighting in Afghanistan was consuming NATO's attention. Why spend time on future threats when you're fighting a present-day one? But, as with the Marine Corps, I didn't want America's allies to have tunnel vision. Eventually they'd be out of Afghanistan and facing different kinds of threats.

I knew I had to be persuasive. Sovereign nations do not take kindly to being ordered around. NATO was necessarily a consensus-driven security organization, with the military subordinate to the political component. I had to gain political agreement on the solution. I couldn't do that if no one could agree on the problem. If we wanted the nations in on the landing of our effort, we had to get them in on the takeoff.

So I asked all NATO nations to send their best strategic thinkers to Norfolk to define the specific military problem facing our alliance. After many months of work together, the NATO Secretary-General and I convened a meeting in Europe with the senior political and military representatives of the NATO countries. I knew it would be messy. But as President Lyndon Johnson put it, it's far better having people inside the tent pissing out than outside pissing in. I had a sense of urgency. We had to seize the opportunity to adapt the alliance while it stood strong.

"If you want your militaries to transform," I said, "we must have a starting point. We must—political and military representatives together—define the problem: What are the future threats our forces must be prepared to overcome? Wars don't wait until you're ready. The way you win or deter wars is by being ready. You can't be dominant in the last war and irrelevant in the next. Here's a document prepared by officers from all your countries. You all sent your best and brightest; if you have questions, speak now. But we need to get this problem statement out there so we're all working on the same problem."

After days of debate, the group agreed upon a set of threats and security trends. The result—entitled Multiple Futures—comprised the problem statement against which each European state could measure the adequacy of its country's contribution to NATO's forces.

This was in 2009. We had already opened the door and solicited ideas in various European capitals, and now there were only two days of debate. We foresaw that Russia, in particular, despite all of our efforts to work with them, would emerge as a new sort of threat. At one point, to emphasize this concern, the Polish Minister of Defense Bogdan Klich flew me in a helicopter from Warsaw to the Baltic so I could see with my own eyes the lack of natural obstacles in his country.

NATO could not cling to legacy forces designed for a World War II–type industrialized war against a nonexistent Warsaw Pact, nor could it adopt simply one preclusive form of warfare. If NATO did so, as Colin Gray cautioned, an enemy would choose a different form. We could not be focused solely on border defense, or counterinsurgency, or nuclear deterrence. While we couldn't get the future exactly right—no one ever can—we sure couldn't afford to get it totally wrong.

Because of the fight in Afghanistan, NATO recognized the need to make irregular warfare a core competency. But the Russian invasion of Georgia highlighted an emerging threat. A bright U.S. Army major we sent to examine both the Israeli-Hezbollah fight in south Lebanon and the Georgia case pointed to a confluence: Hezbollah in 2006 used largely nonconventional tactics leavened with conventional capabilities; conversely, in 2008 in Georgia, the Russians used conventional forces buttressed by irregular tactics. Together these signposts pointed to an emerging character of warfare, a hybrid sort of fight. As history teaches us, the character of warfare adapts to new circumstances. And as the saying has it, "Only the dead have seen the last of war."

Conviction doesn't mean you should not change your mind when circumstance or new information warrant it. A leader must be willing to change and make change. Senior staffs sometimes need pruning. It's easy to get into a bureaucratic rut where things are done a certain way because they're done a certain way. That seems absurd when you read it in print—but it's the norm in large organizations. Every few months, a leader has to step back and question what he and his organization are doing.

As I made the rounds of European capitals, I recognized that I would forever be the outsider, the non-European always urging for change. I stood back and asked, "Why is an American in charge of the transformation of NATO transatlantic forces?" I saw advantages to instead having a European commander in Norfolk making the argument for the forces required to meet the threats identified in the NATO document.

Until this point, both of NATO's two supreme commander positions had always been filled by Americans, in deference to our extraordinary commitment. But America ultimately could not care more about the freedom of Europe's children than the Europeans themselves.

I broached the subject with Admiral Mike Mullen, then the Chairman of the Joint Chiefs of Staff. Mike was a quick thinker with an attentive demeanor. Years earlier, when I was at Quantico, he had been Chief of Naval Operations. An admiral had been complaining that we Marines were adding too many heavier weapons, like tanks and artillery, to what we expected the Navy to carry. This extra bulk and weight required more amphibious shipping that the Navy couldn't afford. The message was clear: The Marines were forgetting they were a naval force and pricing themselves out of sealift. We discussed it over lunch.

"You have it backwards," I replied. "Appearances may be masking the reality. Our afloat units are actually becoming lighter, largely because naval air support is providing more precise firepower. Matter of fact, since Desert Storm, we Marines have cut nearly in half the amount of our artillery. We are not putting more on ships." Mike listened intently and then agreed. He dropped the issue.

Now I was pointing out that I was spending nearly all my time mastering the details of dozens of European militaries. The effort was diverting me from sustaining any attention to my U.S. Joint Forces Command functions. There was no reason, I concluded, for an American to continue as *el supremo*. Mike laughed and agreed that a European officer might well be a better fit for persuading Europeans to carry more of the burden. I recommended that France take over the post, because of my confidence in the strategic thinking of that nation's officers and its demonstrated political willingness to intervene militarily to protect its own interests. And since the French at the political level had frequently been the most difficult to persuade to make necessary changes to the NATO command structure, I thought it best if their generals dealt with the transformation issue.

When Secretary Gates and I were together on the sidelines of the next NATO meeting, in Brussels, I laid out my case. The issue clearly had the secretary's attention, and he had obviously discussed it with Admiral Mullen.

"If we turn NATO transformation over to a European," I said, "that brings European pressure on the nations to address their own shortfalls."

Secretary Gates usually gave no visible feedback. He's a born poker player. In this case, he brightened and nodded right away. In the fall of 2009, I turned over my NATO duties to a superb French Air Force officer. No Frenchman since Lafayette has been more warmly embraced than General Stéphane Abrial was when he lifted the NATO duties off me.

· · ·

I believed then and believe today that NATO is absolutely necessary for geopolitical and cultural solidarity among Western democracies. Friends who share enduring historical values are needed as much today as when we stood united against fascism and communism. Those values are foundational to our Declaration of Independence and our Constitution. If we didn't have NATO today, we would have to create it in order to hold on to our Founding Fathers' vision of freedom and rights for all. We must remember we are engaged in an experiment called democracy, and experiments can fail in a world still largely hostile to freedom. The idea of American democracy, as inspiring as it is, cannot stand without the support of like-minded nations.

At the same time, I strongly believe that Europe must contribute more.

In my judgment, NATO cannot hold together if the burden-sharing continues to be so unequal. Europeans cannot expect Americans to care more about their future than they do. Without adequate resources, even the most brilliant European plan for transformation to meet very real threats will remain a mirage. And if Europe's moral voice is not backed up by a capable military, their geopolitical and moral leadership will become nothing more than empty words on a piece of paper.

For those who question the post–Soviet Union value of NATO, it was telling that an alliance designed originally for the defense of Western Europe fought its first combat campaign in response to the 9/11 attacks on America. It must not be forgotten, in our too often transactional view of allies, that these nations offered up the blood of their sons and daughters in our common defense. As Churchill said, "There is only one thing worse than fighting with allies, and that is fighting without them!"

CHAPTER 13

Disbanding Bureaucracy

B ECAUSE I WAS DOUBLE-HATTED, while I was spending most of my time at NATO, my American command was left largely in the hands of my deputy. He had to be a flag officer who shared my views about allies, warfighting, and leadership. In essence, he would be my co-commander. I turned to my comrade in arms Navy SEAL Bob Harward, who was now a one-star admiral. With Admiral Mullen's support, Bob jumped to a three-star vice admiral, the established rank for the deputy position. I believed we had to import the agility of Special Operations Forces (SOF) thinking into the very top of the U.S. military. I was convinced that Bob, the quintessential fighter, had the combination of SOF experience, persuasiveness, and force of personality to drive my agenda home.

As soon as I figured out what that was. At our headquarters in Norfolk, and spread across other bases, JFCOM had a staff of several thousand and an annual budget of hundreds of millions of dollars. I focused on grasping the essence of JFCOM's mission. The four service chiefs are responsible for recruiting, training, and equipping their forces, taking a longer-term view of what the nation will need in the future. At the direction of the Secretary of Defense, JFCOM allocates their forces to the combatant commanders who conduct current and near-term operations around the world—the Pacific, Atlantic, and other commands.

The Joint Forces Command had been established in 1999 to harness service doctrines into a joint approach. The intent was to nur-

Abu Risha, leader of the Anbar Awakening, 2006
(BING WEST)

Side by side with Bing West in Iraq, 2007
(OWEN WEST)

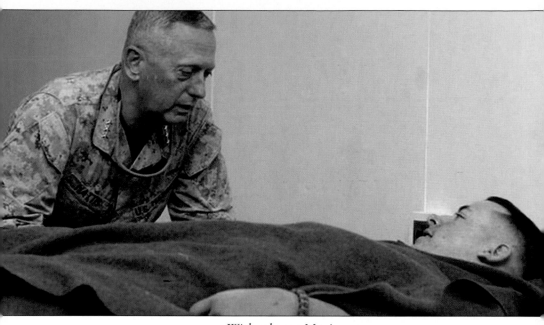

With a brave Marine, 2007
(U.S. MARINE CORPS)

Pre-patrol briefing, Afghanistan, 2010
(BING WEST)

Platoons in enemy contact need sensible rules of engagement
(BING WEST)

Patrol in Afghanistan, 2009
(BING WEST)

At an Afghan outpost, 2010: the troops always motivate me
(BING WEST)

In Marjah with Brigadier General Larry Nicholson and
British MP Tobias Ellwood (face hidden), 2011
(BING WEST)

"Living the dream," Afghanistan, 2011
(BING WEST)

Co-author Bing West with then–Major General John Toolan, Afghanistan, 2011
(BING WEST)

On patrol, finding the enemy
(BING WEST)

Engaging with the troops, Nawa, 2012
(BING WEST)

With stalwart 10th Mountain Division soldiers in Afghanistan
(TONY PERRY)

One of a million patrols in Afghanistan
(BING WEST)

Grunts
(BING WEST)

Listening to learn
(ALEX WONG, GETTY IMAGES)

ture service interoperability in concepts, training, and ultimately war. I understood that JFCOM was supposed to add the glue called "jointness," but what did that mean in practice? What was our core output? What was JFCOM teaching, and how did this add value in making U.S. forces more lethal?

Understanding what made this organization tick meant dissecting its culture, not just what was written down in its charter. Culture is a way of life shared by a group of people—how they act, what they believe, how they treat one another, and what they value. Peter Drucker, the business guru, criticized business executives for devoting too much time to planning, rather than understanding the nature of the corporation itself. As he put it, "Culture eats strategy for lunch." The output of any organization, driven by its culture, must reflect the leadership's values in order to be effective.

Early in my tenure, I visited a brigade headquarters. On the bulletin board were slogans exhorting initiative, like DECIDE THEN ACT! SEIZE THE DAY! and JUST DO IT! These sounded inspiring, reflecting an ethos that valued initiative, until a battalion commander directed my attention to his commanding general's division-wide order. It prescribed the exact attire required for physical training that every soldier had to wear while working out—including the color of their safety belt. By prescribing such minutiae from the top down, the actual culture of the organization contradicted its own declarations and stifled any kind of real initiative. Initiative has to be practiced daily, not stifled, if it's to become a reality inside a culture. Every institution gets the behavior it rewards. We had to reward battlefield behavior, not what in an earlier time we called garrison Mickey Mouse, or worse.

After I encountered numerous such instances of command from the top, I stood back to reflect. When asked how he would order his thoughts if he had one hour to save the world, Einstein sagely responded that he would spend fifty-five minutes defining the problem and save the world in five minutes. Well, how did JFCOM define the joint problem? What guiding vision had formed its culture over the past decade? I knew the service chiefs knew best how to guide the Army, Navy, Air Force, Coast Guard, and Marine Corps in preparing for warfighting. But was JFCOM providing the same guidance for the joint team? The answer was no.

Unlike service doctrines, JFCOM's joint doctrine did not tell me how to fight. I was mostly reading the equivalent of bumper stickers embellished with useless, even confusing, adverbs and adjectives. I talked to hundreds of officers of all ranks and listened to assorted briefings. The concept I heard constantly was "effects-based operations." In its original design, EBO was, and remains, a sound Air Force targeting concept. By employing a "system of systems" approach to attacking certain target sets and by forecasting the degradation in enemy capabilities, some air operations could be precisely calculated to work based on predicted effects. Effects-based targeting had worked well when targeting physically defined, closed systems such as power grids and road networks. For instance, by destroying certain railroad bridges, we could force the enemy to, predictably, move by motor vehicles along certain highways. By bombing road choke points, we could curtail enemy movement.

But JFCOM had bastardized this Air Force doctrine, generalizing it to open systems like warfighting, where adaptation and unpredictability are the norm. In my view, JFCOM's transformation effort was wrongheaded and not anchored in any valid theory of war, in all its messy, violent unpredictability. The only thing predictable about EBO was that it would fail, and so it did, even in jury-rigged exercises and, tragically, in combat.

Five years after JFCOM's adoption of EBO, Israel practiced it in Lebanon and suffered its first defeat in war. The Israelis believed that the enemy could be immobilized by air attacks alone and that, as historian Matt Matthews wrote, "little or no land forces would be required since it would not be necessary to destroy the enemy," and the results were disastrous. The enemy used small-unit initiative, electronic warfare, and irregular tactics to attack Israeli units from the front, sides, and rear. Without "precise" intelligence, "precise" targeting was impossible. An Israeli general complained that the EBO "terminology used was too complicated, vain, and could not be understood by the thousands of officers that needed to carry it out."

The Israelis had learned a bitter lesson. Coming out of a meeting with the IDF in Norfolk, an Israeli colonel remarked to me with regret, "We thought you Americans had done your homework."

After reflection, I concluded that EBO had two fatal flaws. First, any planning construct that strives to provide mechanistic certainty is at odds with reality, and will lead you into a quagmire of paralysis and indecision. As economist Friedrich Hayek cautioned, "Adaptation is smarter than you are." The enemy is certain to adapt to our first move. That's why in every battle I set out to create chaos in the enemy's thinking, using deception and turning faster inside his decision loop, always assuming that he would adapt. War refuses any doctrine that denies its fundamentally unpredictable nature. EBO could not take into consideration enemy cunning and courage, a grievous omission. "Every attempt to make war easy and safe," General Sherman wrote, "will result in humiliation and disaster." Short of a nuclear exchange, war will not abide a mathematical equation of cause and effect. The EBO approach, misapplied, was a mechanistic, even deterministic view that ignored the simple fact that conflict is ultimately a test of wills and other largely nonquantifiable factors.

Second, EBO required centralized command and control to amass the precise intelligence and assess in real time the precise effects of strikes. So the top-level staffs needed a continuous flow of exact battlefield data. Besides requiring uninterrupted communications, our battlefield commanders had to become reporters rather than focus on breaking the enemy's will. This was the surest means of surrendering initiative and creating a critical vulnerability. Having been joined by Bob Harward, with his SOF approach to war, we took the bull by the horns, cutting every shred of EBO wrongheadedness out of our joint doctrine.

Interestingly, everything I was briefed on regarding EBO came to me on PowerPoint, reinforcing a long-standing concern. EBO played well on PowerPoint slides, but I have always urged the avoidance of "death by PowerPoint." In that, I was guided by what General George C. Marshall had written: "The leader must learn to cut to the heart of a situation, recognize its decisive elements and base his course of action on these. The ability to do this is not God-given, nor can it be acquired overnight; it is a process of years. He must realize that training in solving problems of all types—long practices in making clear unequivocal decisions, the habit of concentrating on the question at hand, and an elasticity of mind—are indispensable requisites for the successful practice of the art of war. . . . It is essential that all leaders—from subaltern to commanding general—familiarize themselves with the art of clear, logical thinking."

PowerPoint is the scourge of critical thinking. It encourages fragmented logic by the briefer and passivity in the listener. Only a verbal narrative that logically connects a succinct problem statement using rational thinking can develop sound solutions. PowerPoint is excellent when displaying data; but it makes us stupid when applied to critical thinking.

I abolished EBO as downright dangerous to American warfighting. (See Appendix G.) In a letter to all hands, I wrote, "JFCOM will no longer use, sponsor or export the terms and concepts related to EBO. We must define the problems we are trying to solve and propose value-added solutions. We will return clarity to our operational concepts. My aim is to ensure leaders convey their intent in clearly understood terms that empower their subordinates to act decisively." Whenever militaries build a physical or intellectual Maginot Line, they set themselves up for failure. We must make sure EBO does not return in a new guise, disconnected from war's reality.

If JFCOM had the wrong cultural mindset, and EBO was the wrong approach, what should replace it? What would guide our approach to fighting future wars? I determined to bring back historically informed principles rather than algebraic formulae. We would adhere to those principles. The approach had to be balanced and dexterous, adapting to unforeseen challenges and using history, experiments, and war games to gain insight into the enduring nature of war in its possible future forms.

"The trinity of chance, uncertainty, and friction [will] continue to characterize war," Clausewitz wrote, "and will make anticipation of even the first-order consequences of military action highly conjectural."

My goal was for our joint forces to move against the enemy with a spirit of collaboration among the services, displaying what I had learned to call a jazzman's ability to improvise. I wanted a joint service culture based upon a philosophy of independent alignment and operational decentralization, guided by the commander's intent. The character of the war—its tactics, political reality, technology, weapons—constantly changes. But war's fundamental nature remains, even as its changing character demands that we urgently adapt.

Again employing Einstein's fifty-five-minute rule, I pointed out to my staff that no military had successfully transformed without first defining the problem. That problem was three-tiered: maintain a safe and credible nuclear deterrent so that those weapons are never used; sustain a compelling conventional force capable of deterring or winning a state-on-state war; and make irregular warfare a core competency of the U.S. forces. Concurrently, we had to incorporate two new domains, cyber and space, for in the future those domains will be contested. The course of this effort was not easy, but any leader, whether a commander or a CEO, must guide his or her organization around the rocks and shoals. I took JFCOM off the shoals of EBO and steered in what I determined was the right course. If you don't do that as a leader, you're along for the ride; you're not steering the ship.

In the ten years since JFCOM was established, the idea of "jointness" had expanded into an ever larger circle of tasks. By the time I arrived, the Secretary of Defense had charged JFCOM with carrying out twenty-three formal tasks, with nearly a dozen generals and admirals on board. You name it and JFCOM seemed to have a hand in it. In some cases we were doing well. For example, our joint training was top-notch and highly sought after by the services. I decided to help teach the classes for newly selected admirals and generals. Most generals were promoted because they performed well in operations. They now had to shift their perspective to the strategic level and embrace skills that had played little or no role in their promotion to flag rank. I wanted to convey, in personal, concrete terms, the complexity of dealing with civilian policymakers and how their current skill set was incomplete for what lay ahead.

Above all, I cautioned them that their natural inclination to be team players could not compromise their independence of character. They had to be capable of articulating necessary options or consequences, even when unpopular. They must give their military advice straight up, not moderating it. *Avoid what George Kennan*

called *"the treacherous curtain of deference." Don't be political.*
They had to understand that their advice might not be accepted.
Then they must carry out a policy, to the best of their ability, even
when they might disagree. Recognize, too, that ultimately any President gets the advice he desires and deserves, but in the dawn's early
light you need to be able to look in the shaving mirror without
looking away. As Secretary Shultz had said before Congress, to do
our jobs well, we should not want our job too much.

At inflection points, as history has made clear, change must
come at the speed of relevance. This meant that now, right now, we
had to pick up the tempo. It could not be business as usual. I wanted
disciplined but not regimented thinking. Commanders must encourage intellectual risk taking to preclude a lethargic environment. Leaders must shelter those challenging nonconformists and
mavericks who make institutions uncomfortable; otherwise you
wash out innovation.

I told my one-star admirals and generals: "You're still low
enough in rank to be in touch with your troops, but senior enough
to protect our mavericks. That's your job." If you're uncomfortable
dealing with intellectual ambushes from your own ranks, it'll be a
heck of a lot worse when the enemy does it to you.

By the end of 2009, I had made major changes. The NATO command for transformation had passed into European hands, and JF-
COM's direction had been altered. I now had the time to wander
among the 2,800 servicemen and federal workers and the 3,000
contractors on my staff, soliciting their questions and gaining their
input. Our largest building was 640,000 square feet. I could get lost
in there for days.

My fundamental questions were always the same: "What do
you do? What impact does your team make?" Some junior officers
with a wicked sense of humor sent around an email saying that
people were locking their doors or leaping out of windows when I
came down the corridor. At the same time, the candor of many
answers was refreshing. "General," one young officer said, "I don't
know the value my section is bringing to the military." I heard that
repeatedly from young officers chafing at not being in the fight. I
found great people who wanted to do great things but were more

often frustrated by the convoluted processes and other obstacles internal to JFCOM. The feedback both troubled and goaded me.

Anything that built lethality for those at sea or in the field, I encouraged. For instance, Rear Admiral Ted Carter had an element called the Joint Enabling Capabilities Command (JECC), composed of top-notch planners plus wizards who could swiftly patch different communications systems into our global command system. JECC provided "Flyaway" teams that set up robust connectivity immediately for any commander assigned to command a crisis response. When a task force was dispatched to Haiti after the 2010 earthquake, Ted and his JECC team deployed overnight to provide the commander, Army Lieutenant General Ken Keen, with communications, knitting together thousands of civilian and military personnel from various countries. They were clearly "best of breed."

Within JFCOM, there were other bright spots. I witnessed enormous value in our joint training exercises, but I had to balance that against the huge price tag JFCOM was costing the American taxpayer. While back in 1999 the case could be made that the services weren't operating jointly, by 2010, after a decade of war, arguing that case was no longer sufficient. "Jointness" had been achieved, and the Chairman of the Joint Chiefs and service leaders were the agents to sustain it in the mainstream, not JFCOM. I thought back to a Baghdad dinner I'd had with Dave Petraeus when I was visiting my Marine forces in Iraq in 2007.

"Jim, can you recall any positive impact, other than joint training," he said, "that JFCOM has had in six years of war?"

After two years, I became convinced that our staff of thousands and our large budget were largely redundant. Other existing organizations could perform several of our functions better. Further, I had to accept that much of our work was not adding capability to our forces.

In the spring of 2010, I was in the Secretary of Defense's conference room for a budget meeting. Sitting at the long mahogany table with Secretary Gates and Admiral Mullen were the Joint Chiefs and my fellow combatant commanders. Secretary Gates's message was that we had to take cuts in lower-priority areas so we could maintain readiness while investing now for the future.

The combatant commanders had felt the budget pain of two

wars being fought in the Middle East, with DoD cutting back on support everywhere else. Yet our treaty obligations had not been reduced, even as our forces were being cut back. The services were providing forces to our current wars, but they were also responsible for anticipating and preparing for threats coming over the horizon. In effect, we were mortgaging our future. Secretary Gates and our Joint Chiefs were determined to solve the shortfall.

We had to free up funds. After several hours of discussion, the lack of good options was apparent. I listened attentively, not wanting to add my gripes to the litany already heard. I got up to get a Coke in the back of the room, where I stood listening. I thought for a few seconds and decided, *What the hell.* I took a napkin and scribbled on it:

Disband JFCOM—Mattis.

As I walked past Admiral Mullen, I put the crumpled napkin down so he would see it. When he finished speaking, he unwrapped the napkin and raised his eyebrows. *Are you serious?* I nodded, and Mike nodded back. A major command eliminated? Hundreds of millions of dollars a year saved and thousands of personnel slots reduced . . . Not a halfway measure, even by Washington's accounting standards. It was a seemingly spur-of-the-moment offer, but it was based on many months of reflection and the experience of decades spent looking at what delivers real capability.

Once established, a government bureaucracy provides steady jobs and steady routines. It grows deep roots in the community, attracting the protection of influential politicians. It becomes a self-perpetuating entity. But the American taxpayer is footing the bill, so every organization must serve a worthwhile purpose or it should go away. Who can best judge whether an organization adds value to the lives of the American people? In this case, I was the commander who had studied this organization for two years. I was confident that I'd made the right recommendation.

Secretary Gates was not a leader who sat on decisions. It was done. Over the next months, the valuable parts of JFCOM were moved elsewhere, and the rest of the command was disestablished. I had succeeded in firing myself.

PART III

STRATEGIC LEADERSHIP

CHAPTER 14

Central Command:
The Trigonometry Level
of Warfare

IN JUNE 2010, THE PRESS WAS BUZZING about a shake-up at the top of the military. General Stan McChrystal, our four-star NATO commander in Afghanistan, was in trouble. A magazine had quoted Stan's staff cavalierly making derogatory statements about our elected officials. Those staff officers had demonstrated shocking immaturity and a straight-up lack of professionalism. They cost us a superb leader, as Stan was rightly held responsible and fired.

To replace him in Afghanistan, President Obama appointed General Dave Petraeus, who at this time was commanding the U.S. Central Command, in charge of all of our operations across the Middle East and Central Asia. I thought Petraeus was a wise choice, especially because his stepping down from a broader job sent a message of commitment to our many allies fighting and dying alongside us.

This shift left a vacancy at CENTCOM. In Norfolk, I was packing away my uniforms when the senior military assistant to the Secretary of Defense called. "Sir, Secretary Gates wants you to come to Washington," he said. "You're to bring your dress uniform." I assumed he was interviewing several flag officers to replace Dave at CENTCOM. I figured the odds still favored my getting home by fall, in time to hike the high country before the snows hit the Pacific Northwest.

When I arrived at the Pentagon, I checked in with the Chairman, Admiral Mullen. He told me I was Secretary Gates's choice. I went upstairs and reported to Gates. In his succinct fashion, he confirmed that he was recommending me to replace Dave. But the final decision lay with President Obama. I glanced at the picture of Mount Rainier Gates kept as a reminder of our home state. I guessed I wouldn't be seeing it for a while. When asked to stay in the fight, a Marine has only one answer. I didn't really have to think about it. I told Secretary Gates I could do the job.

Secretary Gates sent me to the White House, where my meeting with President Obama was much like a standard job interview. He asked questions about my previous commands and my views of the Middle East, without commenting on my answers. His thoughtful and reserved side was on full display, so much so that I left not knowing whether I'd been hired. Another four-star job held no appeal to me, because I didn't draw the same energy from high command as I did from the infectious high spirits of the troops. But I reminded myself that I had been educated in war, and it was my responsibility to be ready to apply what I had learned.

A couple of days later, the President called me back. In brief, pleasant terms, he said he had chosen me for CENTCOM, light-heartedly adding that he trusted me to be discreet. Secretary Gates had also touched on my reputation for being outspoken. Twice heard, even a Marine gets the message.

I prepared extensively for my confirmation hearing in front of the Senate Armed Services Committee: I read intelligence updates, spoke with officers recently returned from the fighting, listened to foreign ambassadors, and called on members of the committee. I had never gone in front of a hearing without a "murder board," where I rehearsed succinct answers to complex questions. As long as you are candid and have done your homework, such hearings are not an intellectual challenge. The hearing went well and I was unanimously confirmed, taking responsibility for a region that had spawned much of the world's misfortune over the preceding decade.

The vote closed the circle, so to speak, of my service in the Middle East. I'd first sailed into those waters as a captain in 1979, deployed there by President Carter. Now, three decades later, I was dealing with the ramifications that had grown out of that momentous year, commanding our 250,000 troops in the region.

For thirty-eight years, my role had been leading and coaching, as a tactical or operational commander executing policy. Now my role was to inform policy and support our diplomats, engaging with political leaders and heads of state while guiding my subordinate military commanders. It was to prove a time for fighting, and not just for our troops on the ground. At my level, the next several years would be a fight to keep faith with our troops and the rules of engagement under which we sent our young women and men into combat; faith with our allies and friends who had stood with us; and faith with coming generations, to whom we owed a responsible strategy by which to build a better peace despite the existence of implacable enemies. It was to be a time when I would witness duty and deceit, courage and cowardice, and, ultimately, strategic frustration.

The Central Command area of responsibility encompassed the twenty countries stretching from Egypt to the Arabian Peninsula, up through the Levant, Iraq, and Iran, eastward to Afghanistan and Pakistan, and then north into the Central Asian former Soviet republics—a region accurately called "the arc of crisis." The Ottoman Empire had collapsed during World War I, replaced in many Arab states by European colonialism. Following World War II, the European colonialists left, Israel was established, and indigenous Arab leaders came to power. Some states had enormous oil wealth, and others were impoverished. Across the region, communications technology and petrodollars enabled violent strains of Islam, previously isolated, to gain regional traction in the 1990s. Combined with widespread unresponsive governance, the situation was a powder keg.

Under CENTCOM, U.S. troops and aircraft were deployed across the region, plus vessels at sea, from the Suez and the Red Sea across to the North Arabian Sea and the Persian Gulf. In both Iraq and Afghanistan, an American four-star general commanded the coalitions. From one level up, I would be directing and integrating all U.S. military activities across the greater Middle East and Central Asia.

At CENTCOM, I had to inform and design strategies to carry out the President's policies while enabling operational execution by field commanders. Preparing for my Senate hearing, I had written

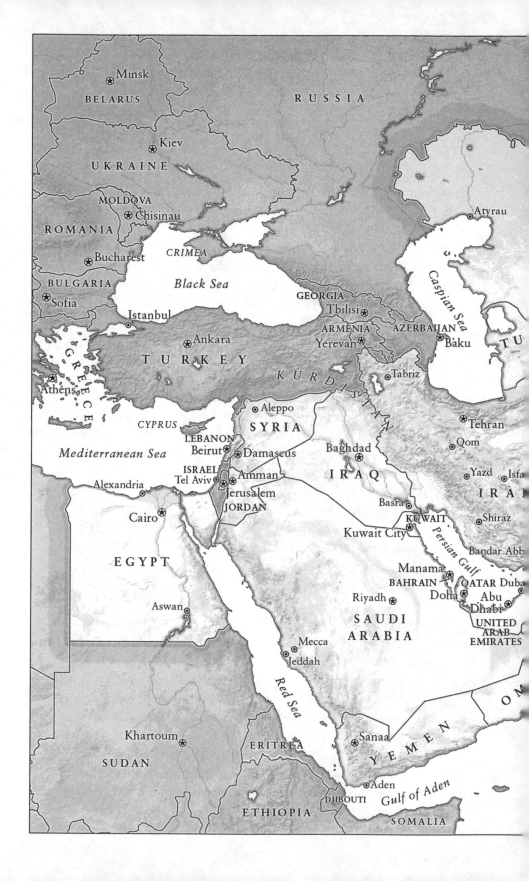

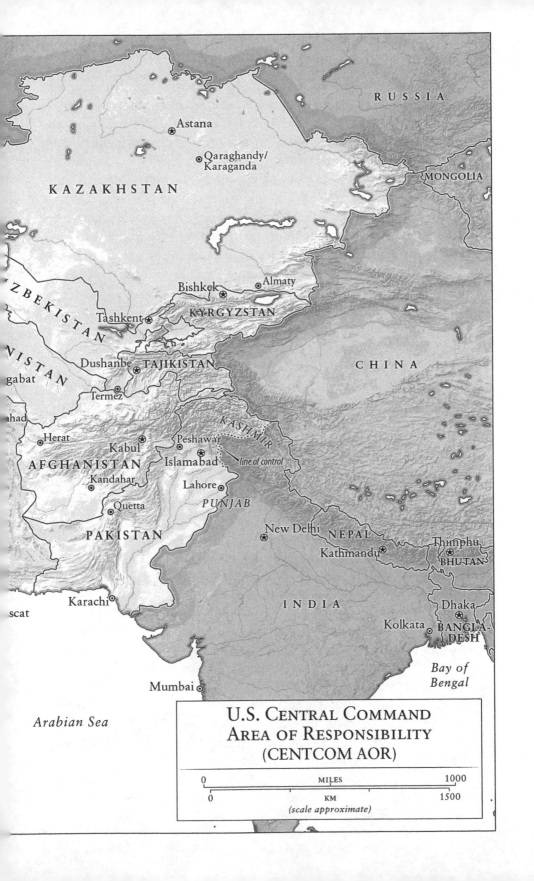

RUSSIA

Astana

Qaraghandy/
Karaganda

KAZAKHSTAN

MONGOLIA

Bishkek   Almaty

Tashkent   KYRGYZSTAN

ZBEKISTAN

NISTAN

gabat

Dushanbe   TAJIKISTAN

CHINA

Termez

had

KASHMIR

Herat   Peshawar

Kabul   Islamabad   line of control

AFGHANISTAN

Kandahar   Lahore

Quetta   PUNJAB

New Delhi   NEPAL   Thimphu

Kathmandu   BHUTAN

PAKISTAN

Karachi   INDIA   Dhaka

Kolkata   BANGLA-
DESH

scat

Mumbai   Bay of
Bengal

Arabian Sea

U.S. CENTRAL COMMAND
AREA OF RESPONSIBILITY
(CENTCOM AOR)

0   MILES   1000

0   KM   1500
(scale approximate)

out succinct answers to anticipated questions. The discipline of writing always drove me to be more exact, even at times driving me to different conclusions than I had originally held. A concern began to gnaw at me: I found myself grasping to define the policy end states and the strategies that connected our military activities to those end states. In the back of my mind rang the adage "If you don't know where you're going, any road will get you there." What I had seen in Baghdad and Fallujah had taught me the dangers created by a lack of strategic thinking. Based on both experience and study, I could not identify a sustainable vision for our diplomatic and military efforts across the Middle East. In some cases, I could see what our policymakers *didn't* want to happen—we didn't want Israel attacked, didn't want Iran with nuclear weapons or mining the Straits of Hormuz, and so on—but I couldn't find an integrated end state we were trying to achieve: What does it look like when we're done?

Again I sought advice from both inside and outside government. Dr. Kissinger, in particular, was most insistent that I concentrate upon the foreign policy horizon before diving into military details or deciding on the correct application of our military power. I also understood that many disputes defied resolution in crisp form or on an expected timetable. Some crises could be solved; others could only be managed; and our military approach had to accommodate both.

On my two-day drive alone from Norfolk to Tampa, I had time to reflect on the mission awaiting me. From combat in the desert to my duty at NATO, the inestimable value of allies was deeply imprinted on me. I was heartened that more than sixty nations worldwide were represented at my U.S. military headquarters and living in Tampa, a reminder of America's unique and invaluable strategic leadership role.

I saw my job as conveying respect to those who had stood by us and foiling the designs of those who opposed us. Living in the toughest neighborhood since Poland in 1939, our friends in the Middle East were understandably anxious. The alternative of American disengagement in this region, due to its unending violence, could only result in vicious enemies or competitors stepping into any leadership vacuum we gifted them. I decided that, while my official job was to coordinate the activities of our U.S. and allied troops across the region, my real role was to fight for a better peace—or what passed for peace—in the region for one more year, one more month, one more day . . . until diplomats could direct us to a better path.

No one contributes money to a presidential campaign to be assigned ambassador to a Middle East country. We military leaders in CENTCOM realized that we had a varsity team of diplomats. We had the best, the most proven, and the most experienced. Ambassadors like Jim Jeffrey in Iraq, Ryan Crocker in Afghanistan, Anne Patterson in Egypt, Stu Jones in Jordan, and Elizabeth Richard and Gerald Fierstein in Yemen.

My overarching, guiding concern was the terrorist threat, because it was growing. It manifested itself in two different groups. First was the Iranian-regime-supported Shiite terrorists, with Lebanese Hezbollah and other associated groups, who declared war on us in 1983, four years after Khomeini took power in Tehran. The 1983 attacks on our Beirut embassy (killing 46, including 17 Americans) and the French and U.S. Marine peacekeeper barracks in Beirut (which killed 58 French military personnel, 241 Marines, and 6 civilians) were the opening salvos.

Second was the Sunni brand of jihadist terrorists—Al Qaeda and associated movements—who declared war on us in the mid-nineties, eventually culminating in the 9/11 attacks on our homeland. This was followed by a metastasizing of its brand globally, from Africa to Southeast Asia.

To date, only the Shiite terrorists have a state sponsor, namely Iran. While we have shredded Al Qaeda's core leadership in Pakistan's North-West Frontier and Al Qaeda's Middle East offshoot ISIS in Iraq and Syria, Shiite militias have a steady stream of financial, military, and diplomatic backing from the revolutionary regime in Iran and as a result have been left virtually unscathed by our counterterror campaign.

While our intelligence community's and military's successes had prevented additional terrorist attacks on our soil emanating from overseas following 9/11, I did not patronize this enemy. I had dealt with them long enough to know they had not arrived rationally at their hateful, intolerant worldview, and they would not be rationally talked out of it. We had to fight, or there would be worse to come.

Our enemies had made clear that they intended to attack us, our friends, and our interests. So, while our tempo of operations had kept them on their back foot and protected our country against overseas terrorists, many other nations had not been spared. In the years following 9/11, terrorism was a growing reality, from London to Bali, Mumbai to Paris, across the Middle East and beyond.

Back in 1984, returning to the States after my first two deployments to the region, I read a speech given by then Secretary of State George Shultz in New York City. In following years, I often referred to this speech because it gave clarity to what I'd been studying. His words guided my approach to dealing with terrorism from those days forward. Secretary Shultz made a cogent case that passive defense against terrorism would not suffice. Active prevention would be needed. He highlighted the "moral right, indeed a duty" to defend our populations and values. Seventeen years before the city where he was speaking would lose thousands of innocents in the 9/11 attack, he made two points: that our public needed to be made aware that we would lose lives among our troops fighting this enemy as well as innocents, and that public support would be "crucial if we are to deal with this challenge."

When I reread his speech yet again just prior to my 2010 Senate confirmation hearing, his emphasis on public support caught my attention. It had been nine years since 9/11 and many Americans had since forgotten their sense of vulnerability in the days and months following what had struck Manhattan and Washington. Further, the war in Iraq had cost us international and domestic support by muddying the waters. Yet fighting a global menace required an international effort.

Putting such a campaign together started with answering one fundamental question: is political Islam in our best interest? That policy question had to be answered if we were to craft strategies fit for our time. The most direct, thoughtful response I received was from the Crown Prince of the UAE. He said, "Absolutely not. Religious leaders should not be running countries." Sustaining a coalition in this war would call on every lesson I had learned over the preceding four decades. I would be dealing with friends and allies who had stuck with us through good times and bad, nations and leaders with whom we had trusted relations and with whom we knew we could work.

I would also need to back up the State Department and be prepared to treat roughly those who supported or employed terrorism. At the same time, we would be using suasion and even transactional methods to work with those in the middle.

With many Middle East states only a generation or two beyond being European colonies or Soviet satellite states, I had to recognize that they often lacked the institutional enablers for democracy. But if our counterterrorism efforts were to be successful, I still had to work with them. I would help them to maintain their territorial integrity against terrorism or Iranian threats while advocating more inclusive and participatory forms of government that would strengthen civil society, making their countries more resistant to terrorism.

When I arrived in Tampa, I called in my staff to give them my three priorities: support our commanders in Iraq and Afghanistan; reassure our friends across the Middle East; and have military options ready for the President in case of Iranian or other aggression.

I spoke weekly with our commanders in Iraq and Afghanistan to ensure we were working in tandem. In Iraq, General Ray Odierno had shifted to a training and equipping mission. In Afghanistan, General Dave Petraeus was leading the broadest wartime coalition in modern history: fifty nations fighting together under NATO command, half of those militaries not even members of NATO. At Joint Forces Command, I had sternly dealt with too much second-guessing of requests from battlefield commanders. I was determined that CENTCOM would be an advocate, not an obstacle, in getting our warfighters what they needed in a speedy manner.

"Let me be clear," I told my staff. "We back up our commanders. Whatever they ask for, we deliver immediately. Ask enough questions to clarify what the field commanders need. Then make sure they get it when they need it. That's our role."

I emphasized that our job was to keep the support aligned to their needs at the speed of relevance, so that it would make a difference to our troops in the fight. I didn't want requests languishing. I consider myself the most reluctant person on earth to go to war. But once at war, our field commanders must be given what they need without delay. We could not have them fighting a two-front war, one against the enemy in the field and the other against us in the rear, extending from Tampa to Washington. A former boss, Navy Captain Dick Stratton, who was held in the Hanoi Hilton for 2,251 days as a "prisoner at war," had taught me that a call from the field is not an interruption of the daily routine; it's the reason for the daily routine.

As it is for any senior executive, time was my most precious commodity. At my headquarters in Tampa, my staff was coordinating contingency plans and directing ongoing operations. Additionally, an unrelenting drumbeat of unforeseen matters had to be dealt with. Further, representatives from sixty nations had pressing issues to discuss. Most had only a small number of troops deployed in combat or support across the region—but some were taking casualties for the first time in a generation. Naturally, they wanted their voices heard.

For a commander, fighting in a coalition is the trigonometry level of warfare. This is because coalition warfighting denies what is considered axiomatic in military circles: that when you assign anyone a mission or duty, you must also provide them with sufficient authority over everyone assigned to execute that mission. Coalitions, however, combine many nations' forces, and those forces still belong to their home nations. Most nations, our own included, place "caveats" on the forces they assign, in effect restrictions that lessen the command authority a coalition commander has over some of his assigned troops, even to the point of denying their use in certain missions. In this environment, the persuasive power of a high-level commander is tested, as is his staff's imagination as they work to identify missions that can be assigned. My direction to my American officers was to concentrate on what allied forces could do, rather than moan about what the allies' home governments or low levels of training prevented them from doing.

An oft-spoken admonition in the Marines is this: When you're going to a gunfight, bring all your friends with guns. Having fought many times in coalitions, I believe that we need every ally we can bring to the fight. From imaginative military solutions to their country's vote in the United Nations, the more allies the better. I have never been on a crowded battlefield, and there is always room for those who want to be there alongside us. Speaking with young generals and admirals, I would explain that in coalitions, I could not give them sufficient military authority to override an ally's decision. "Nonetheless," I explained, "your nation expects success from you." Nothing new under the sun: this was the same challenge Marlborough and Eisenhower had to deal with.

One of my predecessors at CENTCOM, General Zinni, had taught me to break information into three categories. The first was housekeeping, which allowed me to be anticipatory—for example, munitions stockage levels and ship locations. The second was decision-making, to maintain the rhythm of operations designed to ensure that our OODA loops were functioning at the speed of relevance. The third were alarms, called "night orders." These addressed critical events—for instance, a U.S. embassy in distress or a new outbreak of hostilities. "Alarm" information had to be immediately brought to my attention, day or night.

Sorting out the way ahead found me in many meetings in Kabul. Following one with my friend of many years General Abdul Wardak, the Afghan Minister of Defense, I quietly took him aside.

"You look terrible, absolutely exhausted," I said.

He half smiled and looked back at me, two old soldiers who had both fought for years.

"You're one to talk," he said. "I know I'm tired, and I'm getting snappish with my staff."

As I was flying home, my friend's comment stayed with me. Here I was, the advocate for command and feedback, but I was constantly tired, too. Was I getting "snappish" with my staff? What kind of feedback did that encourage? (Note to self: I wasn't immune.) Are my manners deteriorating? Was I becoming an impatient tyrant rather than a coach? The tougher the situation, the more I needed to choose to set a calm example, not allowing long hours and wicked issues to dictate my behavior around a team doing their utmost.

Whether in Tampa or overseas, my schedule included videoconference sessions, assorted briefings, and meetings with heads of state, ambassadors, generals, policymakers, and foreign affairs experts. My daily calendar began shortly before 4:00 A.M., when I reviewed intelligence reports and overnight updates. My schedule, even though broken down into fifteen- and thirty-minute intervals, was frequently interrupted by calls from Washington, others from ambassadors in the region, and discussions with subordinate commanders.

Each morning, I tried to go through my emails before working out and having a light breakfast. I knew in many cases that if I didn't answer promptly, a delayed response could result in weeks of work for staffs undoing hasty decisions made by someone without a full appreciation of the problem.

In our military, lack of time to reflect is the single biggest deficiency in senior decision-makers. If there was one area where I consistently fell short, that was it. Try as I would, I failed to put aside hours for sequestering myself outside the daily routine to think more broadly: What weren't we doing that needed to be done? Where was our strategy lacking? What lay over the horizon? I had fine officers working hundreds of issues, but a leader must try to see the overarching pattern, fitting details into the larger situation. Anticipating the second- and third-order consequences of policy decisions demanded more time than I was putting aside.

It's easy for an outsider to say, "Well, tell your chief of staff to be more efficient." But some unforeseen issues had to end up on my desk due to their gravity. Not two hours into any given day, some commercial ship might report a pirate attack. A foreign leader had read a news report and had urgent questions. Or a cruiser had to go into port for emergency repairs, meaning that a priority mission would have to be dropped or we'd have to request another ship. An ambassador called needing refugee support via military channels. The Special Forces commander needed to brief me on a sighting of a leading terrorist in a sensitive location. The Chairman was calling about a troop request and he needed my input before the Secretary of Defense left on a trip or the decision would be delayed past the deadline. A foreign chief of defense had sent an officer to brief me on a sensitive matter, and, no, he wouldn't tell anyone else what it was about . . . And so it went.

In Tampa, I had sixteen admirals and generals directing operations and staff activities. Having been engaged in two wars for almost a decade, CENTCOM was a magnet for top talent. The services were sending their best officers. This experienced crew was all in, seven days a week. I quickly warmed to them and encouraged them to use their initiative, keeping me informed following my mantra "What do I know? Who needs to know? Have I told them?" I repeated it so often that it appeared on index cards next to the phones in some offices.

Early on, a staff officer, thinking I was in Tampa, sent me a short email asking if he could come by the office regarding a sensitive issue. I typed back, "Hard for you to pop up to 30,000 feet over Saudi Arabia, where I am now. Understand what you want to do. You are cleared hot. Run with it and next time you know this sort of matter is your call. / M."

Every few weeks, I was in Washington to meet with Pentagon, intelligence, and State Department officials, National Security staff, and elected officials and their staffs on the Hill and at think tanks. I needed an understanding of diverse points of view and to be alert to what was coming. Conversely, I had to be able to explain to others our military needs and concerns. I also had to ensure that my command's stance was consistent with that of the political realm above me. You can't carry out those tasks sitting behind your desk.

Wherever I was, I was directing military activities across a zone that extended 2,500 miles east to west, and the same north to south. Scattered across that region were dozens of admirals, generals, American ambassadors, and CIA station chiefs. I recalled Secretary Gates at a breakfast sharing his perspective about teamwork. "The only thing that allows government to work at the top levels," he said, "is trusted personal relations." Within my theater, the American team—diplomats, intelligence, and military officers—exhibited a high degree of trust in one another. You can't achieve this leading by email.

My senior operational commanders met with me every two to three months at our forward headquarters in Qatar. This was our "Knights of the Round Table" get-together: the five component commanders (Army, Navy, Air Force, Special Forces, and Marines); representatives of the Iraq and Afghanistan commanders; my leading officers in Pakistan, Yemen, and Lebanon; the cyber commander; and officers representing adjacent commands in Europe and Africa.

In these meetings, our main focus was warfighting—who would do what, and who would support—examining the details and reordering the priorities, senior officers presenting their war plan and "what if?" thoughts, all the while walking over a map the size of a basketball court, nicknamed the "BAM"—the Big-Ass Map. Meals were taken together, with commands intermixed at stand-up tables so that they conversed with one another across all ranks.

I recognized that if we tried to tightly control and synchronize warfighting from a single headquarters across a far-flung command, we would create a critical vulnerability, even a single point of failure. One disruption could bring the whole system down. Instead, I intended to unleash loosely coordinated but aligned offensive attacks by commands in the air, on land, and at sea. An intimate working understanding of one another's anticipated responses to various war-game scenarios would build synergy and give our team the edge. Our new "jersey drills" walked us all through the maneuvers of our air, land, and sea forces, building confidence across the force. As I had learned, visualization or "imaging" is a critical team-building skill in any command, especially in an age when we anticipate that our communications could be disrupted by the enemy.

Every month, I flew thousands of miles to meet with heads of state and military commanders of two dozen nations. My first stop was always with the American ambassador and the CIA station chief. I didn't want to come off as a plenipotentiary or proconsul acting on my own agenda. Every time I visited, I first asked our ambassador how I could best help his or her diplomatic efforts. In keeping with George Washington's approach to leadership, I would listen, learn, and help, then lead. Secretary Shultz and General Zinni had both strongly urged me to cultivate my foreign counterparts. "The U.S. military," Zinni said, "has been focusing huge attention on the two theaters of war—Iraq and Afghanistan. Don't lose sight of the anchor states in the Middle East. Get out there and spend time in Egypt and Saudi Arabia. And don't forget our other friends. Everyone wants a personal visit to be reassured. You're a bachelor; sleep on your aircraft."

His advice aligned with my strongest conviction: I had to gain the trust of foreign leaders, civilian and military. If regional leaders didn't know me and didn't feel comfortable with my understanding of what they faced, I'd be nothing more than a place card at the dinner table. The intimate conversations and the sharing of confidences would flow around me as if I didn't exist. I'd be irrelevant, treated with indifferent courtesy as a tourist instead of a player. To avoid that, I was determined to be a good listener and to be direct in laying out my thoughts, explaining the courses of action I was considering and asking for their views. I represented the world's most powerful military. But they lived in the Middle East, and I wanted them to know that, where our interests overlapped, their problems were my problems.

Wherever I went during my tenure at CENTCOM, I heard blunt questions about our reliability as a security partner. The impression of many Arab leaders was that we might abandon them. America was emphasizing "rebuilding at home." The lack of constancy in American foreign policy left them unsettled. Many were now openly doubting our word. I understood their concerns but explained that we had enduring interests in the region.

In these countries, we could not insist on the same level of democratic achievement as the United Kingdom had, six hundred years after the Magna Carta was signed. In the meantime, our enemies were not taking a holiday as they moved against our imperfect partners and against us. So, while I unhesitatingly reinforced our State Department's efforts supporting inclusive government, I was also determined to work with our friends on critical, time-sensitive security matters.

In late 2010, WikiLeaks began to release classified State Department cables exposing to the world our diplomats' assessments of foreign leaders. A new kind of adversary had inflicted deep harm to our interests, and of course many friends whose secrets had been compromised were livid. I encountered several who said they would no longer be candid with me, because they didn't trust that Americans could keep secrets anymore. I assured them that I had not written "cables," emails, or after-action reports containing sensitive information. Instead, if I considered an issue sufficiently important to report, I would either pick up a secure phone or meet personally with the Chairman of the Joint Chiefs or the Secretary of Defense. Initially, I encountered silences and superficially brittle discussions. In some cases, the damage was so severe that only with the appointment of new ambassadors could we start rebuilding trust. Instituting on the strategic level what I had learned at the tactical level, "hand-con" became the order of the day, with handshakes cementing trust.

After a few months, the broader complaints about America stopped, and specific disagreements were discussed more productively. But I wasn't naive about relationships and hand-con. Partners were beginning to hedge their bets, now engaging with countries that were competing with us. I had returned to the region even as the dynamics of the Middle East were changing. As Heraclitus put it, you never step into the same river twice. My former commander and predecessor at CENTCOM, General John Abizaid, cautioned me, "This is not the same CENTCOM you and I served in four years ago. Ever since CENTCOM was created, America was seen as an ascending power. Today some see us as a descending power."

America's lack of strategy in setting priorities that would earn their trust resulted in a growing sense that we were proving unreliable. This would cause a series of challenges for me in the Middle East and would later concern me on a global scale.

CHAPTER 15

Snatching Defeat from the Jaws of Victory

DURING MY THREE YEARS AT CENTCOM, American policy errors compounded the turmoil in the Middle East, especially in Iraq and Afghanistan.

After investing seven years of blood and treasure in Iraq, the American-led war effort had by 2010 at last succeeded in establishing a fragile stability. Large-scale combat had ended. Thanks to Secretary Gates's keeping the bulk of our forces there as long as possible, we had driven AQI to its knees. Now, with the end of combat operations, Al Qaeda was on the run or in hiding, and the Sunni-Shiite civil war had died down. In my view, Iraq had entered a post-conflict, pre-reconciliation phase of stability. But the passions unleashed in the civil war still smoldered.

The question was: what to do now? If we pulled out abruptly, intelligence reports warned, Iraq would fall back into civil war, allowing the jihadist terrorists to regenerate. The residual American force was the glue holding Iraq together and helping prevent terrorist resurgence. American advisers still circulated at every level inside the Iraqi police and army. Our officers and troops were the trusted intermediaries among competing factions.

Retaining some U.S. troops required the Iraqi government's agreement. At the same time, the incumbent prime minister, Nouri al-Maliki, was fighting to stay in power, though his party had garnered fewer votes than the opposition in the elections of 2010. The National Security staff in the White House believed that Maliki offered a continuity that, in their minds, would facilitate the withdrawal of U.S. troops. I was opposed to that logic. I increasingly considered sectarian Maliki the politician least capable of unifying Iraq and continuing the process of reconciliation.

In the late summer of 2010, I flew to Baghdad for a change of command. General Lloyd Austin was taking over from General Ray Odierno. Ray had given Secretary Gates and me a carefully calculated plan to leave a residual force of eighteen thousand troops. We met privately to discuss the key issue: Who would be the next Iraqi prime minister, and how would that choice affect U.S. troop withdrawals and stability inside the country? President Obama had said we would maintain a residual force "to advise and assist" the Iraqis. Generals Austin and Odierno and I assumed this would be a sufficient number to hold the gains we had achieved at great cost, a number we'd reduce as Iraqi capabilities increased.

After the change of command ceremony concluded, on a hot Baghdad day, Ambassador Jim Jeffrey invited Vice President Joe Biden, White House staffers, and the American generals to dinner. Jeffrey was one of those diplomats bred for tough times, and he encouraged a frank exchange of views around the table. During and after the dinner, I reminded the others that Maliki had not received the most votes. I was reviewing in my mind reports of Maliki striking candidates' names off election rolls and slow-rolling government formation for months, subverting the Iraqi constitution.

"Prime Minister Maliki is highly untrustworthy, Mr. Vice President," I said. "He looks at our ambassadors and military advisers as impediments to his anti-Sunni agenda. Leaders across the region have warned me that he is set on disenfranchising the Sunnis. He wants to purge or marginalize Sunnis and Kurds from the government. He's devious when he talks to us."

I was thinking of the training wheels on a bicycle: We shouldn't suddenly pull off those wheels. We should slowly inch the wheels up, allowing the Iraqis to wobble but not crash as they slowly pedaled down the path to self-sufficiency. If we pulled out too early, I noted, we would have to bring our troops back in. I argued that we had to stay and emphasized what our intelligence community assessed: our progress was not yet ingrained, and it was "reversible" if we didn't stay. At this point, our casualties were very low. While political considerations rightly guide strategic decisions, political decisions are unsustainable when they deny military reality. Properly aligned, political considerations and strategic decisions are the keys to a better peace.

Vice President Biden and his assistants listened politely. But as we spoke, I sensed I was making no headway in convincing the administration officials not to support Maliki. It was like talking to people who lived in wooden houses but saw no need for a fire department. I saw that the die was already cast. I could understand that I was viewed as a military man, perhaps not attuned to political subtleties, but frankly I was dumbfounded that our diplomats also seemed totally outside of the decision-making loop. The open exchange of views encouraged by Ambassador Jeffrey turned awkward and then trailed off.

"Maliki wants us to stick around, because he does not see a future in Iraq otherwise," Biden said. "I'll bet you my vice presidency."

I liked the Vice President. After dinner, he kidded me about my command. "Know why you're at CENTCOM?" he teased. "Because no one else was dumb enough to take the job." I found him an admirable and amiable man. But he was past the point where he was willing to entertain a "good idea." He didn't want to hear more; he wanted our forces out of Iraq. Whatever path led there fastest, he favored. He exuded the confidence of a man whose mind was made up, perhaps even indifferent to considering the consequences were he judging the situation incorrectly.

Over the following months, messages from my Iraqi and regional contacts and our own intelligence reports were ominous. Maliki was stepping up the purge of Sunnis from all government posts, degrading the military in the process. Each time Maliki grossly overreached, anxious Iraqi officials complained to our advisers as if they were a court of appeals. In 1994, after the collapse of the apartheid government, Nelson Mandela had exercised his wise, calming authority to reconcile the people of South Africa. But Maliki was no Mandela. In my view, a sufficient number of U.S. military simply had to stay in order to sustain our gains.

In Washington, the debate swirled throughout 2011 about how many, if any, U.S. troops should remain in Iraq. Central Command, the Chairman of the Joint Chiefs, and the new Defense Secretary, Leon Panetta, who had replaced Bob Gates, continued to recommend to the White House retaining a residual force, as did Secretary of State Hillary Clinton. Pentagon Under Secretary Michèle Flournoy—thinking strategically—fought long and hard for the department's position. But she was talking to the wind. Beginning with President Bush and continuing through the Obama administration, the White House was set on a total troop withdrawal, for political reasons. The National Security staff put no stock in our forecast that if we pulled out, the enemy would resurrect. They dealt with Iraq as a "one-off," as if the pullout of our troops there would have no regional implications, reinforcing our allies' fears that we were abandoning them. I argued strongly that any vacuum left in our wake would be filled by Sunni terrorists and Iran.

From Syria, on Iraq's western border, Bashar al-Assad's Baathist regime was facilitating the recruitment and training of Al Qaeda and Sunni terrorists. From the eastern border, Iran was supporting the Shiite militias and death squads. The mullahs in charge of Iran intended to draw Iraq into their orbit as an obedient client state. Iran was playing the long game. In my judgment, regardless of where one stood on the decision to invade Iraq back in 2003, securing the gains of seven years of war would require keeping troops and diplomatic engagement in Iraq.

On one of my trips to Iraq, officials repeatedly told me they needed us there to help them "avoid the suffocating embrace of Iran." At the level below Maliki, I heard this same quote often enough to recognize an agreed-on "talking point": senior Iraqi officials wanted us to stay, even if their fractious parliament could not say so publicly, for domestic political reasons.

In White House meetings, we constantly quibbled about numbers, seldom delving into the alternate end states and what was realistically needed to achieve them. The National Security staff would ask why I needed 150 troops to guard an embassy in a stressed Middle East country, or ninety troops to provide logistics at a base outside Baghdad. I would respond that the numbers were based on the specific tasks those troops had to carry out. But this was a kabuki dance. The discussions were designed to give the appearance of consultation, but they were not genuine. I was having none of it. As I was leaving the White House Situation Room one day, I spoke bluntly to a high-ranking National Security staffer.

"Those of us in uniform earnestly want to know," I said. "What do you want us to do?"

I received no answer. I had no issue about obeying orders from the Commander in Chief elected by the American people (no one had elected me), but agreeing that this precipitous withdrawal was a wise course of action was a wholly different matter. After studying the issue, General Austin agreed with Odierno, who was recommending that we retain eighteen thousand troops. I carefully reviewed the numbers and the advisory tasks, knowing that Secretary Panetta needed my independent assessment of the tasks and the troop strength necessary. I told the secretary that I agreed with General Austin. From the perspective of America's strategic interest, I saw no viable alternative.

But instead of eighteen thousand troops, the White House half-heartedly offered a token presence of 3,500 (a number with no analytic basis that I knew of), provided that the Iraqi parliament voted for strict terms protecting our forces from Iraqi judicial prosecution. That proviso was a poison pill. The White House knew that the fractious Iraqi parliament could never unite and agree to those terms. We had other legal ways of protecting American troops from such prosecution. But that made no difference. In October 2011, Prime Minister Maliki and President Obama agreed that all U.S. forces would leave at the end of the year.

"Today, I can report that, as promised, the rest of our troops in Iraq will come home," the President said. "We're leaving behind a sovereign, stable, and self-reliant Iraq."

The words "sovereign, stable, and self-reliant" had never been used by the Pentagon or the State Department, and I had never seen them in any intelligence report. After all we went through and all the casualties we suffered, I thought, surely we were not just giving up.

"You know I say what I mean and I mean what I say," Obama said in the fall of 2012. "I said I'd end the war in Iraq. I ended it."

Rhetoric doesn't end conflicts. With America's influence effectively gone, Prime Minister Maliki imprisoned numerous Sunnis, drove their representatives from government, and refused to send funds to Sunni districts, virtually disenfranchising a third of his country. Iraq slipped back into escalating violence. It was like watching a car wreck in slow motion. Soon the Sunnis were in full revolt and the Iraqi Army was a hollow, powerless shell, allowing the terrorists to return like a barbarian horde, exactly as the CIA had predicted. In the summer of 2014, the medieval scourge called ISIS rose like a phoenix and swept across western Iraq and eastern Syria, routing the Iraqi Army and establishing its murderous caliphate. It would take many years and tens of thousands of casualties, plus untold misery for millions of innocents, to break ISIS's geographic hold. All of this was predicted—and preventable.

Supporting a sectarian Iraqi prime minister and withdrawing all U.S. troops were catastrophic decisions, based on the conditions at the time. I had seen this same dynamic—ignoring reality—in 2001 when we allowed Al Qaeda and bin Laden to escape into Pakistan, and again in Fallujah in 2003, when we were stopped midway in the attack. Now I was seeing it again. This wasn't a military-versus-civilian flaw, or a Democrat-versus-Republican error. It went deeper. At the top, then as now, there was an aura of omniscience. The assessments of the intelligence community, our diplomats, and our military had been excluded from the decision-making circle.

After the fact, some political leaders called it an intelligence failure; that was scapegoating, because we had been warned that an Al Qaeda–aligned terror group would come again. That assessment was ignored. It's frustrating to listen to any leader blame his predecessor, especially a political leader regarding a situation that he knew existed when he ran for office. A wise leader must deal with reality and state what he intends, and what level of commitment he is willing to invest in achieving that end. He then has to trust that his subordinates know how to carry that out. Wise leadership requires collaboration; otherwise it will lead to failure.

After the dinner with the Vice President, I flew on to Kabul. We had been fighting that war for ten years, with little sign of lasting progress. In the decade after Al Qaeda had escaped from Tora Bora into Pakistan, the Taliban had regained control over swaths of southern and eastern Afghanistan. Under the command of General Dave Petraeus, 32,000 Americans troops and 17,000 allies were heavily engaged, alongside 150,000 Afghan soldiers. I wanted CENTCOM to do all it could to help the war effort.

In short order, Dave called me with a disturbing report.

"Jim, you're not going to believe this," he said. "We have sound rules of engagement. But every lower echelon of command has tightened them. The troops going on patrol are discouraged. They think the rules prevent them from firing back. So I'm putting out the word that I establish the rules of engagement and no subordinate command can add additional restrictions. The press may write that I'm not protecting civilians, so I'm giving you a heads-up."

I immediately understood his problem. In the infantry, Dave and I had grown up in an environment where, if the corporal on point shouted back that he needed fire support, he got it. Now the corporal faced a convoluted decision cycle. When I had direct command of those going into battle, my touchstones set the conditions for the use of force: *Engage your mind before your trigger finger. First, do no harm to the innocent. Identify your target before you shoot.* In the rare cases, like Haditha, where poor judgment had occurred, I made my decisions public, ensuring that every grunt would know how I came to conclusions, which reinforced the ethical stance I expected from my disciplined troops.

But now, every complaint about a civilian casualty, however vague, was investigated. The enemy had learned fast how to make spurious allegations, and they grew accordingly. Investigations required interviews by lawyers and investigators and resulted in disruptions to our operations, bringing tension into our ranks. Having been investigated myself, I knew it was no small matter for those involved. Lawyers reached conclusions and wrote instructions. Various Afghan officials, including the mercurial President, Hamid Karzai, railed about civilian injuries, both those that were real and those put forward in Taliban propaganda. Rules to restrict our firepower grew, even when our troops were attacked by the enemy. These one-size-fits-all restrictions did not accord with the reality faced by our grunts.

Rules of engagement are what separate principled militaries from barbarians and terrorists. At the same time, a democracy, no matter how high-minded, has a moral obligation to ensure that its soldiers are permitted—no, encouraged—to effectively carry out their appointed task of closing with and destroying the enemy. The Geneva Protocol codified the application of lethal military force, stipulating that destruction be proportionate to the situation and that diligent efforts be taken to protect noncombatants. Having seen our troops up close in repeated fights, I doubt any military in history could match their efforts to avoid injuring the innocent.

Increasingly stringent rules had evolved gradually, over several years. I believed that, lacking coherent policy objectives, and in the face of growing criticism over a long and inconclusive war, in the field we had tightened our rules of engagement to fight "the right way." These tightened rules were imposed in a vain effort to compensate for the lack of a sound strategy that could show progress. Instead of straightening out the strategy, we tried to remove any criticism of the manner in which we were fighting. In doing so, we were hobbling ourselves militarily, losing the confidence of our troops in the process. Dave Petraeus was aligning military necessity with the absolute need to protect the innocent.

We cannot have our grunts look upon their seniors as setting rules that in effect hamstring our troops while seemingly giving the enemy the advantage of a "fair fight." Our commanders must be the coaches and team captains for our own team, building trust with the grunts in the fight. When the brass lose influence over their troops because their rules are out of touch, the discipline that binds all ranks together is undercut. Discipline, in turn, protects the innocents caught up on the battlefield, which must also be seen as a humanitarian field. We must sustain trust, from the general to the private, as the most effective route to winning battles with the lowest cost to noncombatants.

We have a moral imperative to protect our troops. I unreservedly supported Dave's decision to fix the rules of engagement, necessarily giving more authority to those directly engaged. These rules should not be written by lawyers; they must be written by commanders, with the advice of lawyers schooled in the law of war, not humanitarian issues alone. The rules of engagement must be reflexive, not reflective, so that troops can react swiftly and legitimately when time is of the essence. If a democracy does not trust its troops, then it shouldn't go to war.

Even with sensible rules of engagement, where was the engine of war headed? What was our policy end state, and the strategy for getting there? Ends, ways, and means would be critical. President Bush had declared, "Our goal in Afghanistan is to . . . establish a stable, moderate, and democratic state." That expansive policy goal proved unattainable during his eight-year presidency.

President Obama, however reluctantly, agreed to send in more troops in 2010. "It is in our vital national interest to send an additional thirty thousand U.S. troops to Afghanistan," he said. "After eighteen months, our troops will begin to come home." In his first sentence, the President raised the hopes of the anti-Taliban forces in Afghanistan; in the second sentence, he raised the hopes of the Taliban by giving them our departure date. After President Obama's speech, I asked my Pakistani military liaison officer what he understood to be the message. He was quick to say, "You're pulling out." As Dr. Kissinger had taught me years before, we should never tell our adversary what we will not do.

Much talk has been given to having an "exit strategy." My thought was that "exiting" a war was a by-product of winning that war. Unless you want to lose, you don't tell an enemy when you are done fighting, and you don't set an exit unrelated to the situation on the ground. Dave Petraeus now faced a very short window in which to turn around a deteriorating war effort. It would take months to even get the additional troops on the ground, and more months to make an impact. Nevertheless, he thought he could show progress. The challenge was threefold. First, the Taliban were a zealous and determined foe. Second, the Taliban enjoyed a sanctuary in Pakistan, Afghanistan's neighbor to the east. Third, Afghanistan's government lacked capable functionaries. Three decades of fighting since the Soviet invasion had destroyed the country's social fabric and much of its economy, while reducing its educated class to a fragmented minority.

After coalition troops cleared a district, Afghan soldiers had to move in to hold what had been gained. The time needed to do this proved as indeterminate as it was critical. In a torn-apart society, Dave Petraeus had to choose where to deploy his coalition and Afghan troops to gain the most before time ran out. Near the top of his list was the district of Marjah, the epicenter of the opium trade. In the spring of 2010, it had taken an assault by more than seven thousand Marines and Afghan soldiers to wrest it from the Taliban. Afghan officials were then flown in to set up what was called "government in a box," a governance team with directors for health, water, agriculture, schools, police, and education. But once the "box" was opened, only a few scared Afghan officials appeared. When those officials stepped inside Marjah's marketplace, they faced menacing farmers furious at losing the lucrative poppy trade. The officials fled, leaving governance to the coalition.

When I visited—a year after the initial assault—both an American battalion and a Special Forces advisory team were still there. In the summer of 2011, President Obama declared, "The tide of war is receding. . . . These long wars will come to a responsible end."

But I had been assigned two contradictory objectives: The forces under my command at CENTCOM were to degrade the Taliban while building up the Afghan army. They were also to withdraw on a strict timetable, independent of circumstances on the ground. We could do one or the other, but not both.

I told Secretary Gates when I took command that I would give him my independent judgment of progress and challenges. To do that, I knew I needed a balanced risk assessment that included outside perspectives. Perhaps I and our combat commanders in that country were too close to the people and their problems, grasping every success as a sign of impending victory, even if only transient. After all, our military is hardwired with a can-do spirit; otherwise we could not take on what war requires of us. Further, with repeat tours, some of our battle-tested leaders had developed a fondness for the Afghan people that could reasonably cloud their judgment. I sensed that I needed someone to stand back and scan the horizon. Twenty years earlier, during Desert Storm, I had first dispatched experienced officers to observe the battle and report back, outside my chain of command. They were my "focused telescopes" or "Juliet officers." Now, at the strategic level, I turned to three accomplished, savvy friends: David Bradley, chairman of *The Atlantic* magazine, retired Army General Jack Keane, and my old mentor, retired Marine General Tony Zinni. I knew they would tell me without reservation what they perceived to be ground truth. Separately, they flew to Afghanistan, licensed to talk to leaders and troops at all levels. They returned and gave me their individual assessments of our counterinsurgency effort.

They saw real progress, steps in the right direction, but cautioned that it was an enormous undertaking and would take a lot of time. Tony Zinni later wrote that counterinsurgency "can be expensive in treasure and casualties, require large numbers of troops, fall on an unreceptive populace, and fail to implant permanent change. Buyer beware!" After hearing their reports, I had a chance meeting with retired General Colin Powell. I explained what I was hearing, and he cut to the heart of the matter: "Jim, the central question is: Will all your successes just be transient, because you don't have the forces or the time to solidify them?" The question rode in the back of my mind in every briefing and in every visit to Afghanistan.

Although Regional Command East, under the U.S. Army, provided the most complex geographic and tribal challenges, it was there that I also saw the unique value of allied forces. King Abdullah of Jordan, ever our ally, had allocated one of his most capable battalions to support us in Afghanistan, despite the pressing need for them at home, along his Syrian border. The commander, Colonel Aref al-Zaben, was a resourceful leader who brought fresh ideas to bear. He deployed his men on frequent patrols, and his interpreters kept him updated on the Taliban's hateful messages going out over the airways to isolated communities in the mountain valleys. Using his own Muslim clerics, he began a daily radio barrage contradicting the fundamentalists' misinterpretation of the Koran. The program was titled "Voices of Moderate Islam." His troops distributed small radios to the families, and his clerics took to the air, challenging the Taliban's ideology in a manner only fellow Muslims could. In call-in shows, it was clear that the Taliban were losing their hold on the people. On patrol, female soldiers wearing camouflage head scarves actively engaged with Afghan women in the villages in a manner that men or non-Muslims could not. Aref arranged for Afghan village elders to be flown to the Jordanian capital. In Amman, King Abdullah would address them in person, standing in front of a mosque but across the street from a Christian church in full view. The message of tolerance was clear, from the valleys of Afghanistan to the mosques of Jordan.

From his infantrymen's patrols in the district villages to moderate Islam broadcasts on the radio fighting the "battle of the narrative" to the king's talks as a leader of his faith and his people, the Jordanian unit batted well above its weight, bringing strength beyond numbers to our NATO-led coalition.

NATO's key operational vulnerability for our allies like Jordan and for all our forces across Afghanistan was the terrorist havens provided by neighboring Pakistan.

In the days following 9/11, American officials had insisted that Pakistan align with us. Pakistan initially cooperated. But the country's leaders soon returned to playing a double game, providing the Taliban with a sanctuary. When we cleared them out of Afghan villages, they could retreat across the border to lick their wounds, rest, resupply, and bide their time to come back in again. The history of counterinsurgency teaches us that an enemy who can roll in and out like waves on a beach is devilishly hard to beat.

To understand how we found ourselves in that box, we have to look back. In 1949, as the era of colonialism ended, England returned sovereignty to predominantly Hindu India and Muslim Pakistan, separating them in a bloody partition that cost approximately a million lives. Since then, they have fought four wars, and both now have significant numbers of nuclear weapons. Pakistan views all geopolitics through the prism of its hostility toward India. Afghanistan lies to the rear of Pakistan, so the Pakistan military wanted a friendly government in Kabul that was resistant to Indian influence. This is why, after Russia left Afghanistan in 1988, Pakistan nurtured and supplied the Afghan Taliban movement.

We were now providing substantial economic and military aid and paying large sums for the passage of goods to Afghanistan. These payments did not reassure me. Pakistan was a country born with no affection for itself, and there was an active self-destructive streak in its political culture. I was uneasy that more than 70 percent of NATO's logistics lifeline depended upon one route, via Pakistan. I took one look at the map and decided we had to change the pieces on the chessboard.

I heard a bit of grumbling about why CENTCOM had not attended to this weak link before. While I wanted honest feedback, we needed to focus on removing the vulnerability, not whining about the problem. I had great confidence in our logisticians, directing them to work with our diplomats and develop alternatives. Our ambassadors and U.S. Transportation Command worked zealously with countries to the north and west of Afghanistan to open supply routes from the north. In addition, I directed a buildup inside Afghanistan of ninety days' worth of all critical supplies— ammunition, food, medical replenishment, and fuel. The northern route was more expensive, and I didn't want to use it if I could avoid it. But in conditions of high uncertainty, you must develop alternatives that may or may not come into play: always keep an ace in the hole.

Then, in September 2011, General John Allen, having replaced Dave Petraeus as our NATO commander in Afghanistan, gave a warning to the Pakistani military: he'd learned the Haqqani terrorist group, harbored in Pakistan, was preparing a massive truck bomb. General Ashfaq Kayani, the Chief of Staff of Pakistan's army, said he would take action. Two days later, that bomb detonated at a U.S. base near Kabul, wounding seventy-seven American soldiers and killing five Afghans. A few days later, Haqqani terrorists attacked our embassy in Kabul. At a diplomatic function in Washington, I bumped into the Pakistani ambassador, Husain Haqqani (no relation to the terrorist group). My diplomatic skills were lacking.

"You have a Pakistan Army division headquarters," I said, "in the same city as the terrorist headquarters. You say you're not on their side, but now they attack our embassy in a raid coordinated from your side of the border. You're supporting the very people who will kill you one day."

My obscenity-laced message was overheard by a U.S. diplomat, who sent me a congratulatory email.

My numerous frank talks with General Kayani in Rawalpindi had little effect. By October the U.S.-Pakistan relationship had reached a low ebb. In late November, a night fight broke out between an Afghan company with American advisers and a Pakistani unit, which initiated the fight, using mortars to fire on us. When efforts by the advisers to identify themselves did not stop the firing, they called in an air strike, killing twenty-four Pakistani troops. The Pakistani leadership reacted with outrage.

To confirm what had happened, I sat down with the senior American who had been on-scene, an experienced Special Forces warrant officer. He explained how he had repeatedly radioed to the joint NATO-Pakistan coordinating headquarters to stop the shooting. He even called an F-15 to fly low-level, dropping flares and illuminating the Pakistani position. The Taliban do not fly F-15s, and our on-scene commander was making every effort to stop the firing from the high ground. When the incoming Pakistani fire continued, becoming more concentrated, we bombed the mountaintop position. I explained this all to General Kayani on the phone, offering a joint investigation. He declined my offer. His military was still smarting over our killing Osama bin Laden without informing them, and Kayani could not show any willingness to work with us.

Using the F-15 bombing as an excuse, Pakistan abruptly closed its supply route into Afghanistan. The Pakistani leadership had chosen to turn a battlefield tragedy into an indictment of America. No doubt they thought they had us logistically over a barrel and in a political corner. Fortunately, by that time our ninety days of supplies had been stockpiled and the northern network was tested and ready. We shifted to the north, canceling payments to the Pakistani shippers. Caught by surprise, the Pakistanis could only wait, hoping the northern route could not be sustained through the icy winter and muddy spring.

It didn't work. After a year of brinkmanship, Pakistan backed off the cliff. Both sides acknowledged coordination "mistakes that resulted in the deaths of Pakistani soldiers." Pakistan quietly reopened its supply lines, and the truck convoys to Afghanistan resumed.

To me, the episode illustrated the unpredictable twists and turns of war. It demonstrated the importance of never having only one course of action to achieve your aims. If in a crisis you find yourself without options, you will be pushed into a corner. Always build in shock absorbers. It was my military duty to help our diplomats by anticipating the negotiating strategy of our adversary, and provide options so our State Department would not be hamstrung in negotiations due to a lack of military alternatives.

The Pakistan military had lost more of their own troops fighting terrorists on their side of the border than the NATO coalition has lost in Afghanistan. Yet they thought they could control or at least manipulate the terrorists. But, once planted, terrorism was growing in ways that no one—not even Pakistan's secret service, the ISI—could predict or control. I concluded that our military interactions with Pakistan could only be transactional, based upon the specific issue at hand and what each side had to offer the other. Quid pro quo. Pakistan could episodically choose not to be our enemy, but it chose not to be a trusted friend or ally of the United States or NATO.

Of all the countries I've dealt with, I consider Pakistan to be the most dangerous, because of the radicalization of its society and the availability of nuclear weapons. We can't have the fastest-growing nuclear arsenal in the world falling into the hands of the terrorists breeding in their midst. The result would be disastrous. The tragedy for the Pakistani people is that they don't have leaders who care about their future.

As an illustration of the lack of trust, when we believed we had identified Osama bin Laden's hiding place deep inside Pakistan, President Obama sent in a team to kill him without informing the Pakistanis.

Ultimately, it was in our common interest that we maintain a cautious, mindful relationship, with modest expectations of collaboration. We could manage our problems with Pakistan, but our divisions were too deep, and trust too shallow, to resolve them. And that is the state of our relationship to this day.

With Pakistan continuing to permit sanctuaries for the Taliban, in the summer of 2012 I flew back to Afghanistan. The surge was over, and we were reducing our numbers in accordance with Washington's plan. I visited with John Toolan, my dauntless colonel from the march on Baghdad in 2003 and the Fallujah battle in 2004, who was now wearing two stars and commanded all coalition forces in fierce Helmand Province. Rugby-playing John, with his Brooklyn accent, cut to the essence. After a year in command, he had grave reservations about whether Afghan forces could keep control on their own in the farmlands. Helmand was the Taliban's financial hub, with opium flowing out and finances flowing into the enemy's coffers. The Taliban controlled the villages surrounding the provincial capital, without having to fight to hold them.

"The Muslim religion isn't the barrier to progress here," he said. "The problem is a whole culture that rejects Western concepts of playing by the rules and cooperating with each other."

Decades of violence, ruin, and uncertainty meant that nobody believed in tomorrow. It was every tribe, every subtribe, and every man for himself. Despite pockets of progress and successes in education, public health, and more, the Afghan government lacked the unity, capability, and determination to take back much of the countryside. John and I talked about what bothered us most: How confident were we that the losses among our young men and women—all volunteers—were leading to a satisfactory outcome? Our company commanders told us the Afghan soldiers would not patrol in the Green Zone (the vast farmlands surrounding the district towns) once our troops left. Our troops from dozens of nations had remained steadfast, despite the war's unpopularity in many of the nations fighting there. They evacuated their dead and maimed and went out again the next day to close with the enemy. They gave 100 percent and did their duty.

Strategy links the policy end state with the diplomatic and military ways and means. The policymakers, diplomats, and generals must bargain together, each informing the other, until they firmly resolve that they have a viable policy. That means that if you're going to fight a limited war anywhere, it should be limited in its political end state but fully resourced militarily, to end it quickly. If the policy changes, the strategy and attendant resources must also change, adapted to the new goal. We did not increase our forces to the size needed, nor did we take into account the amount of time needed.

The example of South Korea is instructive. Since the cease-fire in 1953, we have kept tens of thousands of U.S. soldiers there. Our large troop presence and steady diplomacy safeguarded the transformation of that war-torn country from a dictatorship into a vibrant democracy. But it took forty years. In Afghanistan, we were unwilling to devote the resources and time needed to transform the country, decade by decade, into a thriving democracy.

We were trying to do too much with too little.

In light of the Taliban's demonstrated unwillingness to break away from Al Qaeda, it would be foolhardy not to keep the Taliban off-balance and away from the populated centers. In repeated Situation Room meetings, when the White House asked for my judgment, I proposed that at least ten thousand American troops remain in Afghanistan, without any specified timeline for withdrawal, other than one based on the enemy threat to America and the development of the Afghan army. Yet we were pulled in two directions by competing missions: draw down and pull back, whether the Afghans were ready or not, but keep fighting the enemy to protect the population. Without a unified purpose, we would begin losing allies, and we did over the ensuing years, eventually dropping from forty-nine in 2013 to thirty-nine by late 2016. We were losing the very allies that could have carried more of the burden.

At the trigonometry level of warfare, with the absence of a clear policy end state and the resources for a strategy to attain it, it was inevitable that nonstrategic exigencies would win the day.

CHAPTER 16

Friend or Foe

WHILE AFGHANISTAN AND IRAQ received the most attention in the States, I had two superb commanders in charge who kept me fully informed. I spent the bulk of my time dealing with the other nations in CENTCOM's zone.

And there, amid poverty and with scant hope for betterment, resentment on the "Arab street" toward their rulers had built to a breaking point. In 2010, one in every three Arab youths was unemployed. After decades of bad governance, the vast majority faced a bleak future, and in this digital age, they knew they were missing out.

And then suddenly, like a torpedo out of the dark sea at night hitting the side of a ship, the Middle East was convulsed by popular uprisings. They were to shake the foundations of our relationships with every country in the region. In Tunisia, on the North African coast, a fruit seller burned himself to death. He told his wife that for his entire life he had been deprived of human dignity. Television transmitted his despairing self-immolation to half a billion Arabs in the winter of 2011. Soon after, a near total breakdown of the social contract between Arab governments and their people swept across the Middle East. Every day, I looked at maps showing the rapid-fire spread of the protests. It was like a match thrown into a pool of gasoline. In the Western press, we read about the "Arab Spring," implying that the riots would result in the overthrow of autocrats and democracy would flower.

After a rebellion, however, power tends to flow to those most organized, not automatically to the most idealistic. Many Arabs wanted democracy. But the revolt was against unjust and unresponsive governments more than it was a pell-mell rush to democracy and inclusive government. I was certain it was unrealistic to believe that, in a region lacking democratic traditions or civil society institutions, the path to liberal democracy could be swift or free of violence. The French Revolution unleashed six years of terror and trial by the guillotine, ending with the rise of the Napoleonic militaristic state. During World War I, the Russians rebelled against czarist rule, but that ultimately ushered in Stalin's totalitarianism and the deaths of millions. Rebellions, no matter how idealistic in origin, can as often as not produce chaos that often leads to tyranny.

Secretary Gates signaled to me at CENTCOM to continue engaging, encouraging me to keep in close contact with my counterparts in the region. He was wary about the consequences of the uprisings, and I shared his concern about what the new order would look like. Democracy was not preordained to emerge from what was unfolding. I didn't have a crystal ball, but a quick glance at history reminded me that every society has its own carrying capacity for making change. I was concerned that if traditional Arab societies proved unable to assimilate sudden political change, something worse would erupt.

In determining how to deal with a hostile and powerful England in 1807, President Jefferson wrote, "What is good in this case cannot be effected. We have, therefore, only to find out what will be least bad." That struck me as sound advice during the Arab Spring.

As it remains the traditional center of Arab learning and culture, how Egypt went would be critical to the region and to our interests. In February 2011, massive protests erupted in Cairo against President Hosni Mubarak, who had ruled for thirty years and had steadfastly supported our policies. But he and his regime were now the focus of widespread discontent and protests.

It seemed to me that we should now be measured in our approach. In Egypt, I thought we should use quiet diplomacy to urge inclusive government. Our government was divided on how to support the Egyptian people without throwing Mubarak under the bus. But in early February, President Obama came out vocally against Mubarak, insisting that in Egypt, "we were on the right side of history." Having read a bit of history and found that events, good and bad, had been "written" by both good and evil characters, I put little stock in the idea that history books yet to be written would somehow give yearning Arabs what they fervently desired today.

During the tumultuous occupation of Tahrir Square, in Cairo, in January 2011, General Sami Anan, commander of the Egyptian armed forces, called me one evening. He was in Washington but had to return to Egypt. His commercial flight from New York City was leaving in four hours. I met him at Andrews Air Force Base on a gusty, chilly night. We spoke just before I put him on a military plane to get him to JFK Airport on time. "Thank you," he said. "I promise you, military to military, that my soldiers will not fire upon their fellow Egyptians." He was true to his word. There was violence in the street, but the Egyptian military stood aside and Mubarak was removed from power in a bloodless coup.

The political situation now dictated outcomes. For decades, Mubarak had permitted only one opposition party, the Muslim Brotherhood, thus strengthening his hold on the government, since it was either him or the radical Brothers. Their disciplined organization enabled them to surge to power in the aftermath of what was a leaderless revolution.

In my Cairo meetings with prominent Egyptians in and out of power, they were furious with the Brotherhood policies, which included anti-Christian decrees and the sanctioning of marriage for nine-year-old girls. The Brotherhood rapidly lost favor among the people. In the largest public demonstrations in world history, twenty million Egyptians took to the streets and conducted what amounted to a national plebiscite. Within a year, the Egyptian Army had shouldered the Brotherhood out of power, and, in an imperfect election, its military commander was elected president.

Understandably, a military-dominated Egyptian government fell short of our ideals. But had the military not stepped in in response to twenty million Egyptians demanding the removal of the Muslim Brothers, the specter of an implosion loomed large. Yet the Muslim Brotherhood's values made them our enduring adversary, because they were ultimately more restrictive of the human rights of the Egyptian people, a fact made clear by the public's overwhelming rejection of their rule. When we go abroad, our noblest instinct—to champion democracy—must be guided by prudence and humility: as difficult as it is to understand our own political life at times, hoping for a full understanding of another country's politics is outright fanciful.

During this tumultuous time, on my frequent trips, I had three lines of effort. First, I reassured our traditional friends that we stood with them in defending their security against the terrorist threat, which was taking no holiday. Second, I made it clear that we would not tolerate any threat of Iranian incursion violating their territorial integrity. Third, I reinforced our ambassadors' efforts and encouraged regional leaders to be responsive to and inclusive of all their people. I saw all this as buying time for them to make reforms aligned with their societies' carrying capacity.

Cooperation, too, occurs at the speed of trust. I don't know how many tens of thousands of miles I logged during the Arab Spring. Conversations with Arab leaders, civilian or military, usually began with a litany of complaints about American leadership. A common refrain was "We love Americans, and we hate your foreign policy." I think Americans are subject to more lectures about our shortcomings than any other people, because more is expected of us. I listened to my full share. My ironclad rule was to never imply by silence that I agreed with any criticism of the policies of my Commander in Chief. On one visit to a kingdom in the region, after Mubarak had been deposed, the reigning monarch began voicing harsh criticisms of our policies.

"Your Highness," I finally interrupted, "my loyalty is absolute to my country and my Commander in Chief, President Obama. I will not agree by silence when they are criticized. I'm here to help ensure the security of your kingdom. I carry out the last six hundred meters of American policy. Believe me, I know how to do that, and I will do that. Where our interests overlap, your problems are my problems. And I'm here looking for the overlap so I can help."

He sat back and stared at me for a minute while his counselors sat silent. Then he smiled and we had a long and extensive talk. There is no shortcut to taking the time to listen to others and find common ground.

Some responses were refreshing. In the United Arab Emirates, Crown Prince Mohammed bin Zayed and his military were so firm in their commitment to fighting terrorism that we at CENTCOM referred to the UAE as "Little Sparta." When several NATO allies were pulling troops out of Afghanistan due to domestic political pressure, the crown prince sent in more Emirati F-16s and Special Forces, taking the pressure off the U.S. military to backfill the departing forces. Friends like the UAE stood with us when we needed them, even when our country confused or disappointed them. No nation standing alone can sustain its security. When tensions develop between friends, extraordinary effort must be made to keep those friends close. Washington was badgering nations to adopt swifter change to inclusive government without the benefit of candid appraisals from our most knowledgeable diplomats that might have cautioned against moving too fast and derailing the real change that was necessary. Friendly nations that had stood by us grew resistant to reforms they might otherwise have made.

In Jordan, the ever resolute King Abdullah was standing staunchly by us. He assured me he would keep Jordanian soldiers fighting alongside us in Afghanistan. On one occasion, we were meeting alone on his patio discussing what CENTCOM could do to help Jordan with the refugees pouring in from Syria. Always curious, I decided to ask the king about his job.

"What's it like being a king?" I said. "I've never been one."

He laughed and waved his hand at a stack of papers.

"Actually, I've been writing op-eds," he said. "I have to explain to my people why they should vote independently in a way that supports how they judge their best interest . . . I can't just give an order to get things done. I need my people with me."

For those who doubt that reform can happen, here I saw a servant leader in action.

The turbulence from the Arab Spring of 2011 spilled over into the next year. By mid-2012, Syria was in the throes of a bloody civil war, and Libya, next door to Egypt, was in total chaos. Sensing the opportunity, Al Qaeda was on the move in Yemen, while the Taliban were continuing to attack in Afghanistan. Iran was stirring subversion and terrorism throughout the region, from the Mediterranean to the Arabian Sea, while reinforcing Assad's genocidal campaign in Syria. The hope of the Arab Spring had shown itself to be a mirage, disappointing so many.

Secretary Panetta's staff requested that I give an update to a meeting of his Defense Policy Board, a select group of former officials cleared personally by the Secretary of Defense for sensitive classified information. I didn't initiate these sorts of meetings, but I benefited, because I could solicit their wise, discreet advice about broader issues I would not bring up routinely with my subordinates. Former Secretary of Defense James Schlesinger questioned me when I was explaining some force deployments.

"Excuse me," he said, "but I'd like to hear about the larger strategy behind those deployments. Where are we going, and what is the end state?"

Believing we were colleagues addressing the common defense, I replied directly.

"I don't know what our integrated strategy is," I confessed, "or specifically what it is for my region."

Out of two hours of discussion, somehow that quote alone shot directly to the White House, and ricocheted back to the Pentagon, causing severe upset.

Later, when a high-ranking DoD official attempted to chew me out for talking "openly with the chattering class" (a strange description of the Secretary's trusted policy board from one of his own staff), I ignored him. It had become too clear that I was supposed to sit quietly in the back of the bus as it careened off a strategic cliff.

In turbulent times, sound policy and clear strategic principles are especially necessary for achieving our objectives. After they'd stood by us in our time of need after the 9/11 attacks, I didn't want to publicly assail our Middle East friends. With friends, I believe we should praise in public, stating our own values unapologetically, and in private be totally frank about the potential benefits of change. This is the most productive way to allow others to embrace what we propose and represent.

I constantly had to argue with those in our government who wanted human rights to be the singular criterion of our foreign policy. We do not always live up to our ideals. The Arab monarchies and strongman leaders were not reforming at the pace our human rights idealists insisted upon. But those nations that had stood by us after 9/11 had records far better than those of hostile, oppressive regimes like Iran and Syria. Expecting countries with no democratic tradition, only recently coming out from under the yoke of colonialism, to embrace democracy at the level demanded by some in Washington was based on a wholly unrealistic view about the pace of cultural change. We had to be thinking in terms of generations, not months. Pushing change too fast could result in total chaos; better for us to quietly and firmly support a pace of change that would not incite a predictably violent, even volcanic, response—the opposite of what we intended. At the same time, I championed the values America stands for, even when it made our partners uncomfortable. If I wanted them to listen to me, I had to respect their dignity in public. But I'm known for blunt speaking, and I was very blunt—in private.

Public humiliation does not change our friends' behavior or attitudes in a positive way. In international affairs, we have often had to choose between the lesser of two evils, a balance between idealism and pragmatism. It is better to have a friend with deep flaws than an adversary with enduring hostility. We remain convinced of the strengths of our own democratic model. America has two fundamental powers: the power of intimidation toward our adversaries and the power of inspiration toward our friends and like-minded people everywhere. Nothing can inspire others more than our ability to make our own democracy work.

To see what might have happened had the Egyptian military not acquiesced to the will of millions of Egyptians in the streets, we need only look at Syria. In 2011, Sunnis and Kurds—the vast majority in Syria—rose up and demonstrated against the tyrannical rule of the Assad regime. The military, loyal to Assad rather than to the people, fired on unarmed demonstrators and continued with a wholesale slaughter for the rest of that year. Estimates had it that more than a hundred thousand civilians were killed and millions were fleeing.

In the spring of 2012, I visited the refugee camps Jordan had erected for those who had managed to escape. Jordan had been forced to contribute 20 percent of its entire military budget to provide tents and food for 150,000 poor souls who had nothing but the tattered clothes on their backs. In row after row of canvas tents, I saw the human consequences of the Assad regime's brutality. Perhaps two out of every five were wounded. I'd seen refugees in many parts of the world, but never as traumatized as the ones I saw in those camps.

CENTCOM had kept a keen eye on Assad's stockpile of chemical weapons, and we were picking up indications that he was preparing to use them against his own people. As horrific as his murderous crackdown already was, using chemical weapons was even more repugnant. After the awful damage they caused in World War I, even Hitler was unwilling to use them on the battlefield in World War II. Decades earlier, Assad's father had used chemical weapons to put down a revolt. To prevent this from happening again, in August President Obama issued a firm warning. "That's a red line for us," he said. "There would be enormous consequences if we start seeing movement on the chemical weapons front or the use of chemical weapons."

A short time later, Assad did employ chemical weapons, killing hundreds of civilians. Obviously, the President's warning had not impressed the murderous dictator. At CENTCOM, I had assumed we would be the ones to provide the President's "enormous consequence." We prepared options to hold Assad harshly accountable, with NATO and Arab allies in support, from single strikes to more extensive operations, depending on the President's judgment. We were ready, and I awaited the orders.

Instead, the President decided not to strike. We never responded militarily. This was a shot not heard around the world. Old friends in NATO and in the Pacific registered dismay and incredulity that America's reputation had been seriously weakened as a credible security partner. Within thirty-six hours, I received a phone call from a friendly Pacific-nation diplomat. "Well, Jim," he said, "I guess we're on our own with China."

"Dynamite in the hands of a child," Winston Churchill wrote, "is not more dangerous than a strong policy weakly carried out." Over the next several years, Syria totally disintegrated into hell on earth. The consequences included an accelerated refugee flow that changed the political culture of Europe, punctuated by repeated terrorist attacks. And America today lives with the consequences of emboldened adversaries and shaken allies.

From my first day at CENTCOM, I knew we faced two principal adversaries: stateless Sunni Islamist terrorists and the revolutionary Shiite regime of Iran, the most destabilizing country in the region. Iran was by far the more deadly of the two threats. Its fanatical leadership class, the mullahs, had the revolutionary fervor and the intellectual, industrial, economic, and natural resources to develop nuclear weapons and intercontinental missiles while funding terror activities around the world. For more than three decades, the Iranian regime had been America's implacable enemy. I had to deal with the polarities of keeping an unsteady peace while responding to active Iranian operations against us and our friends in the region. Linchpins such as Saudi Arabia, Israel, Jordan, the UAE, and Bahrain kept a wary eye on Iran. But America's erratic response to the Arab Spring and the nonresponse to Assad's crossing our self-imposed "red line" had shaken their confidence. I heard constant concerns that America was acquiescing to Iranian hegemony.

My job was to provide options for the President, and we conducted frequent war games, testing moves versus countermoves. As the strategist Rear Admiral J. C. Wylie had written, "Nobody other than God can consistently predict the onset, scope, tenor, intensity, course, and consequences of any war. Requirements therefore exist for a rucksack full of plans . . . because planning for certitude is the most grievous of all . . . mistakes." My rucksack had plans that would give the President options to ensure the fewest major regrets if a crisis struck.

My deputy at CENTCOM, Vice Admiral Bob Harward, had grown up in Iran and was fluent in Farsi. We both considered the Iranian theocracy to be cunning and hostile—a malign force that exported mayhem and took advantage of any turmoil. Assad, with his Baathist regime in Syria, was Iran's sole ally in the Middle East. Iranian cargo aircraft routinely flew across Iraqi airspace to land at Damascus. From there, supplies were shipped overland into Lebanon, where the Iran-backed Hezbollah militia maintained a state of war against Israel. For decades, Iran was the principal state sponsor of terrorism in the Middle East, and between 2004 and 2009 the regime's Republican Guards sent assassination teams into Iraq and provided the explosive devices that killed or wounded more than six hundred American troops. The regime shipped weapons and explosives to all corners of the region—Bahrain, Yemen, Gaza, Saudi Arabia, and beyond. They renamed a Tehran street in honor of the man who assassinated Egyptian President Sadat.

. . .

On the evening of October 11, 2011, the duty officer at my head-quarters in Tampa informed me that the Attorney General and the Director of the FBI had just held a press conference. They announced the arrest of two Iranians who were plotting to bomb the Cafe Milano, an upscale restaurant in Washington, D.C. They intended to assassinate the ambassador from Saudi Arabia, who would be dining there among the hundreds of American and foreign citizens who crowd Georgetown every night.

Attorney General Eric Holder said the bombing plot was "directed and approved by elements of the Iranian government and, specifically, senior members of the Qods Force." The Qods were the Special Operations Force of the Revolutionary Guards, reporting to the top of the Iranian government. I saw the intelligence: we had recorded Tehran's approval of the operation. I was puzzled why CENTCOM hadn't been informed beforehand. For America, this wasn't solely a local law enforcement matter; Iran had intended to commit an act of war. Had the bomb gone off, those in the restaurant and on the street would have been ripped apart, blood rushing down sewer drains. It would have been the worst attack on us since 9/11. I sensed that only Iran's impression of America's impotence could have led them to risk such an act within a couple of miles of the White House. Ambassadors are men and women of peace, and even nations at war have traditionally protected them. Absent one fundamental mistake—the terrorists had engaged an undercover DEA agent in an attempt to smuggle the bomb—the Iranians would have pulled off this devastating attack. Had that bomb exploded, it would have changed history.

I believed we had to respond forcefully. My military options would raise the cost for this attack beyond anything the mullahs and the Qods generals could pay. First, though, the President had to go before the American people and forcefully lay out the enormous savagery of the intended attack. The American public—and the global public—had to understand the gravity of the plot.

In March 1917, President Wilson received, via British intelligence, a copy of a telegram sent by German Foreign Secretary Arthur Zimmermann to the president of Mexico. It proposed a wartime alliance between their two countries against the United States, dangling to Mexico the offer of seizing parts of Texas and California. Outraged, Wilson publicized the telegram to alert and mobilize the public. Congress responded by arming U.S. merchant ships against German submarines. Public sentiment turned decisively against Germany. In my judgment, the Zimmermann Telegram provided a clear precedent.

I proposed to the Pentagon that we reprise the Zimmermann moment. As President Wilson had done, so too should President Obama go before the American public, lay out the evidence, denounce the Iranian regime, and hold it to account.

America had done this before. In 1988, a U.S. Navy frigate struck a mine in the Persian Gulf. The evidence pointed to Iran. There were no fatalities, but Admiral William Crowe, the Chairman of the Joint Chiefs of Staff, argued for retaliating by sinking an Iranian warship. They had gone too far. He wrote, "We have to let Tehran know that we are willing to exact a serious price." A week later, we bombed and destroyed three Iranian oil platforms after alerting the crews to evacuate. Iran, cowed, halted its misbehavior for a time.

But Washington was not interested in my Zimmermann analogy. We treated an act of war as a law enforcement violation, jailing the low-level courier. Several months later, I was in Tampa conducting CENTCOM's annual war game. This was the only time each year that staff members from the Pentagon, State, and the White House participated. A few days later, *The Washington Post* reported about the war game. The story was picked up, and additional particulars about the game were published in several newspapers. I was chastised, on the assumption that CENTCOM had leaked the war game. Call me crazy, but if the only time our planning leaked was when we included Washington, I'd bet my paycheck the leak came from the banks of the Potomac River. At CENTCOM, we stayed loyal and kept our mouths shut.

This accusation of a leak came on top of my urging that we expose Iran with a Zimmermann moment and did not raise my popularity inside the White House. But at CENTCOM, I had to deal with an Iran that continued to provoke. In June 2012, Iranian gunboats captured a British Royal Navy small craft. Iranian leaders struck a bellicose tone. Rear Admiral Ali Fadavi of the Iranian Revolutionary Guard Corps boasted, "We determine the rules of military conflict in the Persian Gulf and the Strait of Hormuz." That was nonsense. The strait is globally recognized as international waters. Forty percent of the globally traded oil is shipped through those straits. If that oil was taken off the market, our economy would suffer dramatically and immediately.

The aggressive actions and cavalier remarks of the Iranian military had my full attention. You're not the sentinel for your unit if you don't react to warning signals as clear as that one. I notified the Pentagon that I intended to hold an international naval mine-clearing exercise in the Gulf.

My Fifth Fleet commander invited other like-minded nations to join in the exercise. I anticipated that a half dozen navies might participate. Instead, twenty-nine nations came on board. Every continent except Antarctica was represented. Iran stayed well clear of the exercise. For years afterward there was no more talk out of Tehran about mining international sea lanes. This was a good example of a military action supporting our foreign policy and the economic interests of our allies. Only one navy in the world, the U.S. Fifth Fleet, forward deployed in the region, had both the capability and the trust of so many nations to draw together such an international response.

A few months later, the Iranian regime tested us in a different space. An Iranian fighter aircraft attacked an American drone in international airspace over the Gulf. The pilot was a terrible shot, missing on repeated tries captured on the drone's video. I proposed to Washington that we launch another drone on the same track, position a few F-18 aircraft out of sight, and shoot down the Iranian aircraft if it attacked the drone. The White House refused to grant permission.

"I could sense Mattis did not want to back down," Secretary Panetta later wrote in his memoir, "and that the White House was wary of his resolve. As I knew already, the White House didn't fully trust Mattis, regarding him as too eager for a military confrontation with Iran."

I wanted calculated actions, to restrain the regime so it couldn't thrust us into a war. If you allow yourself to be goaded and trifled with, one of two things will happen: eventually a harder, larger fight will explode, or you will get moved out of the neighborhood.

Secretary Panetta understood this point, but it took all his persuasive power to eventually convince the White House to respond. I sent another drone into international airspace—escorted by two of our fighters. The Iranian aircraft stayed on the ground. Yet once again the Iranians had not been held to account, and I anticipated that they would feel emboldened to challenge us more in the future.

The radical Iranian regime's leaders meant it when they led chants of "death to America" and proclaimed that Israel must be wiped out. Iran's terrorist and belligerent activities were ongoing every day. In my view, we had to hold Iran to account and strike back when attacked. But there was a reason for the administration's restraint. The administration was secretly negotiating with Iran, although I was not privy to the details at the time. What emerged was that if Iran agreed to time-phased restrictions on its nuclear program, Europe and America would lift their sanctions. Eventually that deal was publicly ratified, but without the advice and consent of the Senate. In my military judgment, America had undertaken a poorly calculated, long-shot gamble. At the same time, the administration was lecturing our Arab friends that they had to accommodate Iran as if it were a moderate neighbor in the region and not an enemy committed to their destruction. As long as its leaders consider Iran less a nation-state than a revolutionary cause, Iran will remain a terrorist threat potentially more dangerous than Al Qaeda or ISIS.

My traction inside the White House was eroding. It was no secret in Washington that the White House was wary of my command at CENTCOM and increasingly distrusted me. While I fully endorse civilian control of the military, I would not surrender my independent judgment. In 2010, I argued strongly against pulling all our troops out of Iraq. In 2011, I urged retaliation against Iran for plotting to blow up a restaurant in our nation's capital. In 2012, I argued for retaining a small but capable contingent of troops in Afghanistan. Each step along the way, I argued for political clarity and offered options that gave the Commander in Chief a rheostat he could dial up or down to protect our nation. While I had the right to be heard on military matters, my judgment was only advice, to be accepted or ignored. I obeyed without mental reservation our elected Commander in Chief and carried out every order to the best of my ability.

In December 2012, I received an unauthorized phone call telling me that in an hour, the Pentagon would be announcing my relief. I was leaving a region aflame and in disarray. The lack of an integrated regional strategy had left us adrift, and our friends confused. We were offering no leadership or direction. I left my post deeply disturbed that we had shaken our friends' confidence and created vacuums that our adversaries would exploit.

I was disappointed and frustrated that policymakers all too often failed to deliver clear direction. And lacking a defined mission statement, I frequently didn't know what I was expected to accomplish. As American naval strategist Alfred Mahan wrote, "If the strategy be wrong, the skill of the general on the battlefield, the valor of the soldier, the brilliancy of victory, however otherwise decisive, fail of their effect."

Under our form of government, the President is our Commander in Chief and must be the sentinel for our nation's future generations. This calls for a strategy both embraced by the American people and inclusive of our allies. History is not some great, inanimate river determining its own unchangeable course down the centuries. As President Truman, the great builder of the post–World War II order, put it, "Men make history; history doesn't make the man."

We've fought wars that we should have avoided, and half-heartedly engaged in wars that needed to be won. But we can recover our strategic footing, if we don't squander opportunities to strengthen the international order that is in the best interest of all nations seeking peace and stability on the world stage. America has more tools than its military and CIA to draw upon. In league with our allies, our economic strengths and our use of traditional diplomatic practices can reduce the militarization of our foreign policy. Unilateralism will not work, and we must craft an integrated, multidimensional strategy that incorporates America's deepest wells of power.

Policies can change based on political goals established by our elected leaders. Yet those goals must remain realistic and coherent if they are to enable an achievable strategy. Any war, even a war of limited political ends, must be fully resourced for its mission. Acting strategically requires that political leaders make clear what they will stand for and what they will *not* stand for. We must mean what we say, to both allies and foes: no more false threats or failing to live up to our word. Yesterday, today, and tomorrow, the decision of going to war is too great a matter to stumble into or to half-step toward once the decision is taken.

CHAPTER 17

Reflections

LETHALITY AS THE METRIC

History presents many examples of militaries that forgot that their purpose was to fight and win. So long as we live in an imperfect world, one containing enemies of democracy, we will need a military strictly committed to combat-effectiveness. Our liberal democracy must be protected by a bodyguard of lethal warriors, organized, trained, and equipped to dominate in battle.

The military is all about teamwork. Everyone enters the military at junior rank and rises according to merit. Our legacy of teamwork is rich in precedents. In 1804, black and white men and a Native American woman all voted as equals on the Army's long-range reconnaissance patrol known as the Lewis and Clark expedition. They had reached the headwaters of the Columbia River, north of my hometown in Washington, and had to decide whether to risk crossing against a strong current. They were all literally in the same boats together, so they worked as a team for their common survival.

For me, direct leadership was all about preparing my troops to win in close-quarters combat. When you go into battle, you enter a different world. I set out to engrain in every grunt an aggressive spirit and confidence in winning. "Whatever we learn to do, we learn by actually doing it," Aristotle wrote. "People come to be builders, for instance, by building, and harp players, by playing the harp. In the same way, by doing just acts we come to be just. By doing self-controlled acts, we come to be self-controlled, and by doing brave acts, we become brave." Courage as an act of self-discipline can be infused by coaching a team until every member acquires the skills to have and to share confidence. Group spirit binds warriors together in a necessary way that keeps them distinct from the civilian society they are sworn to protect.

The need for lethality must be the measuring stick against which we evaluate the efficacy of our military. By aligning the entire military enterprise—recruiting, training, educating, equipping, and promoting—to the goal of compounding lethality, we best deter adversaries or, if conflict occurs, win at lowest cost to our troops' lives. The next bullet doesn't care who it strikes, yet troops charge onto battlefields. When I meet with Gold Star families, I feel that all the fallen were my sons and daughters. They deserve more than "Thank you for your service."

Politicians should not arbitrarily change how the services are organized to fight. We no longer use conscription, so our volunteers who sign a blank check payable with their lives must be given every opportunity to return home. Those who choose to not serve, and especially those in civilian oversight roles, must show reserve in directing social changes inside our military. They need to listen to those senior officers and NCOs who know how to compose warfighting organizations. Our military exists to deter wars and to win when we fight. We are not a petri dish for social experiments. No one is exempt from studying warfighting and lethality as the dominant metric, and nothing that decreases the lethality of our forces should be forced on a military that will go into harm's way.

I have seen no case where weakness promotes the chance for peace. A Kipling passage comes to mind about a peace-seeking man (the lama) and an old soldier.

> "It is not a good fancy," said the lama. "What profit to kill men?"
>
> "Very little—as I know," [the old soldier replied,] "but if evil men were not now and then slain it would not be a good world for weaponless dreamers."

THE ART OF LEADING

My warfighting style simply represents the Marine Corps way of war. It stems from a Corps that cannot stomach defeat, even when landed on hostile shores with the enemy to the front and the ocean at its back. It's a naval force limited in its fighting philosophy to what the ships can carry, so it cannot rely on overwhelming numbers or heavy equipment. It's a force that integrates skill, courage, cunning, and initiative into its own form of maneuver warfare, maneuver that takes form in the intellectual, physical, and spiritual realms.

It's well known among Marines that our greatest honor is fighting alongside our fellow sailors and Marines. I know that our soldiers, airmen, and Coast Guardsmen feel the same. No Marine is ever alone—he carries with him the spirit passed down from generations before him. Group spirit—that electric force field of emotion—infuses and binds warriors together. If we're not on the front line, then we're supporting the nineteen-year-old infantryman who is. The Corps recognizes that its success comes ultimately from those on the leading edge. This was the reason I felt misgivings upon each promotion. While I could take some satisfaction that I'd met the standard of promotion, I believed I could not do my job well if I lost touch with those on the front lines who carried out orders at the point of danger.

To turn this broader Marine philosophy of fighting into my own authentic leadership style, I drew upon historical influences and the Vietnam veterans whose experiences imparted a healthy dose of reality. I had been shaped and sharpened by the rough whetstone of those veterans, mentored by sergeants and captains who had slogged through rice paddies and jungles, fighting a tough enemy every foot of the way. I learned then and I believe now that everyone needs a mentor or to be a mentor—and that no one needs a tyrant. At the same time, there's no substitute for constant study to master one's craft. Living in history builds your own shock absorber, because you'll learn that there are lots of old solutions to new problems. If you haven't read hundreds of books, learning from others who went before you, you are functionally illiterate—you can't coach and you can't lead. History lights the often dark path ahead; even if it's a dim light, it's better than none. If you can't be additive as a leader, you're just like a potted plant in the corner of a hotel lobby: you look pretty, but you're not adding substance to the organization's mission.

From the classrooms of Quantico to the training fields to the battlefields, I winnowed information to what proved most beneficial in coming to grips with war's realities. From a leader's perspective, intent is the starting point. "Commander's intent" has a special meaning in the military that requires time and thought. A commander must state his relevant aim. Intent is a formal statement in which the commander puts himself or herself on the line. Intent must accomplish the mission, it has to be achievable, it must be clearly understood, and at the end of the day, it has to deliver what the unit was tasked with achieving. Your moral authority as a commander is heavily dependent on the quality of this guidance and your troops' sense of confidence in it: the expectation that they will use their initiative, aligning subordinate actions. You must unleash initiative rather than suffocate it.

If I were to sum up the leadership techniques I constructed on the basis of the Marine Corps's bias for action, it would be simple: once I set the tempo, the speed I prized was always built on subordinate initiative. This governing principle drove home the underlying efforts that would make speed a reality. Speed is essential, whether in sports, business, or combat, because time is the least forgiving, least recoverable factor in any competitive situation. I learned to prize smooth execution by cohesive teams (those that could adapt swiftly to battlefield shocks) over deliberate, methodical, and synchronized efforts that I saw squelching subordinate initiative. In fact it was *always* subordinate initiative that got my lads out of the jams I got them into, my mistakes being my own.

Such initiative must be specifically rewarded throughout any organization. In my chosen field, the military, this starts by mastering the art and science of war so well that we know when to part with doctrine, which serves only as a start point for decision-making. Like a jazzman with the ability to improvise, you need to know doctrine so that you can shift from a known point.

Mastering the art and science of war also means understanding strategy and planning. Strategy is hard, unless you're a dilettante. You must think until your head hurts. I always stress how to enlarge the competitive space to solve problems. Planning, which is simply another word for anticipatory decision-making, is equally rigorous and, in war, is a constant, never-ending process.

Eventually reaching high rank, I made extra efforts to maintain my connection to those who made the difference in the formations that would close with and destroy our adversaries. The spiritual connection was built on my memory of what it was like for those who would step into enemy minefields or patrol the contested ground where lives were on the line. That connection was essential as I worked to balance risk and avoid gambling with their lives on the tactical and operational levels. I was less successful at persuasively arguing against strategic gambles.

Boiled down to its essence, only battlefield harmony could summon the speed I was looking for in order to shatter the enemy. This harmony demanded clearly articulated intentions from senior levels, reinterpreted at each echelon to make it relevant to their part of the effort. With a commander's aim clearly understood down through the ranks, synergy of effort can be constantly maintained, from the senior ranks—where it is no less needed—down to the youngest troops on the front lines and deck plates. In the framework of this book, that means from the direct or tactical level all the way to the strategic.

I used "touchstones" such as "No better friend, no worse enemy" and "First, do no harm," among others, leavened with history's enduring lessons, to guide subordinates who would face situations requiring them to make instantaneous decisions on their feet. I often chose phrases from antiquity, purposely using broad themes and objectives, leaving maximum opportunity for subordinates to use their initiative and aggressiveness. Clearly stating the operation's purpose and sparsely outlining the methods we'd used, I closed my intent by explaining our desired end state.

But I was not just addressing their tactical thinking: I was also appealing to their spiritual side: Intangibles like will, cohesion, morale, and affection are more important than tangibles. I strove to be the opposite of the château general. By conveying my intent in writing and in person, I was out to win their coequal "ownership" of the mission: it wasn't my mission; rather from private through general, it was our mission. I stressed to my staff that we had to win only one battle: for the hearts and minds of our subordinates. They will win all the rest—at the risk and cost of their lives. Once the intent was clearly conveyed, the mission was left in the hands of our junior officers and NCOs, and their animating spirits coached our troops to achieving my aim.

Trust is the coin of the realm for creating the harmony, speed, and teamwork to achieve success at the lowest cost. Trusted personal relationships are the foundation for effective fighting teams, whether on the playing field, the boardroom, or the battlefield. When the spirit of your team is on the line and the stakes are high, confidence in the integrity and commitment of those around you will enable boldness and resolution; a lack of trust will see brittle, often tentative execution of even the best-laid plans. Nothing compensates for a lack of trust. Lacking trust, your unit will pay a steep price in combat.

Yet it's not enough to trust your people; you must be able to convey that trust in a manner that subordinates can sense. Only then can you fully garner the benefits. From mission-type orders that left subordinates with freedom of action to declining to take detailed briefs if I thought it would remove subordinate commanders' sense of ownership over their own operations, my coaching style exhibited confidence in juniors I knew were ready to take charge. I had also found, in Tora Bora's missed opportunity to prevent Osama bin Laden's escape, that I had to build awareness and trust above me. This takes significant personal effort, and the information age has not made this easier or removed the need for face-to-face interaction.

I found staff visits and daily or weekly visits—reducing reports and getting out more to see units on their turf—essential to building trust. And "hand-con," maintaining relationships, takes time to build, and can be lost in a second—and you may not get a chance to get it back. High morale is reflected by the absence of self-pity. Resourceful leaders do not lose touch with their troops. A leader's job is to inculcate high-spirited, amiable self-discipline. Leaders must always generate options by surrounding themselves with bright subordinates and being catalysts for new ideas.

Command and feedback is a fundamentally different approach than imposing command and control for coordinating teams to work optimally. Critical to the command and feedback approach is the speed of information sharing and decentralizing decision-making. While having commanders physically forward with the troops is important, commanders cannot be everywhere, even while their influence must permeate the entire organization. This meant that imaging the troops in advance through potential upsets and decision points allowed them to anticipate what they must take in stride. Using "eyes" officers to supplement reporting from field commanders locked in combat, we turned out decisions faster than our adversary, permitting us to turn inside the enemy's decision loop. When I fight an enemy, my frontline troops quickly sense enemy strengths and weaknesses. Taking immediate advantage of an enemy's misstep is essential, and the resulting feedback allows an organization's decisions and actions to outpace those of the enemy. But for all this, decentralized decision-making ultimately gave us the edge.

We can decentralize decision-making and gain relative speed over the enemy, however, only if conditions are set to enable subordinate success. Where decisions are decentralized, subordinate-unit-leader discipline must be of a higher level than when decisions are made solely at senior levels. This is due to the need for aligning independent decisions in a concert of actions. The glue aligning these decisions is the commander's clearly articulated intent, firmly setting the operation's aim.

The other necessary condition is the education and training of the subordinate leaders to ensure they have the skills necessary to take intelligent initiative. Various techniques for mental imaging proved enormously useful to ensuring that my intent was widely comprehended. After all, subordinate leaders are as likely as senior officers to make bad calls if they are not properly prepared for the increased responsibility. Training to enable "brilliance in the basics" and educating junior leaders to make sense out of the unexpected (as friction, uncertainty, and ambiguity are war's elementals and nothing ever goes according to plan) are the down payment for subordinate initiative. Only with sufficient investment can an organization expect, even demand, subordinate initiative as the price for attaining a leadership position.

As we rise in rank, our teams are more broadly composed. Multi-service and multinational teams are the norm in our current reality. As organizational complexity grows, I've found that the same leadership principles endure for creating the best teams. Clarity of intent actually becomes more critical when the formative experiences of those on your team are dissimilar. When national caveats reduce (or even remove) command authority over allied nations' militaries sharing the battlefield, persuasive commander's intent and a willingness to adapt one's plans are critical to the success of the mission, taking full advantage of what other nations can do instead of focusing on what they cannot.

We sometimes find that we've grown organizations with echelons that have outlived their value. Allowing bad processes to stump good people is intolerable. When the utility of certain staff or command echelons is lacking, they slow down decisions and can paralyze execution, allowing the adversary to dance around the methodical, process-driven approach. Skip-echelon will generally work to restore the speed of decisions and agility; if not, removing entire organizations can clear the pipes. By employing skip-echelon when a staff function did not add value and displaying only critical data, we can achieve alignment and transparency with less internal friction. While I could never reduce internal friction to zero, I enjoyed the challenge of reducing it to the greatest degree possible.

While processes are boring to examine, leaders must know their own well enough that they can master them and not be mastered, even derailed, by them. In competitive situations, a faster operating tempo than your adversary's is a distinct asset. A smoothly operating team can more swiftly move through the observe/orient/decide/act loop, multiplying the effectiveness of its numbers. Left untouched, processes imposed by unneeded echelons will marginalize subordinate audacity.

Robust feedback loops enabled our operations, but we could continue operating even if feedback was interrupted: our momentum was directed onward by the commander's intent in place of "synchronization" matrixes, which I found slowed operations once we met the enemy and the usual emergencies cropped up. All hands had to be thinking all the time: *What do I know? Who needs to know? Have I told them?* Additionally, by reducing the size of headquarters staffs, we reduced demands for information flow from subordinate units, which could then principally focus on the enemy rather than answering higher headquarters' queries.

In the same spirit, any competitive organization must nurture its maverick thinkers. You can't wash them out of your outfit if you want to avoid being surprised by your competition. Without mav-

ericks, we are more likely to find ourselves at the same time dominant and irrelevant, as the enemy steals a march on us. Further,
calculated risk taking is elemental to staying at the top of our competitive game. Risk aversion will damage the long-term health,
even survival, of the organization, because it will undercut disciplined but unregimented thinking. Because maverick thinkers are
so important to an organization's adaptability, high-ranking leaders need to be assigned the job of guiding and even protecting them,
much as one would do for any endangered species.

Leaders at all ranks, but especially at high ranks, must keep in
their inner circle people who will unhesitatingly point out when a
leader's personal behavior or decisions are not appropriate. In its
own way, this too is part of command and feedback, for none of us
are infallible. Further, the significant authority granted to military
officers requires officers to practice command over themselves, and
that is enhanced by maintaining a counterbalance to the obedience
required to conduct military operations in high-stress environments. As a full general commanding NATO's transformation efforts, I had a Hellenic Navy commander who kept me on the
straight and narrow. At U.S. Central Command with hundreds of
thousands of troops assigned to me, I had in my command group a
U.S. Army Ranger sergeant major and a U.S. Navy admiral who
didn't give a damn what I thought of them: if they thought that I
had made a bad call, with door closed they would quickly make
their point loud and clear. I trusted them to do this, and they never
let me down. Knowing that my own approach to decisions was not
foolproof, they saved me on more instances than I can recall from
walking into minefields of my own making.

THE NEED FOR ALLIES

I've had the privilege to fight for our country in many places. Not
once did I fight in a solely American formation. I fought repeatedly
alongside allies and partners. It should be a source of pride for all
Americans that if we have an "empire," it has been an empire of
ideas and ideals sufficient to draw many like-minded nations to our
side. The World War II generation is referred to as our Greatest
Generation because they defeated fascism, and had it seared into
them that while we may not like everything that happens beyond

our borders, our freedom is inextricably tied to the global situation. They then acted to secure a better peace.

History is determined by choices made. America's record is exceptional, despite some notable lapses. After World War II, instead of turning isolationist as we had following World War I, we facilitated the reintegration of Germany and Japan into the community of nations. In a remarkable display of bipartisanship, Democrats and Republicans pulled together for America to invest, via the Marshall Plan, in the economic resurgence of an impoverished Western Europe. We stabilized the international financial system. We entered the North Atlantic Treaty, pledging to defend our European allies against the Soviet threat, even at the risk of a hundred million dead Americans in a nuclear war. The growth in global wealth and the freedoms enjoyed by so many since 1945 were the direct results of America's willingness to lead. You have to go a long way to find a country more willing to admit its mistakes, listen to its friends, and correct its ways.

History is compelling. Nations with allies thrive, and those without wither. Alone, America cannot provide protection for our people and our economy. At this time, we can see storm clouds gathering. By drawing like-minded nations into trusted networks and promoting a climate of victory that bolsters allied morale, we can best promote the values we hold dear and protect our nation at the lowest cost. A polemicist's role is not sufficient for a leader; strategic acumen must incorporate a fundamental respect for other nations that have stood with us when trouble loomed. In our past, America has offered the example of coming together to prevent or win wars. Returning to a strategic stance that includes the interests of as many nations as we can make common cause with, we can better deal with this imperfect world we occupy together. Absent this, we will occupy an increasingly lonely position, one that puts us at increasing risk in a world that as George Shultz said, is "awash in change."

It never dawned on me that I would serve again in a government post after retiring from active duty. But the phone call came; I went to Bedminster and then in front of the Senate. On a Saturday morning in late January 2017, I walked into the Secretary of Defense's office, which I had first entered as a colonel on staff twenty years earlier. Using every skill I had learned during my decades as a Marine, I did as well as I could for as long as I could. Over the 712 days I served as Secretary, we drafted the first defense strategy in a decade, gained bipartisan support for a budget to implement that strategy, adopted unpredictable deployment schedules to confuse our adversaries, accelerated the destruction of ISIS's geographic caliphate, and worked to reassure allies of our steadfast support.

The other occupant of that office who'd required a waiver, as I did, for insufficient time out of uniform was General George C. Marshall. "Problems which bear directly on the future of our civilization cannot be disposed of by general talk or vague formulae—by what Lincoln called 'pernicious abstractions,'" he stated. "They require concrete solutions for definite and extremely complicated questions." When my concrete solutions and strategic advice, especially keeping faith with allies, no longer resonated, it was time to resign, despite the limitless joy I felt serving alongside our troops in defense of our Constitution.

SECRETARY OF DEFENSE
1000 DEFENSE PENTAGON
WASHINGTON, DC 20301-1000

December 20, 2018

Dear Mr. President:

I have been privileged to serve as our country's 26th Secretary of Defense which has allowed me to serve alongside our men and women of the Department in defense of our citizens and our ideals.

I am proud of the progress that has been made over the past two years on some of the key goals articulated in our National Defense Strategy: putting the Department on a more sound budgetary footing, improving readiness and lethality in our forces, and reforming the Department's business practices for greater performance. Our troops continue to provide the capabilities needed to prevail in conflict and sustain strong U.S. global influence.

One core belief I have always held is that our strength as a nation is inextricably linked to the strength of our unique and comprehensive system of alliances and partnerships. While the US remains the indispensable nation in the free world, we cannot protect our interests or serve that role effectively without maintaining strong alliances and showing respect to those allies. Like you, I have said from the beginning that the armed forces of the United States should not be the policeman of the world. Instead, we must use all tools of American power to provide for the common defense, including providing effective leadership to our alliances. NATO's 29 democracies demonstrated that strength in their commitment to fighting alongside us following the 9-11 attack on America. The Defeat-ISIS coalition of 74 nations is further proof.

Similarly, I believe we must be resolute and unambiguous in our approach to those countries whose strategic interests are increasingly in tension with ours. It is clear that China and Russia, for example, want to shape a world consistent with their authoritarian model – gaining veto authority over other nations' economic, diplomatic, and security decisions – to promote their own interests at the expense of their neighbors, America and our allies. That is why we must use all the tools of American power to provide for the common defense.

My views on treating allies with respect and also being clear-eyed about both malign actors and strategic competitors are strongly held and informed by over four decades of immersion in these issues. We must do everything possible to advance an international order that is most conducive to our security, prosperity and values, and we are strengthened in this effort by the solidarity of our alliances.

Because you have the right to have a Secretary of Defense whose views are better aligned with yours on these and other subjects, I believe it is right for me to step down from my position. The end date for my tenure is February 28, 2019, a date that should allow sufficient time for a successor to be nominated and confirmed as well as to make sure the Department's interests are properly articulated and protected at upcoming events to include Congressional posture hearings and the NATO Defense Ministerial meeting in February. Further, that a full transition to a new Secretary of Defense occurs well in advance of the transition of Chairman of the Joint Chiefs of Staff in September in order to ensure stability within the Department.

I pledge my full effort to a smooth transition that ensures the needs and interests of the 2.15 million Service Members and 732,079 DoD civilians receive undistracted attention of the Department at all times so that they can fulfill their critical, round-the-clock mission to protect the American people.

I very much appreciate this opportunity to serve the nation and our men and women in uniform.

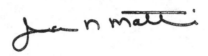

EPILOGUE

America as
Its Own Ally

U NLIKE IN THE PAST, where we were unified and drew in allies, currently our own commons seems to be breaking apart. What concerns me most as a military man, coming out of a diverse yet unified culture, is not our external adversaries; instead, it is our internal divisiveness. We are dividing into hostile tribes cheering against each other, fueled by emotion and a mutual disdain that jeopardizes our future, instead of rediscovering our common ground and finding solutions. At Gettysburg, Lincoln spoke of our nation having a new birth of freedom. Today's disruptive civic climate would confound and sadden the Great Emancipator.

Toward the end of the Marjah battle in 2010, I encountered a Marine and a Navy corpsman, both sopping wet, having just cooled off by relaxing in the adjacent irrigation ditch. I gave them my usual: "How's it going, young men?"

"Living the dream, sir!" the Marine shouted.

"No Maserati, no problem," the sailor added with a smile.

Their nonchalance and good cheer, even as they lived one day at a time under austere conditions, reminded me how unimportant are many of the things back home that can divide us if we let them.

I believe that I and all Americans need to recognize that our democracy is an experiment—and one that can be reversed. I'm all for vigorous debate and vociferous disagreements, grounded in consistent democratic principles and mutual respect. I've developed a love affair with our Constitution. Its purpose, as stated in the preamble, includes, to "insure domestic tranquility [and] promote the general welfare." We all know that we're better than our current politics. Tribalism need not disrupt our experiment.

I'm not singling out one political party. As a military professional, I'm proud that no one knows for whom I vote, and equally proud that I served loyally Presidents of both parties. I was eased out of one job under one party and left another job under the other. I'm politically independent, guided by history's lessons and strategic imperatives.

After he lost his son Robert in Afghanistan, my friend and colleague in arms, General John Kelly, said, "I think the one thing [the parents of the fallen] would ask is that the cause for which their son or daughter fell be carried through to a successful end, whatever that means, as opposed to 'This is getting too costly,' or 'Too much of a pain in the ass,' or 'Let's just walk away from it.' They were willing to go where the nation's leaders told them to go and in many cases gave their lives for the mission. They were willing to see it through literally to their ends. Can we do less?"

Few among our citizenry choose to be warriors. They are our thin red line. No policymaker should ever send them into battle until he has assessed the risks and costs, and is reasonably confident of achieving a clear goal.

I believe that we can get over our current malaise of tribalism. On every coin we've imprinted "E pluribus unum." Out of many, one. That was the motto our forefathers adopted to avoid becoming a nation of immigrants divided into tribes. For the sake of future generations, let us keep the faith.

E pluribus unum.

APPENDIX A

Lieutenant General R. B. Johnston, USMC
Commanding General
I Marine Expeditionary Force

Dear General Johnston:

    I served as the Battalion Commander of 1st Battalion, 7th Marines from February 1990 until June 1991. I am writing to express my extreme disappointment with the performance of the MEF Awards Board in its downgrading of awards I submitted on my men. I am at a loss to determine how else to bring my concerns to your attention other than to lay out the situation and send this via General Myatt. From my meager perspective, there is every reason for concern that the Awards Board is not serving your best interest, nor is it meeting the needs of your subordinate commanders and men. I appeal to you to reconsider several specific cases of downgraded awards.

    To set the general background for these men's actions, I will characterize 1/7's situation as it developed during the Southwest Asia commitment. Nearing the end of a month-long deployment to Bridgeport, the battalion returned to 29 Palms on short notice (6-7 August 1990). Twelve days later we were the first element of 7th MEB to dig in astride the Kuwait Highway. I am sure you recall the uncertainty, heat and challenges of those early days. Throughout September, October and November we served in the desert with occasional breaks for Marines to clean up in oil worker barracks. In the field, the men lived under spartan conditions, sleeping on the ground and, commencing in December, we had no respites in rear areas. The physical cost to our men was obvious over this time; I was by no means unique in my loss of 23 pounds.

    As part of Task Force Ripper, our men moved unhesitantly to breach the two obstacle belts. They were not dismayed by the loss of two of our tanks to mines and incoming artillery during the breach of the second belt which wounded two of my men. The Marines were magnificently led by my subordinate leaders, killing the Iraqis who fought us while shepherding out of danger those who wished to surrender. For example, Captain Bob Hathaway, a mature reflective officer in his second war, led Company A, cross-attached to 3d Tank Battalion. I knew his calm courage would steady his young men. I was totally satisfied at the alacrity with which they moved against the Iraqis, rushing through the breaches on the heels of the gun companies.

    While under fire at the second belt, my fire support coordinator, Captain Jim Horr, coolly shifted our artillery fire to the Emir's Farm. Subsequently, we attacked to clear the Farm during which I gave Captain Horr control of the battalion in order for me to move to where I could best command the attack. Captain Horr performed superbly controlling the fire and maneuver and I recommended him for the Bronze Star. His award was downgraded to a Navy Commendation Medal by the MEF Awards Board.

The danger faced by all my officers and men in the smokey, mine littered battlefield as Iraqi artillery and tank fire was ever present recalls to me that this was not an easy task and I counted on the courage of all hands.

As Ripper moved on towards Al Jaber, my battalion covered the open right flank. As enemy tanks and vehicles appeared out of the Burqan Oil Field's dense smoke, the individuals most responsible for my security were Captain Don Schutt (FAC), in a vehicle equipped with a laser spotter and First Lieutenant Fran Fitzpatrick, who served throughout as my "eyes" on the continually threatened right flank. They ignored all danger and operated consistently from vulnerable locations in order to direct highly effective Cobra fire on the enemy and to keep me informed. I recommended Captain Schutt for the Silver Star. It was downgraded at MEF to a Bronze Star. I recommended Lieutenant Fitzpatrick for the Bronze Star. It was downgraded to a Navy Commendation Medal.

On G+2, 1/7 was again moving north on Ripper's right flank. We maneuvered around a quarried area and were moving back into position to the right of 3d Tank Battalion when we received tank main gun fire from Iraqis to the northeast. Simultaneously, my Combat Train took machine gun and small arms fire from Iraqi troops in BMPs and bunkers we had unintentionally bypassed in the quarried area. I told my exec, Major John Taylor, to take charge of the situation with the Combat Train. He calmly directed the S-4, Combat Train Commander First Lieutenant Jeff Hooks, to extricate the Combat Train while recalling the reserve company to provide support. My Marine Gunner, with extensive combat experience in Vietnam, was impressed with the volume of Iraqi fire and the response of the Marines. Lance Corporal Castleman provided MK-19 covering fire while Lieutenants Raynor (MTO) and Welborn (MMO) crossed open ground under fire to destroy the BMPs with AT-4/LAAW fire. I recommended these three men for Silver Stars and have received no word on the awards to date. I am concerned that the interval has been such that much of the meaning may be lost. Unfortunately Lance Corporal Castleman died in an auto accident in June 1991.

First Lieutenant Hooks extricated and reconstituted his Combat Train as Major Taylor sent the reserve company in to kill the remaining Iraqis. Major Taylor and Lieutenant Hooks' conduct was critical in allowing me and the forward elements of 1/7 to focus on our mission and the enemy to our front. Maintaining their composure under fire, directing well reasoned actions that aggressively engaged the enemy and kept my train intact, they earned my recommendation for Bronze Stars. The MEF Awards Board downgraded both to Navy Commendation Medals.

A short time later we were ordered to continue the attack in order to isolate Kuwait International Airport. Resupplying my lead elements up front while we came under fire, Lieutenant Hooks and his men rapidly provided us the main gun ammo and fuel necessary to cross the LD on schedule. Under terrible visibility and with numerous enemy vehicles and fire coming from our right flank, we moved north with Captain Horr coordinating 23 fire missions in the last five hours. We broke through to Kuwait City just at dark.

When the sun came up, we consolidated our positions, linked up with the Kuwaiti Resistance, and cleared the remaining enemy from our surroundings. One man was hit in the arm by a rifle shot. I could observe Captain Bob Hathaway's cross-attached company clearing an adjacent orchard area on our left flank. During the previous afternoon's attack, Lieutenant Colonel Diggs had the infantry attack into the densely vegetated area. Now as I watched them clearing the orchard and killing the last Iraqi soldier that Task Force Ripper would confront, Captain Hathaway had the respect of all of us. In the usual Marine tradition, he led from up front. Lieutenant Colonel Diggs recommended him for the Bronze Star. It was downgraded to a Navy Commendation Medal by the MEF Awards Board.

Throughout the period I have described, the individual who had planned 1/7's attack so well, Major Drew Bennett, S-3, provided the situational awareness that permitted execution of the aggressive, combined arms attack without sustaining a single friendly fire casualty. His presence of mind, sound tactical judgement under fire, and firm direction guided us. Moving on foot when necessary in mine strewn areas during the assault breach and directing my vehicle forward to speed the tempo of our attack at the Emir's Farm, his combat performance was superb. A pillar of strength in our command, I recommended him for the Bronze Star. The MEF Awards Board downgraded his award to a Navy Commendation Medal.

I must mention here that each of these noted awards was recommended based on direct observation. I understand the difficulty of the Awards Board as it struggles to recognize the contribution of those who faced our combat challenges and overcame them. My Task Force Commander, General Fulford, personally reviewed these recommended awards and concurred. General Draude reviewed them in his role as the Assistant Division Commander/Head of the 1st Division Awards Board. General Myatt forwarded the awards. I doubt that three more experienced, mature and wise combat leaders could be found.

Against this backdrop of downgraded awards, I must mention the recognition approved by the MEF Awards Board for members of the MEF staff. I add this only to provide a comparison; nothing I say here is meant to denigrate the following men or the critical role they played in our Nation's victory. They are fellow Marines and I respect them as such.

I understand that MEF Assistant Operations Officers received Bronze Stars for their roles. The MEF Strategic Mobility Officer received a Bronze Star. The Assistant Public Affairs Officer for I MEF received a Bronze Star. The MEF Ammunition Chief received a Bronze Star also.

The MEF NBC Officer received a Bronze Star. However, the TF Ripper NBC Officer, Warrant Officer Cottrell, who was critical to all of us in 1/7 because he moved the Fuchs vehicle to hazardous areas in order to check for contamination received a Navy Commendation Medal. The MEF Awards Board downgraded General Fulford's recommendation for a Bronze Star for WO Cottrell.

General Johnston, we won a magnificent victory thanks to the competence, valor and unselfishness of all hands. To reach these young men's souls and maintain their affections, we must demonstrate to them our respect for the warriors' greatest virtue, courage. At the very minimum, those who slept on the ground the entire deployment, went without showers for months, and killed or took prisoner all enemy they fought, should have their contributions noted at least equally with those recognized for meritorious service on staffs.

To be parsimonious in awarding appropriate medals to our lead combat elements serves no purpose. On a wider scale, the presentation of Bronze Stars to Officers and SNCOs who served in Riyadh on Centcom and Marcent staffs only lends more disillusion with the penurious awards system as implemented at I MEF. I am unable to comprehend the rationale for award action that downplays the responsibilities and actions of combat leaders who faced danger while recognizing generously those who lived more comfortably and did not face such danger.

Correct or not, there is now a common perception that the level of the staff to which assigned determined the level of award. The results of the MEF Awards Board appears to indicate heavier emphasis placed on meritorious service in important staff positions as opposed to officers who actually led in combat. I do not concur with this. Was my operations officer's contribution lessened because he served in an assault battalion when compared to operations officers at MEF? Was my logistics officer's performance lessened because he did his job under fire while the MEF Strategic Mobility Officer who planned the time phased deployment did not? I believe that we must concern ourselves with an awards system that appears to most highly reward an officer "in inverse proportion to the square of the distance of his duties from the front lines."

I realize that my perspective is a limited one and I may have incomplete information. But all 1351 Sailors, Marines and Kuwaitis in the Battalion lived for months under rugged conditions and selflessly committed themselves to the uncertainties of combat. They did everything I asked of them and their high spirited courage was my daily inspiration. Those men on high level staffs who designed the brilliant mechanics of our battle plan earned their recognition. It is also necessary to recognize the combat leaders whose animating spirits were, in the end, our pledge of success once contact was made with the Iraqi Army. Their loyalty and discipline represented our Corps well both in the fight and in numerous interviews with the media. I protest what has happened since, and request your support in gaining for these men the recognition that any objective evaluation would clearly reveal they earned.

Very respectfully,

J. N. MATTIS
Lieutenant Colonel
U. S. Marine Corps

APPENDIX B

From *Business Insider*

General James 'Mad Dog' Mattis Email About Being 'Too Busy To Read' Is A Must-Read

Source: G. Ingersoll   9 May 2003
http://www.businessinsider.com/author/geoffrey-ingersoll

In the run up to Marine Gen. James Mattis' deployment to Iraq in 2004, a colleague wrote to him asking about the importance of reading and military history for officers, many of whom found themselves "too busy to read." His response went viral over email. Security Blog "Strife" out of Kings College in London recently published Mattis' words. Their title for the post: *With Rifle and Bibliography: General Mattis on Professional Reading*

Dear Bill,

The problem with being too busy to read is that you learn by experience (or by your men's experience), i.e. the hard way. By reading, you learn through others' experiences, generally a better way to do business, especially in our line of work where the consequences of incompetence are so final for young men.Thanks to my reading, I have never been caught flat-footed by any situation, never at a loss for how any problem has been addressed (successfully or unsuccessfully) before. It doesn't give me all the answers, but it lights what is often a dark path ahead.

With [Task Force] 58, I had w/ me Slim's book, books about the Russian and British experiences in [Afghanistan], and a couple others. Going into Iraq, "The Siege" (about the Brits' defeat at Al Kut in WW I) was req'd reading for field grade officers. I also had Slim's book; reviewed T.E. Lawrence's "Seven Pillars of Wisdom"; a good book about the life of Gertrude Bell (the Brit archaeologist who virtually founded the modern Iraq state in the aftermath of WW I and the fall of the Ottoman empire); and "From Beirut to Jerusalem". I also went deeply into Liddell Hart's book on Sherman, and

Fuller's book on Alexander the Great got a lot of my attention (although I never imagined that my HQ would end up only 500 meters from where he lay in state in Babylon).

Ultimately, a real understanding of history means that we face NOTHING new under the sun. For all the "4th Generation of War" intellectuals running around today saying that the nature of war has fundamentally changed, the tactics are wholly new, etc, I must respectfully say ... "Not really": Alex the Great would not be in the least bit perplexed by the enemy that we face right now in Iraq, and our leaders going into this fight do their troops a disservice by not studying (studying, vice just reading) the men who have gone before us.

We have been fighting on this planet for 5000 years and we should take advantage of their experience. "Winging it" and filling body bags as we sort out what works reminds us of the moral dictates and the cost of incompetence in our profession. As commanders and staff officers, we are coaches and sentries for our units: how can we coach anything if we don't know a hell of a lot more than just the [Tactics, Techniques, and Procedures]? What happens when you're on a dynamic battlefield and things are changing faster than higher [Headquarters] can stay abreast? Do you not adapt because you cannot conceptualize faster than the enemy's adaptation? (Darwin has a pretty good theory about the outcome for those who cannot adapt to changing circumstance — in the information age things can change rather abruptly and at warp speed, especially the moral high ground which our regimented thinkers cede far too quickly in our recent fights.) And how can you be a sentinel and not have your unit caught flat-footed if you don't know what the warning signs are — that your unit's preps are not sufficient for the specifics of a tasking that you have not anticipated?

Perhaps if you are in support functions waiting on the warfighters to spell out the specifics of what you are to do, you can avoid the consequences of not reading. Those who must adapt to overcoming an independent enemy's will are not allowed that luxury.

This is not new to the USMC approach to warfighting — Going into Kuwait 12 years ago, I read (and reread) Rommel's Papers (remember "Kampstaffel"?), Montgomery's book ("Eyes Officers"...), "Grant Takes Command" (need for commanders to get along, "commanders' relationships" being more important than "command relationships"), and some others.

As a result, the enemy has paid when I had the opportunity to go against them, and I believe that many of my young guys lived because I didn't waste their lives because I didn't have the vision in my mind of how to destroy the enemy at least cost to our guys and to the innocents on the battlefields. Hope this answers your question.... I will cc my ADC (Lt. Warren Cook) in the event he can add to this. He is the only officer I know who has read more than I.

Semper Fi, Mattis

Among my favorite books are:

Marcus Aurelius, "Meditations"
Max Boot, "Invisible Armies" & "The Savage Wars of Peace"
Robert Coram, "Boyd: The Fighter Pilot Who Changed the Art of War"
Martin Van Crevald, "Fighting Power"
Nate Fick, "One Bullet Away"
Gen U.S. Grant, "Personal Memoirs"
Colin Gray, "Fighting Talk: Forty Maxims on War, Peace and Strategy"
Liddell-Hart' "Sherman: Soldier, Realist, American" & "Scipio Africanus: Greater Than Napoleon"
Laura Hillenbrand, "Unbroken"
M.M. Kaye, "The Far Pavilions"
H.R. McMaster's, "Dereliction of Duty"
Mandela, "Long Walk to Freedom"
Williamson Murray, "Military Innovation in the Interwar Period" & "Successful Strategies"
Anton Myrer, "Once An Eagle"
Hew Strachan, "The Direction of War"
Colin Powell, "My American Journey"
Steven Pressfield, "Gates of Fire"
Guy Sajer, "The Forgotten Soldier"
Michael Shaara, "Killer Angels"
George P. Shultz, "Turmoil and Triumph" & "Issues On My Mind"

Viscount Slim, "Defeat Into Victory"
Nicholas Monsarrat, "The Cruel Sea"
Robert Gates, "Duty"
C.E. Lucas Phillips, "The Greatest Raid of All"
Will & Ariel Durrant, "The Lessons of History"
Ron Chernow, "Alexander Hamilton"
Alistair Horne, "A Savage War of Peace"
Betty Iverson & Tabea Springer, "Tabea's Story"
Sun Tzu, "The Art of War"
Andrew Gordon, "The Rules of the Game"
Paul Kennedy, "The Rise and Fall of Great Powers"
David Rothkopf, "National Insecurity: American Leadership in an Age of Fear"
Barbara Tuckman, "March of Folly" & "The Guns of August"
Vali Nasar, "The Dispensable Nation: American Foreign Policy in Retreat"
Henry Kissinger's, "Diplomacy" & "World Order"
Daniel James Brown, "The Boys in the Boat"
Willaam Manchester, "American Caesar" & "Goodbye Darkness"
Max Hasting's, "Catastrophe 1914: Europe Goes to War"
David Fromkin, "A Peace to End All Peace"
E.B. Sledge's, "With the Old Breed"
Michael Walzer, "Just and Unjust Wars"
Wavell, "Other Men's Flowers" (poetry)
Bing West, "The Village"
Anthony Zinni, "Before the First Shot is Fired"
Malham Wakin, "War, Morality and the Military Profession"
Gail Shisler, "For Country and Corps"
Herman Wouk, "The Caine Mutiny"
Ralph Peter, "Never Quit the Fight"
Max Lerner, "The Mind and Faith of Justice Holmes"
Marine Corps Doctrine Publication 1: "Warfighting"
Albert Pierce, "Strategy, Ethics and the 'War on Terrorism' "
Joseph Conrad, "Lord Jim"
T.E. Lawrence, "Seven Pillars of Wisdom"
Rudyard Lawrence, "Kim"
James McPherson, "Battle Cry of Freedom"
Archibald Wavell, "The Viceroy's Journey"

APPENDIX C

DECLASSIFIED
DOD ltrs.
8 Jan. & 20 June 1974
By ___ LC; Date ___

~~SECRET~~

23 August 1943.

My dear Halsey:

D-day for the operation against Lae has been set tentatively for 4 September, final determination depending upon the weather forecast. The long range forecast, for which our weather men have been running sequences for about three weeks, is excellent and indicates that the operation can go under favorable conditions on D-day or very close to it. You will of course be informed the moment the final determination is made.

It would be highly advantageous if the Lae operation could be supported by deception in the South Pacific. I am writing, therefore, to ask you to consider a movement by an element of your fleet which would attract the enemy's attention and serve to fix in place the hostile air strength in the Buka-Rabaul-Kavieng area. The decision is yours as to the practical feasibility of execution of this plan and of its nature and scope. I would appreciate, however, your careful consideration and an expression of your views.

The action of your forces, ground, naval and air during the course of recent operations has been a source of great pleasure to all of us in the Southwest Pacific Area. Let me take advantage of this opportunity to reiterate my appreciation for your complete cooperation and for the fighting qualities of your command.

Cordially yours,

DOUGLAS MacARTHUR.

Admiral Wm. F. Halsey, Jr.,
Commander, Third Fleet.

~~SECRET~~

COMSOPAC FILE

SOUTH PACIFIC FORCE
OF THE UNITED STATES PACIFIC FLEET
HEADQUARTERS OF THE COMMANDER

DECLASSIFIED
DOD ltrs.
8 Jan. & 20 June 1974
By ___ LC; Date ___

SECRET

25 August 1943.

SECRET and PERSONAL

My dear General:

I believe that I can create a reasonably effective feint and diversion such as you desire in connection with the Lae Dog-Day.

Briefly, my proposal is this:

1. On 30 August strong combined Task Forces will sortie from Espiritu Santo and Efate and commence exercises west of the New Hebrides.

2. On 2 September Fleet will move north of New Hebrides into the Banks-Santa Cruz area with prudent regard for enemy air radii of action, but with the expectation of being sighted by Jap reconnaissance planes on September 3rd.

3. On 2 September Aircraft Solomons will commence a round-the-clock air assault on the Southern Bougainville and associated Jap activities, the assault to continue through the 3rd of September.

I believe that the sudden Fleet and air activities will serve to alert the enemy for some major operation by South Pacific. If the diversion fails to immobilize or divert Rabaul air, I propose to take such advantage of any weakness in the enemy's air defense as may appear profitable.

The details of my proposed diversionary operation were explained to General Eichelberger, and I am forwarding copies of this letter, together with yours of the 23rd, to Nimitz and King.

All success to your D-Day.

Cordially,

W. F. HALSEY.

General Douglas MacARTHUR, U.S. Army,
Commander-in-Chief, Southwest Pacific Area.

Copies sent to Admirals King and Nimitz on 26 August. HC

OOA

01	
02	
11	
12	
15	
16	
17	
20	
22	
25	
26	
27	
31	
52	
75	
80	
90	
95	
05	WES
06	
07	

APPENDIX D

MARINE CORPS BASE CAMP PENDLETON, Calif. (Feb 20, 2004) --
COMMANDING GENERAL
1ST MARINE DIVISION (REIN), FMF
CAMP PENDLETON, CALIFORNIA 92055-5380

February 2004

A letter from the Commanding General to the Families of our Sailors and Marines deploying to the Middle East.

We are returning to Iraq. None of us are under any illusions about the challenges that await out troops there. We also know the understandable anxiety that will be felt by our loved ones when we deploy. We are going to stand by one another, all of us, reinforced by our faith and friendship, and together overcome every difficulty. It will not be easy but most things in life worth doing don't come easily.

Our Country needs us in the struggle to put Iraq back on its feet. Our enemies are watching, betting t heir lives and their plans on America nor having the courage to continue this fight. Our Sailors and Marines, reinforcing the Army and our many allies' forces already in Iraq, will prove the enemy has made a grave mistake. As the division goes back to this combat zone, your loved ones will need your spiritual support so they can focus on their duty.

Our Family Readiness Officers and Key Volunteers stand ready to keep you fully informed. Our Marine Bases have support agencies who, you will find, can provide the tools to deal with every challenge you may face. We will come through these times – seeing one another through, looking out for each other- with our families strengthened, our faith stronger, our friendship cemented for life. This does not imply it will be easy for anyone. But, we must recognize that together we can withstand the strongest storm, dismiss the wildest rumors, and overcome any crisis in confidence. Together, with open communication and trust, we will remain the team that so recently succeeded and proved its resilience during deployment to Afghanistan and Iraq.

Let us know your questions so we can keep you informed. Most importantly, keep the faith and share both your clan strength and your courage with each other and with the American people. We are all enormously proud of our well-trained Sailors and Marines; we know that our country will be safer with our Division deployed against the enemy. We are equally proud of you; remember that you are an integral member of our Marine family as we go back into this brawl and that we will stick together through it all.

God bless you all.

Semper Fidelis,

J. N. MATTIS
Major General, U.S. Marines

APPENDIX E

UNITED STATES MARINE CORPS
U.S. MARINE CORPS FORCES CENTRAL COMMAND
7115 SOUTH BOUNDARY BOULEVARD
MACDILL AIRFORCE BASE, FLORIDA 33621-5101

5800
SJA
AUG 0 g.7n p,

From: Commander, U.S. Marine Corps Forces, Central Command
To: Trial Counsel

Subj: DISMISSAL OF CHARGE AND SPECIFICATIONS IN THE CASE OF <u>UNITED
        STATES</u> V. LANCE CORPORAL JUSTIN L. SHARRATT, XXX XX 1095, USMC

Ref: (a) R.C.M. 306, Manual for Courts-Martial (2005 Edition)
        (b) R.C.M. 401, Manual for Courts-Martial (2005 Edition)

Encl: (1) DD Form 458 Preferred 21 Dec 06

1.   **In accordance with the references, the charge and specifications**
ȵ nhn nnn>n , •ann h ɪ ɪSy ɑɾ ɳo

                              By direct ion

Copy to:
TC
DC

UNITED STATES MARINE CORPS
U.S. MARINE CORPS FORCES CENTRAL COMMAND
7115 SOUTH BOUNDARY BOULEVARD
MACDILL AIR FORCE BASE, FLORIDA 33621-5101

IN REPLY REFER TO:
5810
CG
AUG 0 8 2007

From: Commander

To: Lance Corporal Justin L. Sharratt, U.S. Marine Corps

Subj: DISPOSITION OF CASE

Ref: (a) Commandant of the Marine Corps ltr to Commander, U.S.
          Marine Corps Forces Central Command dtd 06 Jun 2006
          (Subj: Designation as Consolidated Disposition
          Authority for Any Necessary Administrative or
          Disciplinary Actions Relative to the Haditha
          Investigation)
      (b) Army Regulation 15-6 Investigation of Events in
          Haditha, Iraq on 19 November 2005 (MG Bargewell AR
          15-6) dtd 15 June 06 and Forwarding Endorsements
      (c) The Naval Criminal Investigative Service's Reports of
          Investigation Concerning the Haditha Incident from 12
          April 2006 to 25 May 2007
      (d) Uniform Code of Military Justice Article 32 Investigating
          Officer Report ICO United States v. Lance Corporal Justin
          L. Sharratt, U.S. Marine Corps

1. Pursuant to reference (a), and based upon my thorough
consideration of references (b), (c), and (d), I have determined that
the charges in your case will be dismissed without prejudice. I have
made this decision based upon all of the evidence and have
specifically considered the recommendation articulated in reference
(d) from the Article 32 Investigating Officer and his determination
that the evidence does not support a referral to a court-martial.

2. The experience of combat is difficult to understand intellectually
and very difficult to appreciate emotionally. One of our Nation 's most
articulate Supreme Court Justices, Oliver Wendell Holmes, Jr., served
as an infantryman during the Civil War and described war as an
"incommunicable experience.,, He has also noted elsewhere that
"detached reflection cannot be demanded in the face of an uplifted
knife." Marines have a well earned reputation for remaining cool in
the face of enemies brandishing much more than knives. The brutal
reality that Justice Holmes described is experienced each day in Iraq,
where you willingly put yourself at great risk to protect innocent
civilians. Where the enemy disregards any attempt to comply with
ethical norms of warfare, we exercise discipline and restraint to
protect the innocent caught on the battlefield. Our way is right, but
it is also difficult.

3. The event in which you were engaged on 19 November 2005 has been
exhaustively examined by Marine, Army, and Naval Criminal

Subj: DISPOSITION OF CASE

Investigative Service investigators. An independent Article 32
Investigating Officer has considered all the facts and concluded that
you acted in accordance with the rules of engagement. His comments on
the evidence are contained in reference (d). The intense examination
into this incident, and into your conduct, has been necessary to
maintain our discipline standards and, in the words of the Marines'
Hymn, "To keep our honor clean." I recognize that you have been
through a most difficult experience. I am optimistic that you
remained aware that you were, and have always been entitled to, and
received the benefit of, the presumption of innocence that is the
bedrock of our military justice system.

4. You have served as a Marine infantryman in Iraq where our Nation
is fighting a shadowy enemy who hides among the innocent people, does
not comply with any aspect of the law of war, and routinely targets
and intentionally draws fire toward civilians. As you well know, the
challenges of this combat environment put extreme pressures on you and
your fellow Marines. Operational, moral, and legal imperatives demand
that we Marines stay true to our own standards and maintain compliance
with the law of war in this morally bruising environment. With the
dismissal of these charges you may fairly conclude that you did your
best to live up to the standards, followed by U.S. fighting men
throughout our many wars, in the face of life or death decisions made
by you in a matter of seconds in combat. And as you have always
remained. cloaked in the presumption of innocence, with this dismissal
of charges, you remain in the eyes of the law - and in my eyes -
innocent.

(j J. N. MATTIS

APPENDIX F

THE WHITE HOUSE
WASHINGTON

September 28, 2007

Lieutenant General James N. Mattis, USMC
Commanding General
I Marine Expeditionary Force and Commander
United States Marine Corps Forces Central Command
Post Office Box 555300
Camp Pendleton, California 92055

Dear Lieutenant General Mattis:

The Defense Planning Committee of the North Atlantic Council has appointed you Supreme Allied Commander for Transformation. The responsibilities and the authority of the Supreme Allied Commander for Transformation will be contained in the Terms of Reference issued by the Military Committee of the North Atlantic Treaty Organization.

The Senate has now confirmed your nomination to the grade of general while serving as Commander, United States Forces Command and Supreme Allied Commander for Transformation. As you assume command:

    1) The United States Armed Forces assigned to the United States Joint Forces Command will remain under your operational command to the extent necessary for the accomplishment of your mission; and

    2) You are authorized to use officers and enlisted personnel of the United States Armed Forces and civilian employees of the United States Government on your staff as you consider appropriate in the numbers and in grade as necessary, consistent with law and regulation.

Sincerely,

George W. Bush

APPENDIX G

USJFCOM Commander's Guidance for Effects-based Operations

BY GENERAL JAMES N. MATTIS, USMC

Herein are my thoughts and commander's guidance regarding effects- based operations (EBO). This article is designed to provide the US Joint Forces Command (USJFCOM) staff with clear guidance and a new direction on how EBO will be addressed in joint doctrine and used in joint training, con- cept development, and experimentation. I am convinced that the various inter- pretations of EBO have caused confusion throughout the joint force and among our multinational partners that we must correct. It is my view that EBO has been misapplied and overextended to the point that it actually hinders rather than helps joint operations.

Therefore, we must return to time-honored principles and terminol- ogy that our forces have tested in the crucible of battle and that are well grounded in the theory and nature of war. At the same time, we must retain and adopt those aspects of effects-based thinking that are useful. We must stress the importance of mission type orders that contain clear commander's intent and unambiguous tasks and purposes and, most importantly, that link ways and means with achievable ends. To augment these tenets, we must leverage non- military capabilities and strive to better understand the different operating vari- ables that make up today's more complex operating environments.

My assessment is shaped by my personal experiences and the experi- ences of others in a variety of operational situations. I am convinced that we must keep the following in mind. First, operations in the future will require a balance of regular and irregular competencies. Second, the enemy is smart and adaptive. Third, all operating environments are dynamic with an infinite number of variables; therefore, it is not scientifically possible to accurately predict the outcome of an action. To suggest otherwise runs contrary to his- torical experience and the nature of war. Fourth, we are in error when we think that what works (or does not work) in one theater is universally applica- ble to all theaters. Finally, to quote General Sherman, "Every attempt to make war easy and safe will result in humiliation and disaster." History is replete with examples and further denies us any confidence that the acute predictabil- ity promised by EBO's long assessment cycle can strengthen our doctrine. The joint force must act in uncertainty and thrive in chaos, sensing opportunity therein and not retreating into a need for more information. USJFCOM's purpose is to ensure that joint doctrine smooths and simplifies joint operations while reducing friendly friction. My goal is to return clarity to our planning processes and operational concepts. Ultimately, my aim is to ensure leaders convey their intent in clearly understood terms and empower their subordinates to act decisively.

For complete article, see
http://strategicstudiesinstitute.army.mil/pubs/parameters/articles/08autumn/mattis.pdf

ACKNOWLEDGMENTS

JIM MATTIS: This book, over five years in the making, is my attempt to pass to young leaders what I learned over four decades of naval service. Inaccuracies are wholly my responsibility.

Too few of those I owe thanks are named in these pages. Were I to list them all, it would take a companion volume. My parents, West and Lucille, and brothers, Tom and Gerald, do rate special mention. Since leaving home at age seventeen, and during many years of service across the seven seas, I spent little time with them. I trust they know that I carried their love, sense of curiosity, and values with me as I wandered, and I'm forever grateful that they kept me close even when I was far away.

My comrades in arms across our military and among our allies, while too many to mention individually, made invaluable contributions to my life and to the essence of this book. Too many made the ultimate sacrifice in defense of our freedom, and I hold copies of many next-of-kin letters as reminders of the loss felt forever in their families' hearts.

Only with the daily guidance and impressive skill of my coauthor, Bing West, and editor Will Murphy could our book have appeared in print. I am thankful for their mentoring and friendship. I'm also appreciative of Random House's two years of patience when, having been called back to government service, I was delayed in finalizing the book.

I first considered writing this book following my 2013 retirement. Respected friends noted that I had been lucky to have an interesting career and owed it to others to pass on what I had been taught. I was reminded that I wasn't in the Marine Corps for all those years; rather, I was in the United States Marine Corps, serving the people to whom I was accountable. I also carried a strong sense of gratitude that I wanted to share with the country that had paid my tuition to learn all I had been taught. This gratitude was brought vividly to mind when I was a lieutenant general, hosting a Washington, D.C., parade for retired Marine John Glenn. Waiting together to be called to our seats as the lights dimmed, Senator Glenn remarked to me, "I was a Marine for twenty-three years. It wasn't long enough." I was struck by his reflection. Here was a man who had fought in World War II and Korea and was a fighter pilot ace. He was the first American to orbit the earth and a respected senator, with a leadership record respected at home and abroad. Yet he felt his decades of military service weren't long enough. In a similar vein, today I'm grateful and humbled that the Marine Corps allowed me to serve so long in the ranks, beside the finest young men and women our nation has to offer.

In the spirit of keeping our American experiment alive, it will be enough if this book conveys my respect for those men and women who selflessly commit to serving our country—soldiers, sailors, airmen, Coast Guardsmen, and Marines, united in their devotion to our survival as a nation. In the toughest circumstances, they earned my undying respect and admiration. Alongside them I'd do it all again.

BING WEST: Three generations of the West family have fought as Marines in our nation's wars. We were all infantry—grunts—forever marked by a Corps that insisted upon discipline, tradition, mission, and brotherhood. No matter how tough any fight was, Marines before us had faced worse conditions and won. Marines don't fret about who they are or what they're expected to do.

I wrote a few books about my experience in Vietnam. One was a training manual about small-unit action. The other was about a squad that fought for over a year to protect a remote village. Seven of the fifteen Marines died in the village. After a civilian career and with my four children grown, in 2003 I flew to Kuwait to write about the impending invasion of Iraq. Jim Mattis welcomed me and my coauthor, Ray Smith, who was legendary for his exploits in Vietnam. On the march to Baghdad, we saw that Jim was a constant presence, moving constantly to the point of attack and circulating among the battalions.

Over the next ten years, I made dozens of trips to Iraq and Afghanistan. While writing six books and traveling across the battlefields, time after time I crossed paths with Jim. It seemed there was no remote outpost or isolated platoon that he did not visit. I saw him as a two-star, then a three-star, and finally a four-star. While he adapted his leadership style as his span of control broadened, his joy at being with the troops always shone through, and they returned his affection.

Each generation of Marine warriors needs exemplars. In Vietnam, we had Ray Smith, Bob Barrow, and Ray Davis. In the post-9/11 wars, we have Joe Dunford, John Kelly, and Jim Mattis. As a fellow Marine grunt, I am proud to have coauthored Jim's memoir. Hopefully, his lessons about leading will be studied by those in military and civilian jobs where success depends upon taking care of those who follow you.

Jim and I could not have written his memoir without the dedication and brilliance of our independent editor, Will Murphy. Will is a treasure. He stood his ground against two Marines, telling us when we were too technical and reminding us that not every leader finds delight in crawling through mud. He ensured that Jim's lessons were practical for business managers.

This book took over five years to write. Throughout, my beautiful wife, Betsy, was supportive, loving, and infinitely patient. She is also, like Will Murphy, a no-nonsense editor.

I am a lucky guy, grateful to my wife, family, Corps, country, and God.

Semper Fidelis.

NOTES

CHAPTER 1

5   **Lewis and Clark expedition:** In 1805, in a meadow just outside our town, Captain Clark wrote in his journal, "100 Indians Came from the different Lodges, and a number of them brought wood which they gave us, we Smoked with all of them, and two of our Party played on the violin which delighted them greatly." Lewis and Clark, Clark Journal Entry, October 19, 1805. lewisandclarkjournals.unl.edu/item/lc .jrn.1805-10-19.

11 **block and tackle:** I was pleased to read this 2014 post on *Foreign Policy* magazine's website by Marine Captain Jordan Blashek: "Rather than trying to remember 69 different TTPs [Tactics, Techniques, and Procedures], I would suggest that 2nd lieutenants focus on just one: 'Think deeply about your job and figure out the why behind everything.' . . . To face the confusion of the modern battlefield . . . requires a nuanced mind capable of critical thought and the humility to ask the right questions." Jordan Blashek, "68 TTPs Too Many! Or, Why Lists Like That Won't Help Improve Our Junior Officers," Best Defense (blog), *Foreign Policy,* January 29, 2014, foreignpolicy .com/2014/01/29/68-ttps-too-many-or-why-lists-like-that-wont-help -improve-our-junior-officers.

CHAPTER 3

27 **"where no danger is":** George Washington to the President of Congress, February 9, 1776. oll.libertyfund.org/titles/washington-the -writings-of-george-washington-vol-iv-1776.

CHAPTER 4

40 **first to fight:** The Marine Security Guards number approximately a thousand Marines at 174 posts (also known as "detachments"), orga-

nized into nine regional MSG commands and located in more than 135 countries. Wikipedia, s.v. "Marine Security Guard," last modified March 28, 2019, en.wikipedia.org/wiki/Marine_Security_Guard.

45 **"within the overall intention":** Field Marshal Viscount Slim, *Defeat into Victory* (New York: First Cooper Square Press, 2000), p. 542.

CHAPTER 5

51 **"No doubt about it, guys":** General Tommy Franks, *American Soldier* (New York: HarperCollins, 2004), p. 255. See also Nathan S. Lowrey, *U.S. Marines in Afghanistan, 2001–2002: From the Sea* (Washington, DC: Historical Division, US Marine Corps, 2011), p. 134: "On 13 Sept 2011, Gen Franks stated 'Afghanistan untenable for Marine amphibious forces and that ground operations would require US Army combat power supported by US Air Force logistic.'"

51 **"consideration of the Marines":** Lowrey, *Marines in Afghanistan,* p. 34.

53 **"One can call it coup d'oeil":** Napoleon I, 1769–1821, *Mémoires,* cited in Wikipedia, s.v. "Coup d'Oeil," last modified August 19, 2018, en.wikipedia.org/wiki/Coup_d%27œil.

60 **filled sandbags:** Lowrey, *Marines in Afghanistan,* pp. 82–83.

60 **It was a constant dialogue:** Lowrey, *Marines in Afghanistan,* p. 89; Clarke Lethin, interviewed by Bing West, September 4, 2014.

61 **a hundred thousand wounded:** "Gallipoli Casualties by Country," New Zealand History, Ministry for Culture and Heritage, updated March 1, 2016, nzhistory.govt.nz/media/interactive/gallipoli -casualties-country.

61 **advanced land bases across the Pacific:** David C. Emmel, Major, USMC, "The Development of Amphibious Doctrine," master's thesis, Oregon State University, 1998. www.dtic.mil/dtic/tr/fulltext/u2/ a524286.pdf.

61 **"the most decisive maneuver of war":** Robert Heinl, *Victory at High Tide: The Inchon-Seoul Campaign* (Philadelphia: Lippincott, 1968), pp. 346–51.

64 **As they flew northeast over Pakistan:** Lowrey, *Marines in Afghanistan,* pp. 103–10.

67 **"from one of grim hope to hopelessness":** Lowrey, *Marines in Afghanistan,* p. 116.

67 **Again, we sustained no injuries:** Lowrey, *Marines in Afghanistan,* p. 142.

68 **"humanitarian assistance to the people in Afghanistan":** Pentagon press release, November 27, 2001.

68 **"perhaps to the end":** Pentagon press release, November 26, 2001.

69 **"That's not why we put them there":** Pentagon press release, November 27, 2001.

69 **numbers were estimated at twenty thousand:** Lowrey, *Marines in Afghanistan,* p. 133.

70   **"not everyone on your staff"**: Lowrey, *Marines in Afghanistan,* p. 207.

73   **OBL's retreat**: Sean Naylor, *Relentless Strike* (New York: St. Martin's, 2015), p. 184.

74   **twenty-three heliograph stations**: "The Heliograph," National Park Service, updated February 24, 2015, www.nps.gov/fobo/historyculture/the-heliograph.htm. "By August of 1886, Miles was utilizing 23 heliograph stations in Arizona and New Mexico, with each station approximately 25 miles apart."

74   **leaving the terrorists to die inside the caves**: Yaniv Barzilai, *102 Days of War* (Washington, DC: Potomac Books, 2013), p. 317.

74   **we were not called forward**: In the public press, the last mention of bin Laden was by a Delta Force commander who referenced a December 12 radio intercept that he was still hiding in Tora Bora. Pete Blaber, *The Mission, the Men and Me* (New York: Penguin, 2008), p. 195.

75   **"a hell of a Christmas present"**: Mary Anne Weaver, "Lost at Tora Bora," *New York Times,* September 11, 2005.

75   **"armor battalions chasing a lightly armed enemy"**: Franks, *American Soldier,* p. 324. The CENTCOM deputy commander, Lieutenant General DeLong, later explained, "If we put our troops in there, we would inevitably end up fighting Afghan villagers—creating bad will at a sensitive time—which was the last thing we wanted to do." Lieutenant General Michael DeLong, *A General Speaks Out* (New York: Zenith Press, 2007), p. 56.

75   **fast-moving light infantry**: Henry A. Crumpton, *The Art of Intelligence* (New York: Penguin, 2012), p. 259.

75   **"Bush had missed the best opportunity"**: Peter Baker, *Days of Fire: Bush and Cheney in the White House* (New York: Random House, 2013), p. 322.

76   **"the gravest error of the war"**: Weaver, "Lost at Tora Bora."

CHAPTER 6

85   **I commanded the 1st Marine Division**: Lieutenant Colonel Michael Groen, *With the 1st Marine Division in Iraq, 2003* (Washington, DC: History Division, Marine Corps University, 2006), p. 98.

88   **"one tent will be allowed each company"**: Ulysses S. Grant, *The Complete Personal Memoirs of Ulysses S. Grant* (Berkeley, Calif.: Ulysses Press, 2011), p. 153.

92   **"destroy as many military installations as they could"**: Richard Miller, *In Words and Deeds* (Hanover, N.H.: University Press of New England, 2008), p. 133.

92   **"survive only through surrender"**: Ibid., p. 236.

93   **"No Better Friend, No Worse Enemy"**: This expression, "Nullus melior amicus, nullus peior inimicus," is attributed to Roman General Lucius Cornelius Sulla, allegedly a fiercely loyal friend, but cruel, merciless toward his enemies. He supposedly composed the quote to be

inscribed on his own tomb in the Campus Martius, Rome, around 78 B.C.

97   "you have to push through": General John Kelly, interviewed by Bing West, August 16, 2014.

98   "follow you to the end of the world": "William Joseph Slim," Your-Dictionary, updated April 12, 2019, biography.yourdictionary.com/william-joseph-slim. See also Vicki Croke, *Elephant Company* (New York: Random House Trade Paperbacks, 2015), p. 223.

100   "aren't catching up to the maneuver units": Franks, *American Soldier*, p. 511.

100   "I understood the reason for the pause": Donald Rumsfeld, *Known and Unknown: A Memoir* (New York: Penguin, 2011), p. 465.

100   "ready for the push to Baghdad": Rick Atkinson, Peter Baker, and Thomas E. Ricks, "Confused Start, Decisive End," *Washington Post*, April 13, 2003.

CHAPTER 7

104   88,000 gallons of fuel: Groen, *With the 1st Marine Division*, p. 97.

108   youngest Marine to die: *Nashua Telegraph*, April 15, 2003, newspaperarchive.com/nashua-telegraph-apr-15-2003-p-6/.

114   "better state of peace": B. H. Liddell Hart, *Strategy* (1954), cited at Classics of Strategy and Diplomacy (website), posted by Roger Beckett, January 19, 2016, www.classicsofstrategy.com/2016/01/liddell-hart-strategy-1954.html.

CHAPTER 8

116   "beyond the war on terror": "Text of Bush's Speech at West Point," *New York Times*, June 1, 2002, www.nytimes.com/2002/06/01/international/text-of-bushs-speech-at-west-point.html.

116   More than a million Sunnis: "Anbar Province Plagued by Violence," *New Humanitarian*, January 15, 2007, www.irinnews.org/report/64374/iraq-anbar-province-plagued-violence.

116   "classical guerrilla-type campaign": Brian Knowlton, "Top U.S. General in Iraq Sees 'Classical Guerrilla-Type' War," *International Herald Tribune*, July 16, 2003.

118   fair laws and orderly practices: J. R. Fears, "Afghanistan: The Lessons of History," Big Think, October 13, 2011, bigthink.com/learning-from-the-past/afghanistan-the-lessons-of-history. "Alexander, from 330 until 327 B.C., systematically conquered the country by the most ruthless exercise of military force. Then having conquered the Afghans, he won their hearts. Alexander married, as his first wife, Roxanne, the daughter of the Afghan warlord, Oxyartes. Alexander then conciliated all the other warlords of Afghanistan. His firstborn son and heir to his great empire would be an Afghan and Alexander made the Afghans full partners in his great new world. What Alexander did

not try to do was to force Greek customs and Greek values, like democracy, upon the Afghans. He not only allowed them to keep their customs, he adopted the customs of the Afghans and the Persians. Alexander became a national hero to the Afghans, who still invoke with awe the name of Skander (Alexander)."

120   **oath taken by all doctors:** MerriamWebster.com, s.v. "primum non nocere," www.merriamwebster.com/dictionary/primum%20non %20nocere.

122   **Marines would "be bloodied":** Bing West, *No True Glory: A Frontline Account of the Battle for Fallujah* (New York: Bantam, 2005), p. 52.

124   **strong military action must be taken:** L. Paul Bremer, *My Year in Iraq* (New York: Threshold Editions, 2006), p. 332.

124   **"tougher than hell":** Lieutenant General Ricardo Sanchez, *Wiser in Battle* (New York: HarperCollins, 2008), p. 350.

124   **"the might of the U.S. military":** Rumsfeld, *Known and Unknown*, p. 332. See also p. 532: "All of us on the National Security Council recognized that we could not allow an Iraqi city to become a sanctuary for murderers and terrorists. My impulse was not only to find the enemies who had committed the atrocity, but also to send a message across the country that anyone who engaged in acts of terror would face the might of the U.S. military."

124   **300,000 increasingly resentful residents:** "Battle for Falluja Under Way," CNN, November 9, 2004, www.cnn.com/2004/WORLD/ meast/11/08/iraq.main/.

128   **"a source of shock":** Dan Glaister, "US Gunships Pound Falluja," *Guardian*, April 27, 2004, www.theguardian.com/world/2004/apr/28/ iraq.danglaister.

128   **they would resign:** Bremer, *My Year in Iraq*, p. 333.

128   **Bremer called Generals Abizaid and Sanchez:** Ibid., p. 334.

128   **before the end of the Friday services:** Ibid., p. 335.

128   **lost the information war:** General Jim Conway, interviewed by Bing West, Fallujah, Iraq, May 29, 2004.

130   **"I'll have the Hidra mosque":** West, *No True Glory*, p. 143.

133   **"Our orders changed":** I MEF press conference, May 1, 2004.

134   **Bremer objected strongly to the White House:** Bremer, *My Year in Iraq*, p. 345.

136   **was a hooded Zarqawi:** Michael Gordon and Bernard Trainor, *The Endgame: The Inside Story of the Struggle for Iraq, from George W. Bush to Barack Obama* (New York: Pantheon, 2012), p. 113. "The CIA believed that the execution took place in a safe house in the Jolan neighborhood, Tawhid wal-Jihad's base, and that Zarqawi himself slit Berg's throat."

136   **Abu Bakr al-Baghdadi:** Richard DesLauriers, former FBI agent, and Kevin Carroll, Army intelligence officer, Fox News, September 19, 2014.

CHAPTER 9

137   **"find their own way"**: George W. Bush, "5 Step Plan for Democracy in Iraq," speech, Carlisle, PA, May 24, 2004, American Rhetoric Online Speech Bank, www.americanrhetoric.com/speeches/wariniraq/gwbushiraq52404.htm.

138   **"a path to a better future"**: Bremer, *My Year in Iraq,* p. 393.

139   **"in the manner of industrial war"**: General Rupert Smith, *The Utility of Force* (New York: Vintage, 2005), p. 399.

140   **"generals refuse to apologise"**: Rory McCarthy, "US Soldiers Started to Shoot Us, One by One," *Guardian,* May 20, 2004, www.theguardian.com/world/2004/may/21/iraq.rorymccarthy.

140   **"Let's not be naive"**: Ibid.

141   **"access the Marine brass gave me to the enlisted troops"**: Tony Perry to Bing West, July 23, 2016.

142   **"confrontation with the enemy"**: Edward Cody, "Officers Say Target Was Safe House," *Washington Post,* June 20, 2004, p. A01.

147   **"I want insecurity, strife"**: Wikipedia, s.v. "The Paratrooper's Prayer," last modified May 1, 2019, en.wikipedia.org/wiki/The_Paratrooper%27s_Prayer.

CHAPTER 10

150   **"nothing less than recognition"**: Daniel Kahneman, *Thinking, Fast and Slow* (New York: Farrar, Straus and Giroux, 2013), p. 11.

151   **assimilation of knowledge**: Jon Clegg, "How Urban Meyer Took the Buckeyes to School," *Wall Street Journal,* Dec 6, 2014.

152   **"I like brawling"**: David Hancock, "General: It's Fun to Shoot People," CBS News, February 3, 2005, www.cbsnews.com/news/general-its-fun-to-shoot-people/.

153   **"the urge to get something done"**: S. L. A. Marshall, *Men Against Fire: The Problem of Battle Command* (1947; repr., Gloucester, Mass.: Peter Smith Publications, 1973), p. 138.

153   **"speaks with a great deal of candor"**: Esther Schrader, "General Draws Fire for Saying 'It's Fun to Shoot' the Enemy," February 4, 2005, www.latimes.com/archives/la-xpm-2005-feb-04-fg-mattis4-story.html.

153   **second battle to seize Fallujah**: West, *No True Glory,* p. 316.

154   **troops to follow**: Joint Publication 1, Doctrine for the Armed Forces of the United States, www.dtic.mil/doctrine/new_pubs/jp1.pdf.

154   **a guide for small-unit leaders**: "Small-Unit Leaders' Guide to Counterinsurgency," United States Marine Corps, June 20, 2006, www.slideshare.net/marinecorpsbooks/marine-corps-small-unit-leaders-guide-to-counterinsurgency.

155   **"That does away with the Marine Corps"**: Victor H. Krulak, *First to Fight: An Inside View of the U.S. Marine Corps* (Annapolis, Md., Naval Institute Press, 1999), p. 243.

156   "no captain can do very wrong": Admiral Horatio Nelson, quoted in
       "Trafalgar—21st of October, 1805," *Naval Review* XLIII, no. 4
       (1955), p. 388, available at docplayer.net/51746379-The-issued
       -quarterly-for-private-circulation-november-1955.html.

157   "the elemental passions": James Currie, *The Complete Poetical
       Works of Robert Burns: With Explanatory and Glossarial Notes;
       and a Life of the Author* (New York: D. Appleton, 1859), available
       at quod.lib.umich.edu/cgi/t/text/text-idx?c=moa&cc=moa&sid=
       95e3f6e828e116b80d4cccd93c806bc1&view=text&rgn=main&idno=
       ABE9038.0001.001.

CHAPTER 11

162   "I think it will take five years": Mark Walker, "Mattis: Winning in
       Iraq Will Take Five More Years," *San Diego Union-Tribune*, Decem-
       ber 21, 2006, www.sandiegouniontribune.com/news/2006/dec/21/
       mattis-winning-in-iraq-will-take-five-more-years/.

163   "This war is lost": Joel Roberts, "Senator Reid on Iraq: 'This War Is
       Lost,'" CBS News, April 20, 2007, www.cbsnews.com/news/senator
       -reid-on-iraq-this-war-is-lost/.

164   "their own My Lai": John MacArthur, "Semper Why? One More Illu-
       sion Down the Drain," *Providence Journal*, June 20, 2006.

164   "27,000 civilian deaths": "Large Bombings Claim Ever More Lives,"
       Iraq Body Count, October 4, 2007, www.iraqbodycount.org/analysis/
       numbers/biggest-bombs/.

164   "in terms their audience can understand": Walker, "Mattis: Winning
       in Iraq."

165   "Men who take up arms": Frank Freidel, "General Orders 100 and
       Military Government," *Mississippi Valley Historical Review* 32, no. 4,
       March 1946, JSTOR, www.jstor.org/stable/1895240?seq=1#page
       _scan_tab_contents.

167   "lack of due diligence": Paul von Zielbauer, "Marines Punish 3 Offi-
       cers in Haditha Case," *New York Times*, September 6, 2007, www
       .nytimes.com/2007/09/06/world/middleeast/06haditha.html.

CHAPTER 12

170   twelve nations to twenty-six: "NATO Decisions on Open-Door Pol-
       icy," NATO, April 3, 2008, www.nato.int/docu/update/2008/04-april/
       e0403h.html.

CHAPTER 13

180   "little or no land forces would be required": Matt M. Matthews, *We
       Were Caught Unprepared: The 2006 Hezbollah-Israeli War,* Long War
       Series Occasional Paper 26 (Fort Leavenworth, Kans.: Combat Studies
       Institute Press, 2008), p. 26.

180 **"terminology used was too complicated"**: Avi Kober, "The Israel Defense Forces in the Second Lebanon War: Why the Poor Performance?" *Journal of Strategic Studies* 31, no. 1 (June 5, 2008), p. 62.

181 **"Adaptation is smarter than you are"**: Friedrich Hayek, Wikiquote, s.v. "Friedrich Hayek," last modified January 14, 2019, en.wikiquote.org/wiki/Friedrich_Hayek.

181 **"will result in humiliation and disaster"**: Mike Santacroce, *Planning for Planners: Joint Operation Planning Process* (Bloomington, Ind.: iUniverse, 2013), Google Books.

182 **"clear, logical thinking"**: George C. Marshall, *Infantry in Battle,* 2nd ed. (Washington, DC: Infantry Journal Press, 1939), pp. 1–14.

182 **"empower their subordinates to act decisively"**: James N. Mattis, "US-JFCOM Commander's Guidance for Effects-based Operations," *Joint Force Quarterly* (Autumn 2008), p. 25.

182 **"The trinity of chance, uncertainty, and friction"**: www.clausewitz.com/readings/Bassford/Trinity/TRININTR.htm.

CHAPTER 14

191 **twenty countries:** See "The Joint Organization and Staff Functions," *The Joint Staff Officer's Guide* (2000), www.au.af.mil/au/awc/awcgate/pub1/. Note: CENTCOM is a combatant command. "Combatant command (COCOM) is fully defined in Joint Pub 0-2, Unified Action Armed Forces (UNAAF). COCOM is the command authority over assigned forces vested only in the commanders of combatant commands by title 10, U.S. Code, Section 164, or as directed by the President in Command Plan (UCP), and cannot be delegated or transferred. The Congress has given the combatant commander as the authority to give direction to subordinate commands, including all aspects of military operations, joint training, and logistics; organize commands and forces to carry out assigned missions; employ forces necessary to carry out assigned missions; assign command functions to subordinate commanders; coordinate and approve administration, support, and discipline; and exercise authority to select subordinate commanders and combatant command staff."

191 **deployed across the region:** "Combatant Commands," U.S. Department of Defense, www.defense.gov/know-your-military/combatant-commands/.

201 **CIA station chiefs:** "U.S. Central Command (USCENTCOM)," Global Security, www.globalsecurity.org/military/agency/dod/centcom.htm.

CHAPTER 15

206 **"advise and assist"**: Ali Khedery, "Why We Stuck with Maliki—and Lost Iraq," *Washington Post,* July 3, 2014, www.washingtonpost.com/

opinions/why-we-stuck-with-maliki—and-lost
-iraq/2014/07/03/0dd6a8a4-f7ec-11e3-a606-946fd632f9f1_story
.html?utm_term=.5f43adfd99c8i. See also Emma Sky, 336-42.

207   **"I'll bet you my vice presidency"**: Gordon and Trainor, *Endgame,*
p. 643: " 'Maliki wants us to stick around because he does not see a
future in Iraq otherwise,' Biden said, according to the account. 'I'll
bet you my vice presidency Maliki will extend the SOFA.' " See also
Khedery, "Why We Stuck with Maliki": "Maliki would not surrender
power easily. General Austin made clear that he was more comfortable
with the status quo. Jim Mattis, the CENTCOM commander, was
not. The Egyptians, the Saudis, the Jordanians, and the Qataris have
all told him that they did not want Maliki to stay on. If Maliki tri-
umphed, it would send shockwaves across the region, and any exten-
sion of Iranian influence on his government would work against the
United States in the long term. Mattis was reminding the group that
government formation in Iraq would affect relations across the Middle
East. . . . James Clapper, the Director of National Intelligence agreed
with Mattis that the regional impact would be significant."

209   **recommending that we retain eighteen thousand troops**: Howard
LaFranchi, "Iraq Withdrawal: How Many U.S. Troops Will Remain?"
Christian Science Monitor, September 7, 2011, www.csmonitor.com/
USA/Foreign-Policy/2011/0907/Iraq-withdrawal-How-many-US
-troops-will-remain.

209   **offered a token presence of 3,500**: Lauren Carroll, "McCain: Obama
Never Said He Wanted to Leave Troops in Iraq," PolitiFact, September
12, 2014, www.politifact.com/truth-o-meter/statements/2014/sep/12/
john-mccain/mccain-obama-never-said-he-wanted-leave-troops-ira/.

209   **Iraqi parliament could never unite**: While the lack of an Iraqi-
legislated SOFA was given as the administration's reason for leaving
not even 3,500 troops in Iraq, following the 2014 return of Al Qaeda
in Iraq (known as ISIS), the administration reintroduced more than
five thousand troops under the same legal guarantee and protections
the Iraqi government had offered before we pulled out all our troops
in 2011—an executive order that granted U.S. military jurisdiction
over its men simply by affirming our soldier was on duty at the time of
any alleged misdeed. None of our troops would wind up in an Iraqi
courtroom. Why this was sufficient in 2014–16 but insufficient when
offered in 2011 I've never understood.

209   **"sovereign, stable, and self-reliant"**: Mark Landler, "U.S. Troops to
Leave Iraq by Year's End," *New York Times,* October 21, 2011, www
.nytimes.com/2011/10/22/world/middleeast/president-obama
-announces-end-of-war-in-iraq.html?searchResultPosition=27.

209   **"I ended it"**: President Barack Obama, "Barack Obama's Victory
Speech—Full Text," *Guardian,* November 7, 2012, www.theguardian
.com/world/2012/nov/07/barack-obama-speech-full-text.

213 "The tide of war is receding": Mark Landler and Helene Cooper, "Obama Will Speed Pullout from War in Afghanistan," *New York Times,* June 22, 2011, www.nytimes.com/2011/06/23/world/asia/23prexy.html?mtrref=www.google.com&gwh=BF3E31C9DD88A65880999B1C0248021E&gwt=pay.

214 "Buyer beware!": Tony Zinni and Tony Koltz, *Before the First Shots Are Fired* (New York: St. Martin's, 2015), p. 177.

217 "will kill you one day": See, for instance, Missy Ryan and Susan Cornwell, "U.S. Says Pakistan's ISI Supported Kabul Embassy Attack," Reuters, September 22, 2011.

217 closed its supply route: Farhan Bokhari, "Pakistan Blasts 'Unprovoked' NATO Attacks," CBS News, November 26, 2011, www.cbsnews.com/news/pakistan-blasts-unprovoked-nato-attacks/.

219 reducing our numbers: Wikipedia, s.v. "2012 in Afghanistan," last modified April 6, 2019, en.wikipedia.org/wiki/2012_in_Afghanistan.

CHAPTER 16

221 one in every three Arab youths: "Look Forward in Anger," *Economist,* August 6, 2016, www.economist.com/briefing/2016/08/06/look-forward-in-anger?frsc=dg%7Ca.

222 "find out what will be least bad": Thomas Jefferson to Albert Gallatin, December 3, 1807, in Albert Gallatin, *The Writings of Albert Gallatin,* vol. 1 (Philadelphia: Lippincott, 1867), p. 367, Google Books.

222 came out vocally against Mubarak: "Obama Says Egypt's Transition 'Must Begin Now,'" CNN, February 2, 2011, www.cnn.com/2011/POLITICS/02/01/us.egypt.obama/.

222 "the right side of history": Liz Halloran and Ari Shapiro, "Obama: U.S. Is 'On Right Side of History' in Mideast," NPR, February 15, 2011, www.npr.org/2011/02/15/133779423/obama-u-s-is-on-right-side-of-history-in-mideast.

225 resolute King Abdullah: Wikipedia, s.v. "2011–12 Jordanian Protests," last modified April 29, 2019, en.wikipedia.org/wiki/2011–12_Jordanian_protests.

229 "most grievous of all . . . mistakes": Rear Admiral J. C. Wylie, quoted in John Collins, "National Security Career Choices," War on the Rocks, September 16, 2013, warontherocks.com/2013/09/national-security-career-choices/.

229 killed or wounded more than six hundred American troops: Robert Palladino, Department of State press briefing, Washington, DC, April 2, 2019.

230 "senior members of the Qods Force": "Two Men Charged in Alleged Plot to Assassinate Saudi Arabian Ambassador to the United States," Justice News, U.S. Department of Justice, October 11, 2011, www.justice.gov/opa/pr/two-men-charged-alleged-plot-assassinate-saudi

-arabian-ambassador-united-states. See also Mark Memmott,
"'Factions' of Iran's Government Behind Terrorist Plot, Holder
Says," NPR, October 11, 2011, www.npr.org/sections/thetwo
-way/2011/10/11/141240766/reports-terrorist-plot-tied-to-iran
-disrupted.

230 **Zimmermann:** Wikipedia, s.v. "Zimmermann Telegram," last modified April 28, 2019, en.wikipedia.org/wiki/Zimmermann_Telegram:
"The Zimmermann Telegram (or Zimmermann Note) was a 1917
diplomatic proposal from the German Empire offering a military alliance with Mexico, in the event of the United States entering World
War I against Germany. The proposal was intercepted and decoded by
British intelligence. Revelation of the contents outraged American
public opinion, and helped generate support for the United States declaration of war on Germany in April of that year. President Woodrow
Wilson released telegram and immediately proposed to Congress that
American merchant ships be armed to defend against German submarines."

231 **"willing to exact a serious price":** Admiral William J. Crowe Jr., *The
Line of Fire* (New York: Simon and Schuster, 1993), p. 201.

231 **"We determine the rules":** Sean Rayment, "Armada of International
Naval Power Massing in the Gulf as Israel Prepares an Iran Strike,"
Telegraph, September 15, 2012, www.telegraph.co.uk/news/world
news/middleeast/iran/9545597/Armada-of-international-naval-power
-massing-in-the-Gulf-as-Israel-prepares-an-Iran-strike.html.

232 **"White House didn't fully trust Mattis":** Leon Panetta, *Worthy Fights*
(New York: Penguin, 2014), p. 435.

234 **"If the strategy be wrong":** Alfred Thayer Mahan, *Mahan on Naval
Warfare* (Boston: Little, Brown & Company, 1918), p. 12.

234 **needed to be won:** George P. Shultz (ed.), *Blueprint for America* (Stanford, Calif.: Hoover Institution Press, 2016), p. 137.

CHAPTER 17

236 **"What profit to kill men?":** Rudyard Kipling, *Kim,* in *The Writings in
Prose and Verse of Rudyard Kipling* (New York: Charles Scribner's
Sons, 1902), Google Books.

INDEX

Page numbers of maps appear in italics.

ABOUT THE AUTHORS

JIM MATTIS is a Pacific Northwest native who served more than four decades as a Marine infantry officer. Following two years as the Secretary of Defense, he returned to the Pacific Northwest and is now the Davies Family Distinguished Fellow at the Hoover Institution.

BING WEST has written ten books about combat. He served as a Marine grunt in Vietnam and later as an assistant secretary of defense in the Reagan administration. He has been on hundreds of patrols in Iraq and Afghanistan, including many operations with General Mattis. He is a member of the Military History Working Group at the Hoover Institution. He lives with his wife, Betsy, in Hilton Head, South Carolina, and Newport, Rhode Island.

bingwest.com

ABOUT THE TYPE

This book was set in Sabon, a typeface designed by the well-known German typographer Jan Tschichold (1902–74). Sabon's design is based upon the original letter forms of sixteenth-century French type designer Claude Garamond and was created specifically to be used for three sources: foundry type for hand composition, Linotype, and Monotype. Tschichold named his typeface for the famous Frankfurt typefounder Jacques Sabon (c. 1520–80).